AMERICAN ART POTTERY

A collection of pottery, tiles, and memorabilia 1880–1950

Identification & Values

Dick Sigafoose

COLLECTOR BOOKS

A Division of Schroeder Publishing Co., Inc.

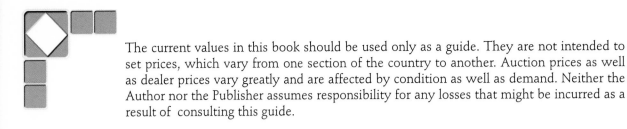

The current values in this book should be used only as a guide. They are not intended to set prices, which vary from one section of the country to another. Auction prices as well as dealer prices vary greatly and are affected by condition as well as demand. Neither the Author nor the Publisher assumes responsibility for any losses that might be incurred as a result of consulting this guide.

Searching For A Publisher?

We are always looking for knowledgeable people considered to be experts within their fields. If you feel that there is a real need for a book on your collectible subject and have a large comprehensive collection, contact Collector Books.

Front cover: (from back left) Hamilton Lion Tile, Rookwood 1922, Roseville Cosmos, Peters & Reed Bowl, Rookwood 1928; background, Weller Dickensware I Jard.

Cover design by Beth Summers
Book design by Terri Stalions

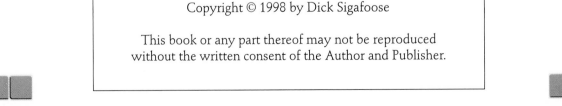

ontents

Introduction

Soon after the end of WW II, when I was 11, I started helping my older brother deliver the Sunday newspaper in the Pleasant Ridge suburb of Cincinnati. We'd rise at about 2:30 a.m. to head for a local automotive shop where we would collate all the sections and inserts on a series of long tables. Jim and I would take turns sitting on the tying machine while the other would roll the bulky package and stick it in the foot operated machine. The contraption was, or appeared to be, a modified bicycle frame. At about 5 o'clock the route man would arrive, and we'd load his sedan to the bottom of the rolled down windows, front and rear. We put the rest in the trunk. Lou, the route man, would drive down the center of the streets while Jim and I, one on each side, would grab two or three papers, jump off the running board and run to each home delivering the paper, and return to the sedan to repeat the process. Many subscribers wanted their paper behind the storm or screen door. We put the rest on stoops or porches. Lou gave Jim $1.50 for this work. Jim gave me the 50¢ for helping.

I usually used some of this money to attend the Saturday matinee at the Monte Vista theater. Sometimes I'd buy a Sunday pass for the streetcars. You could ride anywhere in Cincinnati, all day long, for 35¢. I'd take a couple of Milky Way candy bars to snack on. My favorite trip was to ride through Eden Park to the Art Museum, then down and up the Mount Adams incline railway.

The Rookwood Pottery was at the top of the incline. I'd always think about Cousin Rinny on this trip, because she worked at the pottery. Everybody called her Cousin Rinny, her real name was Lorinda Epply, a Rookwood artist. She was a cousin to my grandmother. I especially remember her at the family Christmas gatherings. She was friendly and cordial, and attracted the children.

Relatives we'd visit had a few pieces of Rookwood sitting around their homes. My parents had several commercial pieces they received as wedding gifts. Giving Rookwood pottery as gifts was a common practice throughout Cincinnati.

My years as a youth have undoubtedly contributed to sustaining my interest in pottery. But it wasn't until 1974 that a purchase of a piece of Roseville aroused my interest in this art form.

4

Collecting pottery and related memorabilia has, from the beginning, been an important part of my interest. There is an abundance of information available through advertising, old articles not referenced by other authors, trade publications, catalogs, and postcards. Many of which are shown or referenced in this book.

Most everything in this book is in my collection, including all references listed in the bibliography, all the articles, ads, and postcards. All the photographs are by the author. All of the ceramics are in my collection, except three shown in the chapter on Cincinnati Art Pottery, along with the Weller Narona jardiniere and Roseville Chloron/Egypto vase, which were at one time in the collection, and the Weller plaque with a maiden, which was never in my collection because I acted too slowly in trying to obtain it. The whereabouts of these six are unknown to me.

My collection represents my interest fairly well. I've sold many objects I wish I still had, but economics, practicality, and changing interests play a role in most collections.

I decided to assemble this book for several reasons. Although the last few years have seen an increasing surge in books on American ceramics, there are still many factories, products, and individuals about which we have little information. I have seen the passing of several very knowledgeable collectors who took with them some valuable information. While contemplating the loss of our mutual interest discussions and companionship, I found myself selfishly regretting I didn't have, couldn't get that lost knowledge. It didn't take long to recognize I too, might take it with me by simply not sharing. I have belonged to several ceramics organizations. Some have failed for the lack of articles submitted for publication. Some have skipped issues, or reduced the frequency of publications because of insufficient participation by the membership. I have also been encouraged to share this collection by several collectors who have seen it. Finally, I felt a need to rectify some misinformation that gets repeated over and over again. My first notes pointed to the sources, thinking this might help to quell the misinformation. This appeared as finger pointing, so I've taken the approach of just supplying the accurate backup data, and letting the readers decide for themselves. However, in a few instances, I felt I had no choice but to identify the source to set the record straight.

Pricing Guide

While visiting with friends, my wife Nancy and I attended our first auction. When I hesitated while bidding on a small Roseville Cosmos vase, my friend said, "You can bid more, the other bidder is a dealer and he won't pay more than half of what it's worth." And so my collection began with my first purchase of art pottery.

Starting a collection without over paying was easy. But assembling a collection of what your changing taste dictates and staying within your budget while maintaining some standards of economic value is difficult. I have, on but very few occasions, paid a price I could not easily justify as a good value. I guess I was giving myself a treat. Why not? Collecting is supposed to be enjoyable.

My friend could have been wrong. Maybe the bidding dealer didn't really know the value of the vase. How do you know the value of your prospective purchase? The system I've trusted for 20 years requires the accumulation of price references.

Price guides offer buyers, sellers, owners, and appraisers a general idea of the value of items from a specific manufacturer or studio. These general price guides are assembled from one or more of several resources. The commonly used resources are the asking prices listed in trade journals, at antique malls, or shops. Others attempt to be more accurate by including some prices realized by dealers or at auctions. There are many books on the market that are, or include, price guides for their subjects of decorative arts, art pottery, American art pottery, or specific American art potteries. All of these resources have some value in assisting with the evaluation of a particular piece of pottery. I

just counted over 90 books on my shelves that fit the categories in this paragraph. About half of these books are on ceramics, the others I use in my general lines antique business. Every one of these books returned my investment within 30 days, without exception. However, there is a better way to evaluate.

The evaluation process for ceramics requires finding items, along with their sold prices, that are very similar to the one you are pricing. Ceramic items are rarely identical. In the case of artist decorated pottery there is never an identical example. Even in a case of two molded Roseville vases, same pattern, shape, size and color, one of a sharp, well defined mold, could be worth twice that of one with poor definition. So the specific challenge is to know what your comparing, and doing it within the largest database you can reference. The more alike the comparable examples are to the one being evaluated, the more accurate the evaluation will be.

Large databases are needed because of the large number of different objects within the ceramics category, and the amount of variables that could be called attributes or degradings when making comparisons. A 7" Weller Hudson vase with a floral should not be used as a comparable piece for evaluating a 12" Hudson scenic. The vast differences of the size or decoration make it nearly impossible because they are so dissimilar. Evaluations for color, artistic execution, artist signature, or condition require some adjustments. Normally, condition would be things like dirt, minor scratches, or maybe stilt pulls on the bottom or a glaze flake. If the condition of either the object in question or one of the comparable pieces includes a hairline or thumbnail size chip or a repair, this evaluation method won't work because the subjects are more different than they are alike.

To qualify as comparable pieces, the items being used to make the evaluation need to be of the same manufacturer, the same line, and nearly the same size. The size also means the decorated area, not just the height. The decoration needs to be similar in subject. Compare portraits to portraits, florals to florals. In a case where the glaze is the most

artistic attribute, as with most Fulper pottery for example, glazes need to be compared to like or similar glazes.

Some variables exist within different types of ceramics. The effect of the condition of tiles on their valuation is different than the effect on most artist-painted vases. A scratch or edge chip on a tile does not have as much overall impact. Collectors have accepted the fact that mint tiles are scarce, probably because by design they were put in harm's way by being subjected to shoes, metal fireplace tools, the weather, and other hazards. A similar judgment has been made by Fulper collectors relative to bottom grinding chips. Frequently, Fulper pottery left the factory with these grinding chips, almost a necessity as a result of obtaining the desired glaze effects. There would be little or no difference in the value between two similar Rookwood vases, one signed by Howard Altman, the other by Virginia Demarest. However, there would be a significant difference if one were signed by Kataro Shirayamadani. Purchasers need to learn the variables within their area of interest that prevent objects from being comparable pieces, and the value of differences between acceptable comparable pieces.

The database! The price guides mentioned are helpful. However, if you're serious about collecting American ceramics, you need to subscribe to at least two of the major auction house or gallery sales catalogs. These catalogs have color photographs, a written description including condition, and the pre-sale estimate of every item for sale. You will also get the post sale results. These catalogs and the information they supply are the ultimate for evaluation because they are written by experienced people, the buyers include dealers and collectors who are the most knowledgeable in the business, and you will get the large, accurate database not available elsewhere.

If, within your database, you find several examples similar to the one being evaluated, add or subtract from the price realized at auction ie; if you believe the example being evaluated to be better than the one sold at auction, add a dollar equivalent and write the number down. Continue this process for each example. Add the total and divide by the number of examples. This figure is the value of the subject. This process is commonly used by antique and real estate appraisers and others.

Most of the catalogs in my collection are from:

Cincinnati Art Galleries
635 Main Street
Cincinnati, Ohio 45202

The Perrault-Rago Gallery
17 South Main Street
Lambertville, N.J. 08530

Treadway Gallery, Inc.
2029 Madison Road
Cincinnati, Ohio 45208

The Perrault-Rago Gallery also has an annual tile sale, and the only tile-exclusive sales catalog of which I'm aware.

Your collection or interests are probably different than mine. You need to determine which catalogs to order. For example, someone who has a major interest in California arts and crafts should identify an auction house whose sales represent those products. That auction house may be one of several on the West Coast.

The values shown in this book are for items in perfect condition, even if the specific item obviously is not. The values were derived from the resources mentioned, in the manner recommended. A guide is just that. Pricing varies over time, and in different parts of the country.

Alhambra Tile Co.

In 1901 the Alhambra Tile Company of Newport, Kentucky, was organized and headed by John F. Sheehy. He had previously been involved in the organization and operation of the Kensington Art Tile Company that failed in 1892.

This time Sheehy was successful in establishing an ongoing business. Production was limited, never expanding beyond four kilns. They manufactured faience and glazed enameled tile. The business continued at least through 1943.

John Sheehy was president of the company as late as 1936, and was succeeded by his son who became the president and treasurer.

(The above information is from the *Bulletin of The American Ceramics Society* of May 1943. Elsewhere in this publication it lists this company as being founded in 1892. Maybe 1901 is an incorporation date.)

The Cincinnati and Northern Kentucky business directory of 1902 – 03 lists "The Alhambra Tile Co., Otto Wolff, President; Phil J. Veith, Vice President; Oscar Reimert, Secretary and Treasurer; J. F. Sheehy, Manager; manufacturers of enameled and embossed tiles, 10th and Monroe."

The 1926 – 27 Covington and Newport city directory lists "The Alhambra Tile Co. Inc., J. F. Sheehy, President and Manager; K. Johnston, Vice President; J. F. Sheehy Jr., Sec. and Tres. Makers of enameled and mat tile, plain and embossed and faience mantels. 10th and Monroe."

The 1942 city directory contains the last listing stating "The Alhambra Tile Co. Inc., John F. Sheehy Jr., Pres.; Mrs. Kathleen S. Johnston, Vice. Pres.; Mrs. Aileen S. Riorden, Sec. and Tres. 16 E 10th."

I have been told by the U.S. Patent and Trademark Office, and the State of Kentucky Trademark Archives that they have no listing for the Alhambra Tile Company, or a record of the "A" trademark shown on these tiles. However, I believe the examples of faience and glazed enameled tiles shown here were manufactured by Alhambra.

In the 1890s the American Encaustic Tile Co. produced a line of tiles named Alhambra. These tiles are usually made of two or three colors, but can be found with as many as five. The pattern name "Alhambra" is marked on the backs of these tiles and they should not be confused with products of the Alhambra Tile Company.

The clay and glaze of these enameled wall, trim, or hearth tiles are similar to that of the many other producers of the period. The in mold marks on the backs are raised, and the same design of that stamped in the faience tile. $4.00 – 6.00 ea.

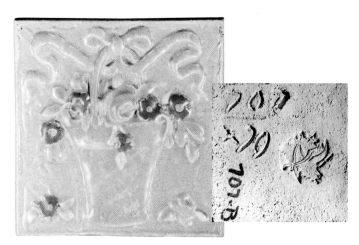

Both the clay and glazes of this 6" square faience tile have the appearance of a product of the Rookwood Pottery, just across the Ohio River from the Alhambra Tile Company. The marks are a die impressed "A" trademark, incised 707 X70, and painted black 707-B. Rare, $300.00 – 500.00.

American Encaustic Tiling Co.

The American Encaustic Tiling Company was founded in Zanesville, Ohio, by Benedict Fischer in 1875, and was incorporated in 1878, with Mr. Fischer as its first president. A.E.T.Co. was the pioneer in the United States in floor and wall tile production.

The plant began small but it grew rapidly. In 1892 an entirely new factory was opened. It was more advanced of any other factory making tile. The old plant was abandoned.

George Stanbury was manager for many years. Herman Mueller, an outstanding modeler and designer in the tile industry, was employed in 1886. Karl Langenbeck was employed as their chemist in 1890. Mr. Langenbeck introduced Parian vitreous bodies. Both Mueller and Langenbeck left in 1893 to participate in the founding of the Mosaic Tile Company.

In 1895 A.E.T.Co. was the first to manufacture white wall tile in the United States.

Mr. Fischer remained as president until his death in 1903, when John Hoge succeeded him.

In 1910, the size of their factory was increased by one third, and they installed the first tunnel kiln in the industry. Mr. Stanbury died and Harry D. Lillibridge succeeded him as manager.

In 1912, A.E.T.Co. purchased the Atlantic Tile and Faience Company of Maurer, New Jersey, and in 1919, the West Coast Tile Company at Vernon, now part of Los Angeles, and placed Frank Philo in charge. Operations under Mr. Philo's management were successful, and the plant expanded to more than double its original size in the next few years.

Mr. Emil Kohler, Mr. Fischer's son-in-law, succeeded Mr. Hoge as president from 1920 to 1924.

On July 29, 1926, the company purchased another factory at Hermosa Beach, California, owned by the Proutyline Products Company. The company continued to operate two plants in this area; the Vernon plant manufacturing ceramics and clay-bodied tile, and the Hermosa plant manufacturing Hermosa tile, which was the talc-body type of tile. Mr. Philo was placed in charge of this operation, as well as the Vernon operation.

In 1930, the American Encaustic Tiling Company with their large Zanesville plant and three branch factories constituted the largest tile industry in the world, and Benedict Fischer's estate was the principal owner. The president at this time was C.E. Diefenthale. The company, during the depression of 1932, got into financial difficulties. About August 1933, they concluded a deal with Gladding, McBean & Company of Glendale, California, to purchase all the West Coast operations.

As their financial position did not improve, they borrowed $500,000 from the Reconstruction Finance Corporation (RFC). This government loan did not get them out of trouble, so in 1936 there was a reorganization with Malcolm A. Schweiker as president and manager of the company. This reorganization only kept them going a little while. The government then stepped in to protect their loan, placing Malcolm A. Schweiker in charge to liquidate the company. He disposed of all of the stock and sold the Zanesville factory to the Shawnee Pottery Company.

Mr. Schweiker, with several others, bought the factory at Maurer, New Jersey. They formed a new company, which they named the American Encaustic Tiling Company, Incorporated.

(The information above is from the *Bulletin of the American Ceramics Society* of May 15, 1943.)

In 1879 A. E. T. Co. became the American Encaustic Tiling Company Limited.

According to the publication, *Zanesville Decorative Tiles,* by E. Stanley Wires, Norris F. Schneider, and Moses Mesre, American Encaustic made their first glazed or enameled tile in 1880. A year later they began to manufacture embossed tile.

There was an industry standard of seventeen 6" square tiles, or the equivalent, for a mantel facing. The seventeen tiles were to be arranged in a six high, seven wide configuration. However, most designs were such that architects, designers, and homeowners could add to, or take away tiles of a set to fit their needs. Shown in the catalog are sets of three 18" x 6" tile panels, or two 18" x 6" vertical side panels with a choice of two different horizontal upper panels. Buyers could choose other tiles to complete their facing, or use the panels alone.

Wild boar head, $125.00 – 175.00.

Shown in a circa 1890 A. E. catalog, this rose decorated 6" square tile is one of a set of seventeen 6" square tiles. The catalog refers to the set as an "Embossed Art Tile Mantel Facing," No.1003 F, and tile #356 B. Two #356 Bs are shown in the complete floral set. $30.00 – 60.00.

This 6" x 18" hunting scene center panel is shown in the catalog as part of a facing with a fox head in the upper left corner and a wild boar head in the upper right. The other 12 tiles shown are a branch and leaf design. Three tile panel, $350.00 – 450.00.

Sometime after single color tiles were introduced, multi-colored mottled glazes appeared. These mottled glazes were not as popular as single colored glazes on mantel facings, but they were very popular as hearth and trim tiles.

Comical or amusing subjects on American tiles are scarce. However, these decorations were popular in England. The 4½" tile character shown here is a companion to another tile of a man with a jester's hat and collar. $125.00 – 175.00 ea. Inset shows back mark.

The backs of this pair of 6" square portrait tiles are signed "A. E. Tile Co. Limited." $300.00 – 350.00 pr.

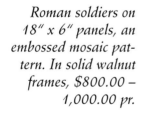

Roman soldiers on 18" x 6" panels, an embossed mosaic pattern. In solid walnut frames, $800.00 – 1,000.00 pr.

These 3″ square relief tiles are a few of many offered in the 1890 catalog. Today, most people refer to "embossed" tiles as relief, low relief, or high relief tiles. $10.00 – 20.00 ea.

Tile #454 is 6″ square It's an example of an embossed tile with mosaic patterns, in the style of earlier encaustic tiles. $30.00 – 60.00 ea.

The 1890 catalog offers this pair of 18″ x 6″ panels with a choice of two different 6″ x 18″ companion center panels to complete a set of three. Buyers could use their own discretion to select tiles to complete the design. These designs are attributed to Herman Mueller. Recently framed, $700.00 – 950.00 pr.

Tiles and panels, individually and in pairs or sets, were purchased by decorators and retailers to be framed for the decoration of homes and offices. Some may have been framed at, or for the pottery. Each of the original frames of these 18" x 6" tile panels is made of 20 machine-carved pieces of solid oak. Finding desirable tiles like these, that have never been installed with cement or plaster, means there is no damage due to being removed from the original installation. These panels are attributed to Herman Mueller. $800.00 – 1,200.00 pr.

These 18" x 6" and 6" x 18" panels are part of a three panel set shown on Plate 31 E of the catalog. Back mark is shown at left. Framed tile, $300.00 – 400.00. Unframed tile, $250.00 – 350.00.

E.A. Barber said of American Encaustic, "Some of the most artistic productions of this factory are the eight, ten, and fifteen tile facings, with raised designs of classic female and child figures."

Mr. Barber describes the intaglio process, "By a peculiar treatment, pictures and portraits are also reproduced on a plain surface. This consists in modeling on a smooth surface of clay in intaglio and filling the carved portions with a colored glaze, the shadows being regulated by the depth of the carving, the high lights being raised to near the level of the tile. The relative thickness of the glaze produces the corresponding depth of tint, and the effect is that of a photograph or flat picture instead of a design in relief. In this manner ideal heads and faithful portraits have been successfully executed."

Complete sets similar to this are rare. A set in excellent condition is very rare. This 12" x 30" multi-tile panel is one of two Barber chose to show in his book in support of his statement. He said this design was done by Herman Mueller. $2,000.00 – 2,500.00 set.

Relief tiles that were hand painted in colored glazes are another variation to the original one-color treatment. These six-color tiles are 18" x 6". Framed, $750.00 – 1,000.00 pr.

 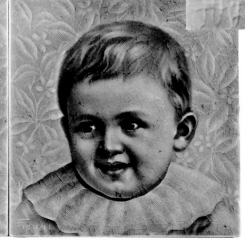

The 1890 catalog, plate 49 E, shows only these four intaglio tiles along with two plain and six small embossed trim tiles. The child portraits and mill scene are each 6" square and signed by the unknown artist Frenzel. The tile with a stag is 4¼"square. Child portraits, $500.00 – 600.00 pr. Mill scene, $275.00 – 325.00. Mill scene framed, $300.00 – 375.00. Stag, $125.00 – 175.00.

Anthony and Cleopatra were offered as 18" x 6" companion tiles. Anthony, $300.00 – 400.00 if perfect.

This 6" x 12" Lioness tile has a companion tile showing a lion facing the opposite direction. Inset shows back mark. $300.00 – 350.00.

The same Lioness tile was used as part of this fireplace or mantel facing. Since an equivalent of only sixteen 6" square tiles were needed, this facing set probably would not have appeared as such in any A.E. catalog. This set was either chosen by the customer or recommended by the dealer or a decorator. The practice of mixing and matching tiles was not uncommon. Some original installations have tiles of two or more manufacturers. The complete mantel facing set, $1,000.00 – 1,250.00.

Tiles with musical subjects were popular in the 1880s and '90s. The 18" x 6" companion tile to the one shown here is of a somewhat shy maiden. Framed, $300.00 – 400.00.

The Parrot and Peacock pair is another example of several colored glazes painted on relief tiles. The tiles measure 12" x 6". If perfect, $450.00 – 600.00 pr.

Herman Mueller designed these 4¼" square tiles to commemorate the opening of A.E.s large new production facility in Zanesville, Ohio. $150.00 – 200.00 ea.

Shown in Barber's 1893 publication, but not in the 1890 factory catalog, indicates this 6" x 18" tile with swallows decoration was probably modeled in the 1890 to 1892 period. Framed, $300.00 – 350.00.

This 3″ diameter stove tile with the portrait of a girl is signed "A.E.TILE Co.Limited" around the perimeter of the concave portion of the back. Framed, $100.00 – 150.00.

Also unsigned and shown in the same publication mentioned below, this 4¼″ x 7¼″ stove tile is decorated with a youthful warrior and his companion bear. The 4″ diameter tile of the same decoration and glaze is mounted in its original metal picture-type frame. The round stove tile is signed "A.E.T.Co. Limited" in a straight line on the back. Rectangular tile, $175.00 – 225.00. Framed circular stove tile, $175.00 – 250.00.

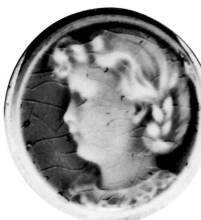

These 2¼″ diameter stove tiles with female portraits are unsigned, but the right facing portrait is identified in Zanesville Art Tile in Color by Evan and Louise Purviance. $100.00 – 150.00 pr.

17

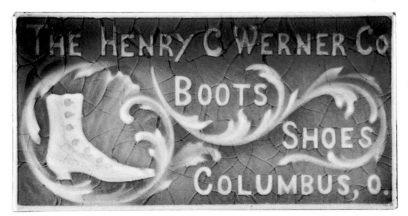

Advertising paperweight calendar tiles were sold for several years around the turn of the century. The Boots & Shoes example is not a calendar, but has more advertising on the applied paper back and edges, along with an 1896 date. The hi-gloss blue AE ad tile has a paper calendar for 1911 on its back. Most of these advertising pieces measure 2⅛" x 4¼" and have high-gloss glazes. However, the green A.E. ad tile is unusual because of its mat glaze. There is a handwritten date of 1910 on the back in red pencil. $125.00 – 175.00 ea.

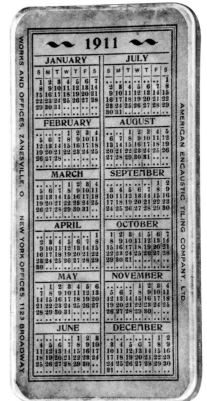

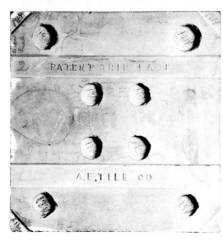

Portrait tiles were made for the presidential campaigns of 1896. All four of the presidential and vice-presidential candidates were featured on 3″ square intaglio tiles with blue glazes. The tiles came with either applied paper backs with printed biographical sketches, or the in mold mark of the A.E.T.Co. as shown here. A.E. also made 6″ square political portraits that were transfers on gloss white backgrounds. Intaglio tiles, $125.00 – 175.00 ea. Transfer printed political tiles, $100.00 – 150.00 ea.

Wedgwood-style oval medallions measuring 3″ x 2″ were produced by A.E. The low relief decorations are of classical subjects. Background colors were in blue, green, or terra cotta. The backs have a hand-incised trademark and date. The medallion shown here is dated 1914. A similar example is shown in Zanesville Art Tile in color, with the full length decoration of a classical woman, and is dated 1913. Scarce to rare, $150.00 – 200.00.

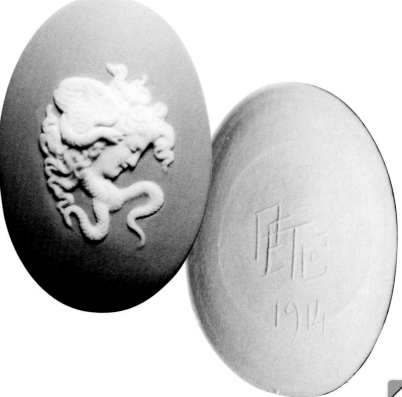

In 1897 Mr. D.W. Caldwell, president of several railroads and an intimate personal friend of Mr. John Hoge, a director of A.E., died. To commemorate his death Mr. Hoge commissioned Mr. Christian Nielson, who replaced Herman Mueller as modeler and designer in 1894, to make a portrait tile of Mr. Caldwell to be presented to friends and associates. The 9" x 7" tiles had the biography and dedication printed on paper applied to the backs. The initials CN appear next to the left shoulder of the portrait. The closest friends of Mr. Caldwell must have received framed examples with the biography signed in ink by Mr. Hoge, and protected by a glass window. Although this is the only framed example of which I'm aware. Framed and with Hoge's signature, $500.00 – 650.00. Others with attached biography, $400.00 – 500.00.

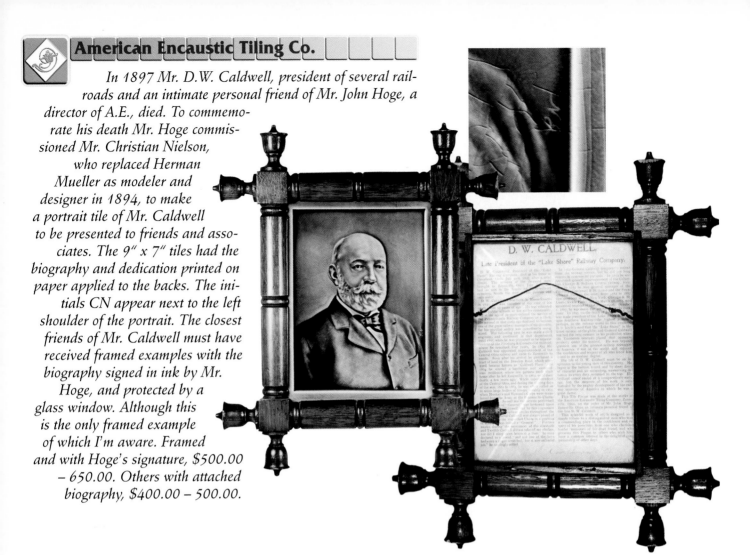

Throughout nearly all of A.E.'s manufacturing existence they offered undecorated tiles for sale. Many of these tiles were utilized by the very large number of amateur decorators 20 years prior to, and long after the turn of the century. These tiles appear in today's market and sometimes, when decorated by a skilled amateur, are difficult to distinguish from factory or professionally painted examples. The amateur decorated tile shown here is a Valentine, commemorating 50 years in 1899. $15.00 – 25.00.

The arts & crafts tile decorated with a peacock and the Art Deco tile of a stag are both 6" square and have the circular mark shown on the commemorative discs. The mark on the buff-colored faience peacock tile was hand stamped with a die. The mark on the white faience stag tile was hand incised. The peacock decoration has an unusual combination of mat luster and iridescent gloss glazes. The unusual peacock tile, $300.00 – 400.00. The black and silver stag tile, $200.00 – 250.00.

A variety of 2" diameter commemorative discs were produced for fraternal groups and other organizations. The discs were worn around the neck on ribbon or string. The A.E. mark used on these discs was introduced sometime after the turn of the century and was used extensively on faience, usually die impressed by hand. $75.00 – 100.00 ea.

A.E. produced a wide variety ceramic items that included statues, paperweights, candlesticks, lamps, vases, plaques etc. Advertising ashtray, $30.00 – 50.00

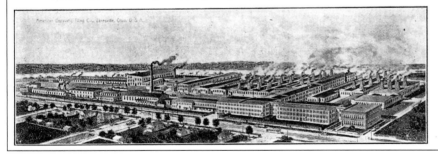

ZANESVILLE, OHIO.—Only Concrete Y Bridge and Largest Tile Works in the World.

Postcard

American Encaustic Tiling Co., Zanesville, Ohio.

Postcard, 1909.

The above illustration of a wainscote frieze
shows the use of insert tiles.

Faience Department

American Encaustic Tiling Co.

16 East 40th Street, New York

Zanesville, O.   Maurer, N. J.

Sept. 1915.

AMERICAN ENCAUSTIC TILING COMPANY,

[LIMITED.]

Patentees and Manufacturers of

Artistic Embossed, Glazed, Inlaid, Enamelled and
Decorated

—Tiles—

for Floors, Walls, Fire-places, Cabinet Work, Architectural Enrichment and general Internal and Exter-
nal Decorative purposes.

Designs and estimates upon application.

SHOWROOMS, 116 West 23d Street, N. Y.
WORKS, Zanesville, Ohio.

Art Amateur, January 1888.

Art Amateur,
January – March 1884.

The
American
Encaustic Tile,

SPACIOUS SHOWROOMS, { **116 WEST 23d STREET,** near Sixth Avenue, } NEW YORK.

(WORKS, ZANESVILLE, OHIO.)

ACKNOWLEDGED BY EXPERTS TO BE THE
BEST IN THE WORLD.

Artistic Embossed, Glazed, and Enamelled Tiles,
For Mantels, Hearths, Wainscoting, Bath-Rooms,
Furniture, and Stove Decorations. Also,

PLAIN TILES FOR AMATEUR DECORATION.

DESIGNS FREE UPON APPLICATION TO

The American Encaustic Tiling Company.

B. FISCHER, President.   GEO. R. LANSING, Treasurer.   WM. G. FLAMMER, Secretary.

AMERICAN ENCAUSTIC TILING CO. LIMITED

PATENTEES & MANUFACTURERS OF

PLAIN, GLAZED, ENAMELED AND RELIEF TILES.

WORKS,
ZANESVILLE, OHIO.
GEO. A. STANBERY,
General Supt.

OFFICE & WAREROOMS,
140 WEST 23RD STREET,
NEW YORK.

Zanesville, O. Dec 3 1890

*Company
letterhead.*

Malcolm and Roy Schweiker decided to go into the tile-making business in 1923. Both men were in the building trade, and on several occasions they had found ceramic tile difficult to obtain. As graduates of the Williamson School in Medina, Pennsylvania, an eminent trade school of the day where young men came to class in starched collars and ties, the Schweikers were familiar with ceramic products and their manufacture and saw no reason why they couldn't make ceramic tile as well as anyone else. There was an obvious market for tile. The economics of it looked fine. And they had some savings and a modest borrowing capacity. In October 1923, they bought an abandon cannery building in Lansdale, Pennsylvania, cleaned up some left-over apple butter, and started what was quickly to become known throughout the local building fraternity as a reliable little place to get quality tile, the Franklin Tile Company.

When Franklin Tile was founded, the capital investment was $55,000 and the total number of personnel, from top to bottom, was eight. It was a shirt-sleeve operation, with Malcolm personally designing the kiln and other equipment and managing the business end of things. Roy was primarily responsible for production and the marketing of the company's products.

It was a successful melding of talents, and within four years the company's capitalization had increased to $1,500,000 and employment to 350. This growth necessitated an addition to the original cannery building, an addition which was soon outgrown. This was followed by a new plant built with a very special capability on a 30-acre site on the outskirts of Lansdale.

It took about five days to produce tile under the original two-fire system, requiring repeated handling and high manufacturing costs. The new one-fire system, developed through their research, would reduce production time to two days and decrease costs dramatically.

In 1934, representatives of the U.S. Reconstruction Finance Corporation asked Malcolm Schweiker to assume the presidency and management of the American Encaustic Tiling Company, the country's oldest and largest tile manufacturing company with five plants, a full range of ceramic products, and a universally good reputation as a quality manufacturer. American Encaustic had not been able to cope with the Depression, now in its fifth year, and the company was perilously close to going out of business completely. Malcolm agreed, and in 1935 American Encaustic was reorganized and funded by a new stock issue and by the continuance of a $600,000 loan granted by the Reconstruction Finance Corporation. Roy then became president of Franklin and Malcolm remained as a director.

One of the first steps taken was to sell the American Encaustic plants that were closed and not operating. The only active plant was in Perth Amboy, New Jersey. The operations and methods used at Franklin Tile were employed at the Perth Amboy plant, and by 1941 American Encaustic had not only survived the rest of the Depression, but was a profitable operation and becoming a growing factor in the tile industry.

Then came the war. Having nowhere near the war production capabilities of the Franklin plant in Lansdale, American Encaustic's Perth Amboy facilities were leased to a war materials producer, tile-making equipment was removed, and American Encaustic was, in fact, no more than a name.

But there was a great deal in that name. For one thing, American Encaustic's capital stock was widely distributed and it was listed on the New York Stock Exchange. This was a desirable situation, and when the managements of Franklin and American Encaustic foresaw a favorable conclusion to the war, they decided to combine the assets of the two companies. Manufacturing was concentrated at Lansdale, the Perth Amboy plant was sold, and by 1948 "American Encaustic Tiling Company, Inc.," was adopted as the new firm's name.

All of this is said easily, but you can be sure it was not an easy decision for the Schweikers to make. Tile made by the Franklin Tile Company was the number one choice of architects and tile-setters — a recognized position that should not be endangered. Franklin's customers preferred the retention of the Franklin name, so did the company's hundreds of employees.

These were good reasons to keep the Franklin name. But American Encaustic, as mentioned earlier, also had *a fine reputation. Furthermore customers were appraised immediately of the merger, and, in some ways, the two-fold reputation of the companies was an advantage. Most important in the final decision was that management could not logically sacrifice the business advantages to be gained by a listing on the New York Stock Exchange. The balance was tipped, very decidedly, in favor of adopting the name of American Encaustic Tiling Company, Inc.*

Since the early thirties, the company's products have been marketed through a separate sales company jointly owned by Franklin Tile and the Olean Tile Company in Olean, New York. Olean produced unglazed ceramic mosaic tiles for floors, a natural compliment to the glazed wall tiles produced by Franklin. The products were not competitive, but were largely sold to the same customer, and management of both companies had seen the wisdom in combining sales efforts. Formerly named American-Franklin-Olean Tiles, Inc., the name of the sales organization was now changed to American Olean Tile Company. The products of both companies were sold under that name — and every facet of its operation was re-examined. Sales and distribution centers reached from coast to coast, but because

of prohibitive shipping costs American Encaustics products were not sold west of the Rocky Mountains. This did not change until 1966, but new distribution outlets were added or updated throughout the rest of the country, and advertising and sales efforts were coordinated to thoroughly penetrate into every corner of what management carefully determined to be American Encaustic's viable market.

In 1958 American Encaustic merged with the National Gypsum Company. The Olean Tile Company, manufacturers of ceramic mosaics, and the Murray Tile Company, manufacturers of quarry tile, were acquired in 1959. This combined merger gave National Gypsum's ceramic tile division a complete line of ceramic tile products, together with mining facilities and distribution and sales systems.

In 1964 the name of the division was changed to American Olean Tile Company, Inc.

(The information above is from the book, *Notes on a 50-Year Revolution*, by Frederic Bell, a profile of the company whose innovations brought ceramic tile into the twentieth century.)

The Olean Tile Company was incorporated in 1913 by O.W. Pierce, Charles T. Fuller, and Gordon D. Phillips. Franklin Tile was founded as the Franklin Pottery Company. The name change occurred during or after 1928. Franklin Tile absorbed the Domex Floor and Wall Tile Co. of Greenburg, Pennsylvania.

Armstrong World Industries purchased American Olean in 1989. On January 4, 1996, Dal-Tile International Inc. of Dallas, Texas, acquired the American Olean Tile Company creating the world's largest manufacturer and distributor of ceramic tile.

This group of Franklin tiles are typical of the company's decorated designs. Several shown appear in the company's 1936 catalog. The 4¼" sq. tiles have raised lines with "painted in" colored glazes. The backs are all marked with the factory name in small raised letters. $20.00 – 30.00 ea.

Ben Franklin in relief decorates this 5¼" tall oval advertising paperweight. Franklin within an oval was the company trademark. The paperweight is signed on the back, "Franklin Pottery, Lansdale, Pa." $50.00 – 75.00 ea.

The bowl of jonquils decoration on this 8½" square tile is also a raised line design. This tile is signed with a black ink stamp, "Compliments of American Encaustic Tiling Company, Lansdale, Pennsylvania." $250.00 – 300.00.

COMPLIMENTS OF
**AMERICAN ENCAUSTIC
TILING COMPANY**
LANSDALE, PENNSYLVANIA

In addition to the regular lines of floor and wall tiles, American Olean also made complimentary tiles commemorating historical places or events. The 6" tiles were supplied in gift boxes that sometimes included a booklet of the subject on the tile. $20.00 – 30.00 ea., with box.

FRANKLIN FAIENCE

DECORATIVE PANELS
CONTINUED

512- LILY POND PANEL

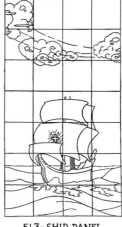

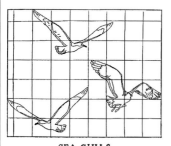

SEA GULLS

510-LEFT FLIGHT   509-RT. FL'T.   508-LANDING FLIGHT

513-SHIP PANEL

507-FISH

368 -DUTCH PANEL

ABOVE DESIGNS, EXCEPT 368, CAN BE MADE ON FAIENCE OR DUST-PRESS

In a two-page ad in the souvenir book for the 25th annual convention of the Tile & Mantel Contractors Association of America held in St. Petersburg, Florida, in February 1928, the Franklin Pottery listed their products, which included frost-proof Franklin Flints, bathroom accessories, lighting fixtures, and faience tiles. Some of the faience tiles are signed Franklin Pottery Faience.

Two pages from a 1936 Franklin Tile Co. catalog.

FRANKLIN FAIENCE

INSERTS
8⅞″x 8⅞″ & 8⅞″x13½″

INCISED SILHOUETTES -DECORATIVE PLAQUES

NO. 105 CAN BE MADE WITH SPOUT FOR FOUNTAIN

 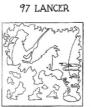 

97 LANCER

98 PEGASUS

102 BOY FISHING

107 MOOSE & GEESE

106 INDIAN

96 POINTER

104 VIKING SHIP

150 LIGHT HOUSE

100 LANTERN BOY

103 SHIP

401 SPANISH

99 PARROT

101 SWAN

105 DOLPHIN

American Terra Cotta & Ceramic Co.

William D. Gates, a lawyer, founded the Spring Valley Tile Works about 1880. In 1885 Gates renamed the business the Terra Cotta Tile Works. The establishment was located in Terra Cotta, Illinois. Gates also had an office on Washington Street in Chicago. He manufactured architectural terra cotta, statuary, vases, building and ornamental tile, pressed and enameled brick, and drain tile. In 1886 he gave up his law practice to devote all his energy to producing terra cotta. A fire partially destroyed the facility in 1887, but Gates rebuilt and incorporated as the American Terra Cotta and Ceramic Company.

The Teco line of art pottery was put into production in 1900 after several years of experimentation by Elmer T. Gorton, with the assistance of two of Gates's sons, William and Ellis. The senior Gates designed many of the shapes. The products of the first 10 years were covered with a mat green glaze which has a silver gray cast. Although other colored glazes had been developed, they were not offered until 1910.

In the publication, *Teco-Art Pottery of the Prairie School,* Sharon S. Darling writes:

During the winter of 1899 – 1900 Teco evolved into three distinct types of pottery, each with a different glaze and clay body. Gates and his chemists concentrated on developing glazes compatible with various clays suitable for firing in the kilns alongside architectural terra cotta. First they used clays in subdued red tones, then in browns, then in buffs. They even developed an experimental high fire porcelain body. A demand for terra cotta with mottled or marbled surfaces led to their trying to obtain similar glaze effects on pottery. Merely by chance one vase emerged with an attractive metallic luster. Efforts to duplicate the odd combination of conditions that had created the shiny surface eventually resulted in the production of a brown glaze speckled with tiny flecks of gold. Applied to small vases with delicate bodies made of porcelain clay, the glossy metallic glaze yielded handsome effects that flowed from deep brown to gold.

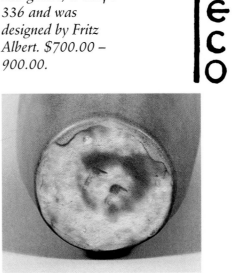

This 8" vase, with one of Teco's green mat glazes, is shape 336 and was designed by Fritz Albert. $700.00 – 900.00.

Sample tiles and advertising paper-weights were made with a wide variety of solid color, mottled, and marbleized glazes of a mat finish. These sample tiles and paperweight measure 3" x 5" and are 1" thick. $50.00 – 75.00 ea. for sample tiles. $150.00 – 200.00 for the frog decorated paperweight.

This belleek 4" tall ewer has a brown high gloss glaze with flecks of gold. The ewer, the tiles, and paper-weight shown here are examples of the products referred to by Sharon Darling. $300.00 – 400.00 for the ewer.

Two other tile collectors who have tiles of the same dimen-sions, clay, glaze, and hand-relieved back, and I believe this tile and those in their collec-tions to be part of a series of six or more tiles, each depicting a boy with a different animal, in low relief. Although all are unsigned, we attribute them to American Terra Cotta. $300.00 – 500.00 framed.

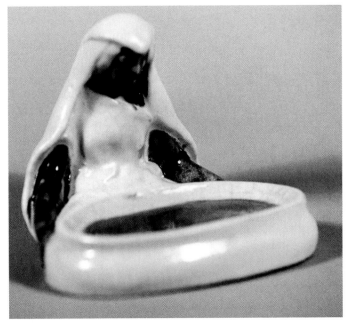

A Don Treadway auction catalog of Arts & Crafts in Chicago, *March 27, 1988, item 25, identifies this rare unsigned pin tray as a product of American Terra Cotta. $200.00 – 300.00*

Art Lovers should send
for Book about

Teco
Pottery

The newest developments in ceramics. Its chasteness of design, new and unique glaze, velvety glossness of finish and soft, moss-green crystalline color, celebrated for its delicate shadings, and the richness of its tones appeal to the lover of the beautiful, and have won for it an enviable place among the world's art wares.

For Christmas

weddings, anniversaries, birthdays, etc., Teco Pottery is the ideal gift.

Sold by all leading dealers

Book sent anywhere upon request.

THE GATES POTTERIES

635 Chamber of Commerce, - - CHICAGO.

Art Lovers should send for Book about

TECO POTTERY

The newest developments in ceramics. Its chasteness of design, new and unique glaze, velvety glossness of finish, and soft, moss-green crystalline color, celebrated for its delicate shadings and the richness of its tones, appeal to the lover of the beautiful and have won for it an enviable place among the world's art wares.

For Christmas

weddings, anniversaries, birthdays, etc., Teco Pottery is the ideal gift.

Sold by all leading dealers

Book sent anywhere upon request.

THE GATES POTTERIES

602 Chamber of Commerce, Chicago

Harper's Magazine, November 1904.

McClure's, *November 1904.*

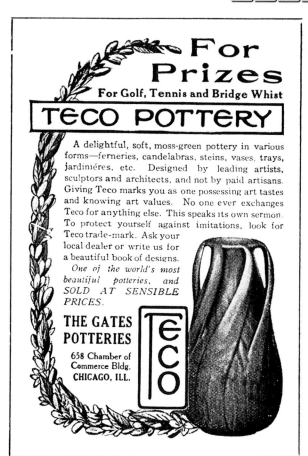
Fine Art Journal,
1909.

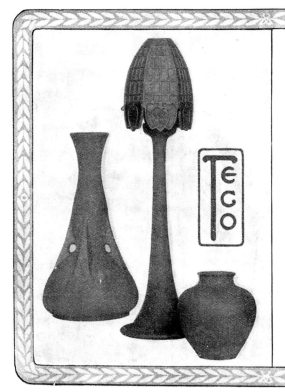
Scribner's, *December 1905.*

177. By F. Albert. Daring Iris Theme. 22 inches in height: **$25.00**

283. By F. Albert. Pompeian; 9 inches high: **$5.00**

269. By W. B. Mundie. Of height 11 inches: **$8.00**

271. By W. B. Mundie. Diameter, 10 inches: **$10.00**

265. By Max Dunning. For Mission interior. 12 inches high: **$12.00**

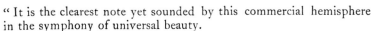

TECO POTTERY

is the most serious contribution that America has yet made to the eternal art of the world.

" It is the clearest note yet sounded by this commercial hemisphere in the symphony of universal beauty.

"It is the most vigorous, and will prove to be one of the most reverberating, of the syllables in which America has sought to give utterance to her immature national æstheticism.

"Teco is really the harmonic and intelligible voice of America at her best—a divine melody of curve and color.

"We are privileged among many generations; we have been at the birth of a new and everlasting classic."

THUS WRITES A TECO ENTHUSIAST.

COLOR:
TECO GREEN is a tone not easily classified by colorists, and is far too elusive for description. Cool, peaceful, healthful, it is a happy and unobtrusive color to live with.

TEXTURE:
The surface of TECO is equally difficult to indicate in words. It has no gloss, is not rough, nor yet solidly smooth. It is itself.

DESIGNS:
The TECO contours, so famous for purity of line, are not the work of dependent artisans nor of employed designers. The great things in art are never done for money, and many of the finest of the TECO conceptions have slipped from some celebrated pencil almost by accident, it seemed. New shapes are constantly being added and each piece bears its designer's name.

TECO is the Gift among Gifts

in every case where inherent beauty and merit may expect to receive intelligent appreciation. Purchase TECO in your own city if possible. Personal examination will be an added pleasure and immediate possession may be desirable. TECO is sold in

New York City: Burns-Mills Co., 36 E. Twenty-first St.
Philadelphia: J. E. Caldwell & Co., 902 Chestnut St.
Washington, D. C.: Dulin & Martin Co., 1215 F St.
Pittsburgh: Hamilton & Clark Co., 416 Penn Ave.
Buffalo: George W. Benson, 656 Main St.
Cincinnati: Hamilton & Clark Co., 126 Fourth St.
St. Paul: Wm. A. French Co., Sixth and Cedar Sts.
Minneapolis: John W. Thomas & Co., 500 Nicollet St.
Los Angeles: Barker Bros., 420 S. Spring St.
New Orleans: John Gauches Sons, 827 Canal St.
Louisville: The Arts and Crafts Co., 658 Fourth Ave.
Atlanta: Davis & Freeman, 47 Whitehall St.
Indianapolis: Arts and Crafts Society, 21 E. Ohio St.
Montreal: Paul Beau & Co., St. Catherine St.
Berlin, Germany: Friedman & Weber, Koniggratzer Strasse, 9.

St. Petersburg, Russia: Alexandre Nevsky, No. 11.
Chicago: Marshall Field & Co.
Brooklyn: Abraham & Straus.
San Francisco: Shreve & Co.
Denver: Daniels & Fisher.
Newport: Herman's Jewelry Store, Thames St.
St. Louis: Scruggs, Vandevoort & Barney.
Baltimore: The Gifts Shop, Walbert Hotel.
Cleveland: C. A. Selzer, Euclid Ave. and Erie St.
Seattle: C. W. Parker & Co., 714 First Ave.
Omaha: H. P. Whitmore, 1517 Dodge St.
Mobile: Julius Goldstein, 5 So. Royal St.
Nashville: K. P. Wright, Belmont Place.
Quebec: Quebec News Co., 27 Buade St.
Hamburg, Germany: M. Herz, Neuerwall, 5.
And by the best store in each of about 500 other cities.

TECO may also be ordered by mail. to be shipped direct from the Potteries

The new TECO PORTFOLIO, de luxe, very simple yet very costly, and showing nearly one hundred pieces, will be forwarded upon proper application to

The GATES POTTERIES, 645 Chamber of Commerce, Chicago.

WHY NOT MAKE IT

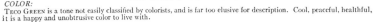

A TECO CHRISTMAS

297. By N. Forester. Hellenic vase; a favorite. 5 inches in height: **$6.00**

250. By William D. Gates. Lamp base; simplicity idealized. Of height 10 inches: **$5.00**

134. By F. Albert. Lilies in low relief. 13 inches in height: **$8.00**

252. By H. M. G. Garden. Vase or lamp base; slight tracery; 12 inches high: **$8.00**

336. By F. Albert. For white daisies or golden-rod. 8 inches in height: **$4.00**

G.500. By William D. Gates. Mission Loving Cup or lamp base. Of height 9 inches: **$10.00**

348. By F. Albert. Punch Bowl; unusually ornate Teco piece. Heavy white glaze within; diam. 14 in.: **$20.00**

355 By W. D. Gates. For the Master's cigars. 4 inches high: **$4.00**

287. By W. B. Mundie. Vase or lamp base. 7 in. high: **$5.00**; 13 in., **$20.00**

Sketchbook, *June 1906.*

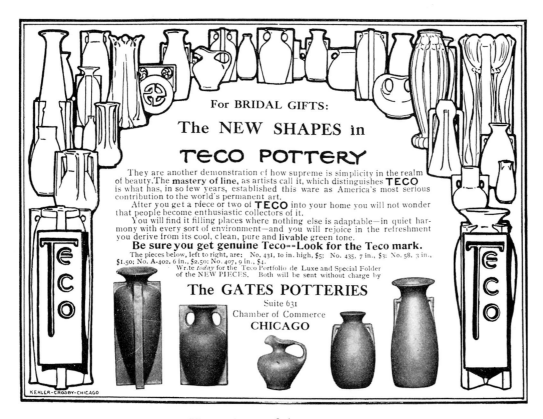
House Beautiful, *June 1907.*

Refinement is Most Clearly Shown in the Home

Large, gaudy vases and highly colored pictures look cheap and commonplace, when compared with the quiet, restful pottery and harmonious surrounding of the truly refined home.

One small Teco vase, costing perhaps but a dollar, will do more to give that touch of elegance and artistic refinement to the home than any other one thing.

TECO POTTERY

is distinctive for its crystalline, moss green color, its grace of form and the beauty of its glaze. It is beautiful, restful, artistic, refined.

Two Gold Medals, St. Louis, 1904

The great variety of designs in lamps, vases, wallpockets, candlesticks, fern dishes, flower holders, punch bowls, cigar jars, trays, etc., etc., gives a range for selection rarely found in pottery, yet each is a work of art that will give greater charm to any home.

A gift that will be in constant use and bear witness of good taste in the giver.

Send for "What to Give"

An interesting book which illustrates and describes scores of Teco designs suitable for gifts or use in your own home.

The Best Dealers Sell Teco

but if your dealer does not, send us his name and we will tell you the name of a dealer who does.

Look for **T**e**co** *on every*
this mark **co** *piece.*

The Gates Potteries

637 Chamber of Com., Chicago, Ill. U. S. A.

House Beautiful, *July 1910.*

It is GOOD NEWS that

TECO POTTERY

is now produced in *YELLOWS, BROWNS, BLUES* and *GRAYS*, all in the soft tones which have made the TECO green so distinctive. Look for the TECO trademark.

TECO—so soft and velvety in finish—is in various forms: ferneries, candlesticks, vases, etc., and is designed by leading artists and architects whose services are not for hire.

Ideal to give to others—and

— why not give yourself a piece?

Ask your leading art dealer or write for book of designs.

THE GATES POTTERIES

631 Chamber of Commerce Chicago

Harper's, *1906.*

Country Life in America,
November, 1910.

No. 375—10in. high—$4   No. 377—13in. high—$10
NEW SHAPES as well as *NEW COLORS*
Everybody who ever gives anybody
anything—or who cares for *home*—is
glad to learn of the *NEW THINGS* in
TECO POTTERY
It is now made in *Browns, Blues, Yellows* and
Greys, as well as the classic "*Teco Green.*"
Ask your art dealer or *write* for *NEW TECO BOOK*
The GATES POTTERIES 634 Chamber of Commerce, Chicago

Tints of Color Hold the Future of Architecture

Our material furnishes them in acceptable,
lasting and cleanly form

Architectural Forum,
March 1923.

Wm D Gates **Pres.**

American Terra Cotta and Ceramic Co.
Chicago, Ill.

35

Associated Tile Manufacturers

This association had its inception at a meeting in Cresson Springs, Pennsylvania, in 1893, that was called to discuss the tariff situation then confronting the industry. The organization was then formed and held its first meeting in October 1893, at Pittsburgh, Pennsylvania.

Francis W. Walker was elected secretary. The association has no record of which companies were the charter members or who the first president was, but I believe that the Star Encaustic Tiling Company, United States Encaustic Tiling Company, American Encaustic Tiling Company, Beaver Falls Art Tile Company, Columbia Encaustic Tile Company, Cambridge Tile Manufacturing Company, Robertson Art Tile Company, Grueby Faience and Tile Company, and the Providential Tile Company were the original members. I think that Mr. Fischer of the American Encaustic Tiling Company was the first president. After his death in 1903 Emil Kohler was president. (In fact, Mr. Kohler may have been the first president.)

For a number of years, the interest of the association was in matters mainly relating to the tariff.

Beginning with 1905, the activities of the association broadened out materially. Many things were undertaken then that later proved beneficial, and in a large measure the association pioneered much of the work now accepted as standard practice by other more powerful associations. Matters of credit, protection, sales promotion, joint advertising, and apprentice training were each, in turn, undertaken collectively. In all it was a service appreciated by those directly intended, as well as by those in the trade it sought to serve.

During the early years of white wall-tile manufacturing, companies making this line were vying with each other to see who could put on the market the handsomest line of caps, borders, and bases, made in many sizes, heavily embossed, and with beautiful decorations.

These lines were costly to produce, so the association appointed a committee of three to meet at Beaver Falls, Pennsylvania, to weed out as many designs as possible and establish standard patterns to which each factory could adhere. Members of the committee were Francis W. Walker, chairman, and secretary of the association; Harry D. Lillibridge, the American Encaustic Tiling Company; and Everett Townsend, the Robertson Art Tile Company.

Each factory sent a full line of samples to Beaver Falls, and worked two weeks to straighten out this problem.

Mr. Walker resigned on December 17, 1927, to give his undivided attention to his new company, the Rossman Corporation.

The office of the association, which had been at Beaver Falls, was then moved to New York, and its present address is 50 East 42nd Street, K. Maloney, Secretary.

The above information was provided by Mr. Everett Townsend and others in the May 1943 issue of *The Bulletin of the American Ceramic Society — Ceramic History*

In a booklet, *Beautiful Association Tiles,* ca. 1925, the association members are listed as Alhambra Tile Co., American Encaustic Tiling Co., Beaver Falls Art Tile Co., Cambridge Tile Manufacturing Co., Grueby Faience and Tile Co., Matawan Tile Co., Mosaic Tile Co., National Tile Co., Olean Tile Co., Old Bridge Enameled Brick and Tile Co., Perth Amboy Tile Works, The C. Pardee Works, United States Encaustic Tile Works, and the Wheeling Tile Co.

The advertising booklet states "The outstanding purpose of the Associated Tile Manufacturers is to insure satisfaction to the users of tiles. The headquarters at Beaver Falls, Pennsylvania, is a clearing house for all kinds of information on tiles, their proper use and methods of application.

It is the desire and aim of this organization to assist home builders, architects, and all others interested in using tiles to have tilework that is artistic and beautiful, to select tiles of the right variety for the use intended, and above all, to satisfy the individual requirements of the owner. Every question pertaining to tiles in any way will be promptly and gladly answered."

Advertising in magazines and trade catalogs indicates changes in membership. In the association's ad in the 1915 Sweets catalog, the Atlantic Tile Manufacturing Co., Brooklyn Vitrified Tile Works, and Robertson Art Tile Co. were added as members. The

This is the Cover of a Book

intended for the owner of a home already built or now building, to prove that the use of tile in a bathroom is not only attractive but also necessary. Tile is the sanitary and inexpensive covering for the walls and floor of the bathroom. This book "Tile for the Bathroom," will be sent free.

Also these other books if you are interested: "Tiles on the Porch Floor," "Tiles for Fireplaces," "Tiles for the Kitchen and Laundry."

THE ASSOCIATED TILE MANUFACTURERS,   Room 4, Reeves Bldg.,   BEAVER FALLS, PA.

Good Housekeeping,
August 1910.

If you do not use Tiles for the floor and walls of your bathroom you will regret it and finally you will come to it. No other treatment is so clean and so cleanable, so artistic and so durable.

Tiles are the most inexpensive treatment in the long run, and no other is so sanitary.

We have four books on the use of Tiles, all handsomely done and very informing. They are free to home owners, present or prospective. Write for those which interest you:

"Tile for the Bathroom"
"Tiles on the Porch Floor"
"Tiles for the Kitchen and Laundry"
"Tiles for Fireplaces"

The Associated Tile Manufacturers
Room 4, Reeves Building, Beaver Falls, Pa.

Good Housekeeping, October 1910.

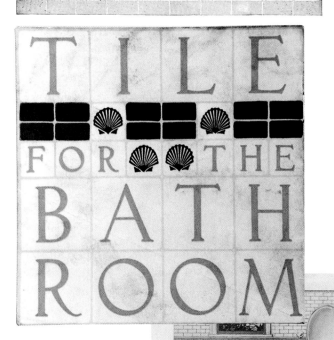

Associated Tile Manufacturers booklet.

TILE FOR THE BATHROOM

THE use of tile for the floor and walls of a bathroom should be considered by everyone who is building a home or who expects to make alterations in his present home.

There are few things which add so much to the real usefulness as well as to the appearance of a bathroom as a tiled floor and walls.

The white porcelain tubs and lavatories of the modern bathroom are now everywhere. Tiled floors and walls are not so common.

[1]

Tiles & their uses

There are a number of places in that new home you are planning where tiles can be used to better advantage than any other material. There are at least four places where tiles are essential: the fireplace, the porch floor, the bathroom floor and walls and the walls and floors of the kitchen and laundry.

We have prepared four booklets:

  "Tiles for Fireplaces"
  "Tiles on the Porch Floor"
  "Tile for the Bathroom"
  "Tiles for the Kitchen and Laundry"

which we send free to home builders. You would do well to read them before perfecting your plans.

THE ASSOCIATED TILE MANUFACTURERS, ROOM 1, REEVES BUILDING, BEAVER FALLS, PA.

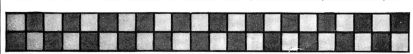

ad in Sweets catalog of 1922 does not list the Olean Tile Company as a member. Magazine advertising in July of 1927 shows the recent additions to membership to be the United States Quarry Tile Co., The Sparta Ceramic Co., and the Federal Tile Company. The Robert Rossman Corporation, Franklin Pottery, and Wheatley Tile and Pottery Co. were added in 1928. The Beaver Falls Art Tile Company, Old Bridge Enameled Brick and Tile Company, and the Perth Amboy Tile Works merged in 1927 to form the Robert Rossman Corporation.

Country Life,
November 1910.

Country Life,
December 1910.

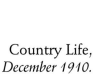

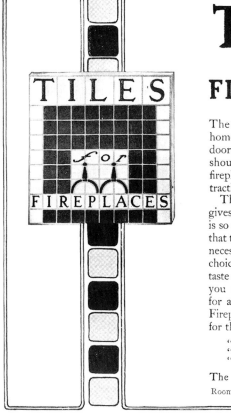

TILES
for
FIREPLACES

The fireplace is the center of the home. You spend most of your indoor life in front of the fireplace. It should be, first, a perfectly good fireplace, and second, the most attractive spot in the home.

The one fireplace material which gives that good construction which is so necessary, and at the same time that touch of beauty which is equally necessary, is tile. There is a great choice of color and texture for any taste and any color scheme. Before you build a single fireplace, send for and read the book, "Tiles for Fireplaces." Other books to be had for the asking:

  "Tiles on the Porch Floor"
  "Tiles for the Kitchen and Laundry"
  "Tile for the Bathroom"

The Associated Tile Manufacturers

Room 1, Reeves Building, Beaver Falls, Pa.

Country Life,
January 1911.

Good Housekeeping,
July 1910.

The American Architect, May 1920.

For interior uses of various kinds—for fireplaces, hallways and vestibules, also for porches whether open or enclosed—Tiles render a complete and distinctive service.

Color effects and decorative treatments of the widest possible range are obtainable with Tiles.

They represent the tone and texture so essential to the creation of agreeable **first impressions.** Moreover they have the practical values of durability and economy of upkeep.

*T*ILES
Add the Artistic Touch of Color and Texture

The Associated Tile Manufacturers Beaver Falls Pennsylvania

Associated Tile Manufacturers booklet.

TILES ON THE PORCH FLOOR

As you step from the walk or lawn to the porch of your house the material that seems to be most natural for the covering of the floor is tile.

Tile is related to the earth. It is made from clay, subjected to tremendous heat until it becomes vitrified, but still its source is the earth.

[1]

Avon Faience Co.

A pottery works established in Tiltonsville, Ohio, in 1880 became the Avon Faience Company in 1902. The original works had gone through about six ownership and name changes when it was purchased by J. N. Vance and Sons in 1900. Vance called the 1900 purchase the Vance Faience Company. They produced a line of art pottery that was skillfully molded in relief with decorations of mermaids, monkeys, or grotesque heads. The forms were painted with shaded colors. Most were done in a brown to orange or yellow, similar to the shaded background of Weller Louwelsa and Rookwood Standard Glaze.

The owners evidently wanted to change the company image, for in September of 1902 they changed the company name to the Avon Faience Co. and hired William P. Jervis to be the manager. Frederick H. Rhead and Albert Cusick were soon hired as designers and artists.

The art pottery products of Avon Faience were artist decorated on solid color backgrounds, under the glaze, in three styles. Art Nouveau motifs were painted in slip, applied white tube lining, or carved outlines done after the greenware was decorated. Some examples were decorated in two or more styles. Avon Faience products were strongly influenced by Rhead and are

VANCE F. CO.

Avon.F.Co. Tiltonville

Avon Faience used two incised marks and two ink stamp marks. One of the ink stamps noted Avon was a division of the Wheeling Potteries Co.

similar to those he designed while employed at Weller and Roseville.

In December of 1902, the Wheeling, West Virginia, pottery of J. N. Vance and Sons and the La Belle, Riverside, and Avon Faience potteries combined and were incorporated as the Wheeling Potteries Company. Art pottery was produced at the Avon Faience plant until it was discontinued in 1905. The firm entered receivership in 1908.

Most authors of the last 30 years continue to mistakenly refer to the Avon Faience Company as Vance/Avon Faience. The Vance Faience

Company and the Avon Faience Company were two completely different organizations with different management, different designers and artists, and very different products that are signed with different marks. E. A. Barber, in his 1904 publication, *Marks of American Potters,* lists these as two separate organizations and makes no attempt to join them in any way.

Similarly, authors confuse the products of the Avon Faience Company and the Avon Pottery of Cincinnati. This is completely unnecessary for the products of these two do not resemble those of the other. See the Avon Pottery chapter.

Both of these products of the Avon Faience Co. show Rhead-type of decorations. They are 4" tall and unsigned. After the decoration on the bulbous vase was painted on the greenware, it was outlined by carving. A similar carving tool was used to cut the number 88 in the bottom of the small vase. Large, bulbous vase, $350.00 – 500.00. Small vase, $100.00 – 150.00.

This 7" pitcher with an embossed and painted decoration of tulips is marked on the bottom with the "Avon, Wheeling Potteries Co." ink stamp. $50.00 – 75.00.

The Avon Pottery of Cincinnati was founded in January 1886, and was in existence for a period of about a year and a half to two years. One variety of ware produced here was made of yellow clay, decorated in colored slips, and modeled or etched in part. This was treated in a "smear" or dull glaze finish. Another variety was made of white clay, decorated with atomized colors and painted designs on the biscuit, and covered with a brilliant transparent glaze. The effect of the atomized coloring was a gradual shading of the ground from light to darker tints, in pink, olive, violet, blue, brown, etc. All of the pieces were thrown on the wheel, while some were furnished with modeled handles. In the Pennsylvania Museum collection are several small vases of this character including two with green tinted ground and covers, and handles in the form of elephants' heads. In the collection of Dr. Marcus Benjamin, of Washington, D. C., is a mug-shaped cup of graceful shape with a tinted ground shading from white to dark pink, and a modeled ram's horn handle. Some of the pieces made at this pottery were marked with the name AVON.

The information above is from *The Pottery and Porcelain of the United States* by Edwin Atlee Barber. Mr. Barber failed to mention the founder of this pottery, Mr. Karl Langenbeck. Others associated with Langenbeck at Avon were David Stern, chemist; James MacDonald, principal artist; Martin Rettig, artist; and Artus Van Briggle, apprentice artist.

Examples of pottery from this Cincinnati company are rare. In 22 years of collecting, I have seen only four pieces, three vases and my own covered candy. One piece was in the Rookwood III auction of 1993. The auction catalog proclaimed that none of the staff at Cincinnati Art Galleries had ever seen an example of Avon Pottery prior to this one offered at auction. The exceptional example offered was an 11" vase decorated with a fish by Martin Rettig. It sold for over $3,000.00.

Of the four examples I've seen, all have been the hand-turned white clay with atomized backgrounds, the variety described by Mr. Barber. However, none of these examples had the stamped or impressed block letter mark shown by him. They all had marks similar to that on the example shown here. Maybe artist-decorated examples were marked by the artists and non-decorated pieces were stamped.

This covered candy is 3" tall and 5" wide. The atomized shaded background is on a hand-turned white clay body. The fruit tree branch and blossom decoration is done in colored slip and covered with a clear glaze. The marks on the bottom were done with a brush or pen in the same color as the atomized background. $700.00 – 900.00

Batchelder Tile

In 1910 Ernest A. Batchelder built a studio in the backyard of his home overlooking Pasadena, California. He started making handmade tiles. In 1912, with business partner Mr. Frederick L. Brown, the rapidly growing operation was moved to a building in Pasadena. This company was called Batchelder and Brown, Inc. The business expanded, and in 1920 Batchelder took on a new business partner, Mr. Lucien H. Wilson. They moved the manufacturing operation to Los Angeles. The name of the business then became the Batchelder-Wilson Company.

Mr. Batchelder admired the tile work of Henry Chapman Mercer of the Moravian Pottery in Doylestown, Pennsylvania, and some of his early tiles depicted the medieval subjects in the style of Mercer. Batchelder used local clays to make low relief tiles that were decorated with colored engobe (mineral slips) which produced non-reflecting surfaces.

Later, tiles and large panels, mantels, fountains, and garden pottery were offered with Dutch or California landscapes. Spanish, Mayan, and classical designs were added to the rapidly expanding line of products. By 1923, the factory catalog was among the largest in the business showing both products and installations, including custom, one-of-a-kind designs. By 1925 Batchelder had 175 employees.

Batchelder-Wilson was another victim of the Depression, closing in 1932.

Batchelder tiles are always signed, an advantage to the collector offered by but a few other manufacturers.

Batchelder wrote many articles on design and decoration that appeared in both trade and amateur publications. He wrote the book *The Principles of Design*. Several recent authors say the book was published in 1908, but my copy says copyright in 1904

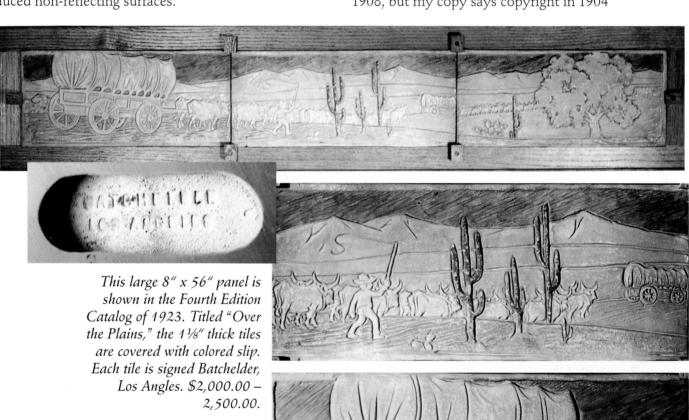

This large 8" x 56" panel is shown in the Fourth Edition Catalog of 1923. Titled "Over the Plains," the 1⅛" thick tiles are covered with colored slip. Each tile is signed Batchelder, Los Angles. $2,000.00 – 2,500.00.

Decorative Tiles for the Garden

*Designed by Ernest O. Batchelder
of Pasadena, California*

This drawing shows an interesting use of the Batchelder tiles in a wall fountain. The figured tiles are placed as a border around the surface of plain tiles, and a square of delicately executed tiles, that compose together a complete motif, are set at the top of the fountain and out of this motif springs the water inlet, the water being caught in the semicircular basin just below. The two low walls, coming forward on either side of the fountain, offer an attractive spot for potted plants, which are recognized, nowadays, as having a distinct decorative value in gardens.

The employment of tiles in the garden—in fountains, walls, summer-house, or in the adjacent out-of-doors living-room—affords the ingenious mind many chances for interesting combinations of figure tiles and of figure tiles with plain. The figure tiles, when used with restraint, add the final touch of interest. The color of these tiles is difficult to describe. Mr. Batchelder says, "Our colors, like those of an old rug, do not admit of positively inharmonious combinations. The effects of our colors have been described as 'luminous, mellow, tapestry like.' We labor under the disadvantage that a single sample tile conveys no idea of the ensemble produced by a completed piece of work."

This beautiful mantel shows a very interesting use of catalog material....photographed in the billiard room of a California home.

BATCHELDER TILES

A BEAUTIFUL home...a charming hostess...a cheerful fire blazing in a friendly fireplace...a wonderful mantel of Batchelder Tile.

Nothing can supplant the mantel as the dominant point of interest in any room.

The colors of Batchelder Tiles are those of a rare old tapestry...soft, subdued, mellowed with age, the textures rich and delicate; the designs, distinctive, many and varied. A Batchelder mantel quietly harmonizes with any decorative motif... any furnishings.

In addition to mantels, Batchelder Tiles are available for fountains, baths and pavements.

More complete information in the Batchelder "Describe-o-Log". Write for a copy.

BATCHELDER-WILSON COMPANY
...ian Street, Los Angeles
...Avenue, New York City

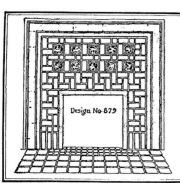

Design No. 879

BATCHELDER TILES

A Fire place in our Tiles is a joy Forever. They are Handwrought, Unique, Distinctive. Let us send you Designs and Estimates. :: :: :: :: ::

BATCHELDER & BROWN
PASADENA : CALIFORNIA

Craftsman,
September 1912.

BATCHELDER TILES

The colors are those of rare old tapestries....
dulled, softened, mellowed by age.

No glaring highlights, no vividly obtrusive
colors....only soft tones that harmonize with
any surroundings.

Tile for mantels, fountains, pavements, wains-
cots and architectural Terra Cotta. See
Sweet's Catalogue or write for complete information.

BATCHELDER-WILSON COMPANY
2633 Artesian Street, Los Angeles
101 Park Avenue, New York City 1-A

⚜ BATCHELDER TILES ⚜

Our new mantel catalog of one hundred pages is available for distribution to architects only. It contains many interesting suggestions for fireplace construction.

A MAYAN FIREFRAME

FROM A FIELD OF ORNAMENT REPLETE WITH INSPIRATION FOR THE DESIGNER WHO DARES STRAY FROM THE EASY PATH OF ACCEPTED STYLES.

A FIREPLACE is a permanent built-in feature of a room and remains long after rugs, furniture and draperies have been replaced. It should be thoughtfully designed, —with distinction of line and form. Its colors should harmonize with any reasonable decorative treatment. A well chosen fireplace is a source of perennial satisfaction.

A fireframe of Mayan derivatives is appropriate for a rough textured wall in a room of unconventional character. The motifs are unique and offer a fertile field of inspiration to the designer. The modelling is in low relief with mellow toned colors. We have tried to catch the spirit of Mayan ornament rather than a mere copy of isolated symbols.

MADE IN U.S.A.

BATCHELDER-WILSON COMPANY

LOS ANGELES	CHICAGO	NEW YORK
2633 ARTESIAN ST.	38 SO. DEARBORN ST.	101 PARK AVE.

12

BATCHELDER
☒ TILES ☒ ☒

A MANTEL OF GENEROUS IMPULSES

 SIZE is not the only thing to consider in the designing of a mantel. Large or small the mantel is the focal point in the decorative scheme of any room. It is invariably the center of interest. It may be large without being obtrusive, or small without being niggardly. It is a matter of scale, form and color. Moreover, the mantel is a permanent, built-in feature and will outlive furniture, rugs and draperies. Therefore, it should be of such character that it is adaptable to any reasonable decorative treatment. If it is really beautiful the next generation will share our pleasure in living with it. BATCHELDER TILES of the mottled finish type are peculiarly beautiful for interior work. They have a mellow, pleasing color effect that may be depended upon to harmonize with fine woods, furniture and rugs.

BATCHELDER-WILSON COMPANY

LOS ANGELES	SAN FRANCISCO	CHICAGO	NEW YORK
2633 ARTESIAN ST.	557 MARKET ST.	38 SO. DEARBORN ST.	101 PARK AVE.

California Art & Architecture, *April 1930.*

BATCHELDER
☒ TILES ☒

PATINA GLAZES

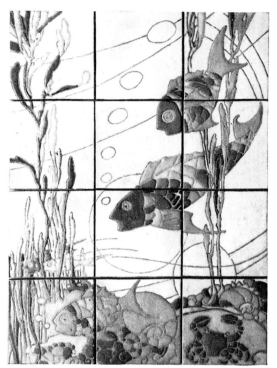

WE SHALL BE PLEASED TO MAIL YOU A
CATALOG DESCRIBING PATINA GLAZES

A TILE INSTALLATION offers endless opportunities for the play of individual fancy in the selection and arrangement of materials. There is infinite choice ---not only in design, but in color and texture as well. Contrasts may be positive, if that is to ones taste, or they may be of closely blended harmonies.

Patina Glazes are peculiarly appropriate for bathrooms, swimming pools and fountains. They are full glazed, fired to high temperatures but without excessive gloss. Their texture is akin to the Patina of ancient marbles---hence the name. They are made in a sequence of color blends permitting many variations of effect through the intermingling of colors with interesting results.

BATCHELDER-WILSON COMPANY

LOS ANGELES	SAN FRANCISCO	CHICAGO	NEW YORK
2633 ARTESIAN ST.	557 MARKET ST.	38 SO. DEARBORN ST.	101 PARK AVE.

House Beautiful, *September 1929.*

Beaver Falls Art Tile Co., Ltd.

The Beaver Falls Art Tile Company of Beaver Falls, Pennsylvania, was organized in 1886 by Mr. F.W. Walker, who was secretary, treasurer, and manager. Mr. John Reeves, a banker, was president. The works started with the manufacture of plain enamels, and a few months later added embossed and intaglio tiles, as well as tiles for stove decorations, which this company made a specialty. The discovery of natural gas and the advantages obtained by its use as a fuel for the burning of all pottery wares was the inducement for Mr. Walker, who had been very much interested in the investigation of tiles and their manufacture, to organize the company. His ability as a chemist soon enabled him to place the works in a position to manufacture a line of glazes of soft, rich tones. Their remarkable freedom from crazing soon won the factory a high reputation in the trade. Their delicate tints of pale blue and greenish and purplish

The pair of 2¼" diameter stove tiles shown here are both signed on the front with the "B" of Broome's monogram. The backmarks are "Beaver Falls" in block letters in a semicircle. $150.00 – 200.00 pr.

This 3" diameter stove tile is also signed with the semicircle mark and is attributed to Broome. $100.00 – 150.00 ea.

Part of a vertical panel, this 6" square tile with a bird is signed "Beaver Falls Art Tile Co. Ltd., Beaver Falls Pa." in raised letters. $75.00 – 100.00

This series of 6" x 18" relief panels, representing poetry, music, and painting is referred to in E.A. Barber's 1893 publication, with the music panel being illustrated. All three panels are signed "Broome" on the front. The back of the poetry tile has an in mold mark of B. F. A. T. Co. Ltd. in raised letters. The other two are unmarked. Framed set, $1,800.00 – 2,400.00.

grays are particularly beautiful examples of transparent colored glazing. The factory specialized in artistic tile designs for wall decorations, in all the leading styles, for libraries, dining rooms, and bathrooms. These works employed the best designers that could be obtained. Prof. Isaac Broome, a sculptor of rare artistic ability, became connected with the factory in 1890.

This firm incorporated in 1906. In 1927 it was one of three companies that were merged to form the Robert Rossman Corporation.

Isaac Broome was one of America's most versatile artists. He was born in Valcartier, Quebec, on May 16, 1835. He first became interested in the subject of ceramics when, as a young man, he visited the museums of Europe to study the collections of Grecian and Etruscan vases for archaeological material for use in his chosen professions of sculpting and painting. After some years he turned his attention to the potters' art, and about the close of the Civil War he established a terra cotta manufactory at Pittsburgh, where he made fountains and architectural designs. His productions, however, were in advance of public taste and the venture had to be abandoned. After a period of portrait-painting, frescoing, sculpting, and modeling, he did architectural terra cotta work in Brooklyn, New York, about 1871, and produced some large pieces of artistic work. He was finally compelled to relinquish this second enterprise by the arbitrary ruling of the City Board of Health which, under the pretext that the firing of his kilns endangered the safety of the adjacent buildings, ordered him to close the works.

Just previous to the Centennial, Broome was engaged by the Etruria Pottery of Trenton, New Jersey, to prepare some special designs for the approaching exhibition. In 1878 he was appointed a special commissioner on ceramics to the Paris Exposition, and, in conjunction with General McClellan, made a thorough study of the ceramics arts as it existed abroad. While connected with the Ott & Brewer Company at Trenton, he made some original drawings on stone for some special and general work which were painted in black, in colors, and in gold, said to be the first lithographic printing on pottery ever done in America.

In 1880, upon his return to Trenton from abroad, he utilized the time from an illness to put into practical application some ideas which he had previously thought out in the production of a variety of ware never before attempted in this country. The body was a well vitrified porcelain with under glaze color effects, the paste, colors, and glaze being thoroughly incorporated together by a single firing. The result was a ware difficult to describe, but most pleasing in its modest tones and the softness and depth of translucent effect. Only about 100 of these vases were made. For the most part they were of small size, ranging from three to ten inches in height, the form being simple but full and rich in outline, and particularly adapted to the peculiar style of coloration in analogous or contrasting harmonies. These pieces were made entirely by Prof. Broome, assisted by his young son. The clays were prepared in the basement of his residence, dried in plaster molds in the sun, thrown, turned, glazed, and colored on the green clay in a second story room, and finally taken to a pottery in Trenton and fired in a regular ware kiln. All of these interesting pieces were sent to a dealer in New York and scattered in collections throughout the country.

In 1883 Broome became connected as designer and modeler with the Harris Manufacturing Company that later became the Trent Tile Company. In 1886 he was instrumental in establishing the Providential Tile Works of Trenton, and designed many of their best works. He was an indefatigable worker and a prolific artist, his sculptures being characterized by exquisite conception and the most painstaking details.

Among the more important works of Prof. Broome are a marble bust of Dr. Ducachet, executed in 1858; a semi-colossal marble bust of Washington, made from the most authentic portraits in the same year; and a ceramic bust of Hon. Joseph D. Bedle, New Jersey's Centennial Governor.

Boys Town Pottery

Ceramic production at Boys Town started in 1940. The first shop was opened in the old recreation building by Bill Wilkins. Mr. Wilkins was an English potter whose family was in the trade for over 300 years.

Ceramics was taught in the vocational school as a trade, and was offered to all boys as a fine arts course.

When the new Vocational Career Center was built in 1948, an extensive ceramic shop and studio were included in the plans. Several hundred thousand small ceramic items were produced over the next 45 years that were sold in the Visitor Center gift shop.

The two 4½″ vases shown here are of the same shape, but are quite different. The root beer aventurine glazed vase is hand turned, heavier in weight, and has a hand incised B.T. on the bottom. The burnt sienna glaze vase came from a three-piece mold and has an in mold mark. $75.00 – 100.00 for the aventurine glazed vase. $25.00 – 30.00 for the sienna glazed example.

Blank china plates were ordered, then decorated with decals representing scenes at Boys Town. These plates, the "He Ain't Heavy" statues, an outstanding Nativity set, and Christmas ornaments were the most popular items.

With the advance of more modern technology, the shop and studio became less able to compete with outside suppliers to provide the needs of the gift shop, and in 1993 the ceramic shop at the Career Center was closed.

A retrospective of the items created is in the Boys Town museum, The Hall of History, and can be seen by request, or when it is occasionally put on public display.

This 5" vase with handles is marked with a hand-incised "Boys Town" and a Boys Town souvenir label. $30.00 – 40.00.

The "He Ain't Heavy" statue is 9" tall and has an in the mold Boys Town mark. This statue was also offered in a smaller size. $25.00 – 35.00.

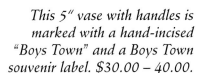

California Art Tile Co.

In 1922, James White Hislop and his sons organized the Clay Glow Tile Company in Richmond, California. The name of the business was soon changed to the California Art Tile Company. They manufactured hand-crafted tile with pastel glazes.

A 65 page factory catalog of later vintage shows an extensive offering of large panels, mantels, sconces, grills and vents, fountains, store fronts and interiors, all in a style similar to their competitors, Batchelder, Claycraft, and Muresque. The catalog emphasizes custom design services and pictures completed installations.

Tiles were press molded, painted with colored enamel slip, then fired at high temperature. Polychrome decorated tiles were also produced. The plant had a rated capacity of 1,000,000 square feet annually.

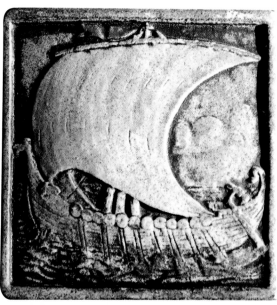

The tiles shown here are 5⅝" square and almost ¾" thick. They have colored slip glazes with a mat finish. All have the same hand-stamped "California Art Tile Co. Richmond, Calif." mark, except the "Ferry to Sausalito" tile, which is unmarked, but pictured in the catalog. $200.00 – 350.00 each

Cambridge Tile Manufacturing Co.

In 1885, a common red brickyard was operated as the Busse Brothers, at 16th and Woodburn Avenue, in Covington, Kentucky. Heinrich Binz, a German tile maker employed at the firm, glazed some brick for decorative purposes and at the same time made some glazed tile in colors. Evidently the tiles were admirable, for in 1886, Busse Brothers started to sell enameled tile. They called this business the Mount Casini Art Tile Company.

In 1887, Messrs. Heinrich Binz, A.W. Koch, and F.W. Braunstein organized a sales company called the Cambridge Art Tile Company.

In 1889, the Cambridge Art Tile Company and the Mount Casini Art Tile Company merged to form the Cambridge Tile Manufacturing Company. The officers were Henry Busse, president; Herman Busse, treasurer; and F.W. Braunstein, secretary. Products manufactured at this time were bright glazed colored enameled tile, decorated tile for mantel facings, and tile used for decorating the exterior of heating stoves. The principal designer and modeler for the works was Mr. Ferdinand Mersman, formerly of the Rookwood Pottery of Cincinnati. Mr. Clement Barnhorn was also employed as a designer and modeler.

By 1900 the company was producing white glazed wall tile, white and colored vitreous floor tile, a bright glazed faience called Kenton Vitrea brick, as well as faience mantels with wrought-iron trim.

In 1906 the Kentucky company was dissolved. The Cambridge Tile Manufacturing Company was incorporated under Ohio laws with a new capitol structure. At this time the company started to produce mat glaze tile.

In 1927, the Wheatley Pottery Company was acquired. The corporate name of this operation was changed to the Wheatley Tile & Pottery Company, with its manufacturing plant on Eastern Avenue, Cincinnati, Ohio. The old Cambridge plant in Covington, Kentucky, with about 20 periodic kilns, was scrapped, but the office staff remained.

In the 1889 factory catalog, this 12" x 6" tile and three companion tiles, each with decorations including two cherubs, are shown with nine 6" square tiles to complete the mantel facing. The tile shown is not signed. $200.00 – 300.00.

A–28

Cambridge Tile Manufacturing Co.

Covington, Ky.

In 1929, Cambridge built a new plant in Hartwell, Ohio, a town in the north of Cincinnati. The building was equipped with modern machinery including two Harrop tunnel kilns. In November, the new plant was in operation, and the office staff moved to its new quarters from Covington.

In 1931, the Wheatley Tile & Pottery Company operation on Eastern Avenue was closed down, and all manufacturing for Wheatley was moved to the Cambridge plant in Hartwell.

In 1942, the plant consisted of three periodic kilns and two tunnel kilns with a combined capacity of 5,000,000 square feet annually.

The portrait tiles shown here are typical of the early relief work at Cambridge. All tiles in this chapter appear in either or both the 1889 and 1890 factory catalogs, except the mat glaze portrait tiles and the Lincoln hexagon tile. All tiles shown here are signed with the script style mark with raised, in the mold letters, except the Lincoln tile.

These 6" square Thistle pattern tiles formed a continuous design using but three different molds to produce the complete 17 tile frieze. $25.00 – 35.00 ea.

A beautiful mottled glaze with very little crazing covers these 1½" x 3" and 1½" x 6" hearth and wall tiles. These tiles are marked with raised, in the die, block letters. $2.00 – 3.00 ea.

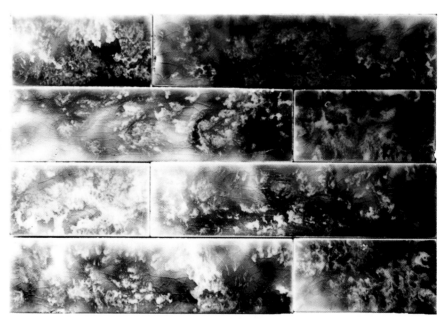

The three pair of 6" square portraits of adults have an interesting similarity. The two right facing bearded men have an identical profile and ear, as do the three figures facing left. This was an obvious cost cutting procedure, or a hurried attempt to get some products on the market fast by modifying existing designs and molds instead of creating totally new products. Similarly, the 1890 catalog shows some 18" x 6" panels with full length female portraits that were offered in both fully clothed or bare breasted. $300.00 – 400.00 per pair of 6" portraits.

Note the "Cambridge" advertising on the 6" square tile with the portrait of a girl with a hat. $350.00 – 450.00 pr.

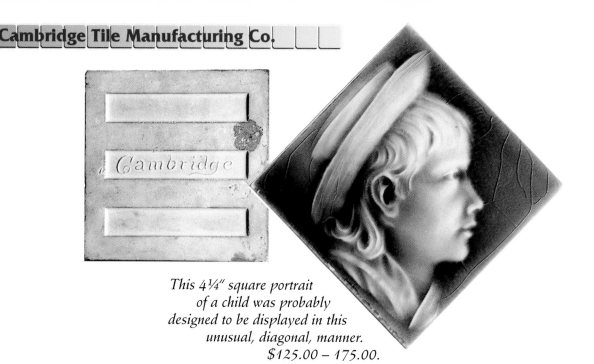

This 4¼″ square portrait
of a child was probably
designed to be displayed in this
unusual, diagonal, manner.
$125.00 – 175.00.

These 4¼″ square portrait relief
tiles are covered with a mat
glaze, a rarity on this type of
tile. Cambridge started producing mat glaze tiles in 1906.
$175.00 – 250.00 pr.

This hexagon tile
appears to be a product
of the Mosaic Tile Co.
However, the blue clay of
this replica is much more
Wedgwood blue than the
original Mosaic products. A paper sticker on the
back reads Lincoln Memorial Paperweight, Manufactured by The Cambridge Tile Mfg. Co., P.O. Box
15071-Cincinnati 15, Ohio. $40.00 – 50.00

Cincinnati Art Pottery Co.

Mr. Thomas J. Wheatley began experimenting in clays and glazes at the pottery of Mr. P.L. Coultry & Co. in 1879. Soon thereafter a joint stock company was organized under the title of the Cincinnati Art Pottery Company. Mr. Frank Huntington was president, and Mr. Wheatley continued his connection with the works until 1882, when he withdrew to engage in other business. For several years the company confined its operations to underglaze work. Later, barbotine ware, an applied work, was manufactured for a time, but was soon dropped for a more artistic style of overglaze decoration on white bodies. The Hungarian Faience made here soon became popular with the purchasing public. They introduced a Portland Blue Faience line in 1884, named after the famous Portland vase because of its rich dark blue glaze, which formed a striking ground for gold decorative effects. The highest achievement of this company, and most distinctive in style, was the Ivory Colored Faience decorated with gold scroll-work and chrysanthemums in natural colors. They named this line Kezonta Ware. Some pottery in the biscuit, in deep blue and in white glazes, in modified ancient Roman and Greek forms, was sold to decorators. The Cincinnati Art Pottery continued operations until 1891.

In 1887 Mr. William Dell, an employee at the pottery, purchased some molds and glazes of the Hungarian Faience line. He manufactured Hungarian-type faience under his own name until he died in 1892. Pottery manufactured under the Dell name are signed with an incised "Wm Dell & Co., Cin. O." mark. The earliest known example of signed William Dell pottery was sold in an Ark Antiques auction in 1985, and is dated 1887.

Three marks were used on Cincinnati Art Pottery products, the first one being the figure of a turtle. About 1886 the Indian name for turtle, Kezonta, was added to the turtle mark. On the finer grades of ware, the mark was printed in red. On plainer wares such as blue glazed and white pottery, the mark "Kezonta" was impressed. About 1890, an impressed mark consisting of the initials of the company was used.

This pilgrim flask with Hungarian Faience decoration is 8" in diameter. The flask is unsigned, but the shape is pictured in the January 1892 issue of Popular Science Monthly, *and credited to the Cincinnati Art Pottery Company and the Hungarian Faience line of products. This flask was also sold in a four footed version. $150.00 – 200.00.*

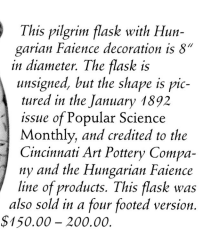

The Portland Blue type glaze on this 8″ Kezonta vase identifies it as one probably destined for the amateur decorator trade. The handles were molded in the form of sea creatures, then applied by hand. Undecorated artistic forms with the Portland Blue glaze are preferred over examples of white glazed or biscuit forms. $300.00 – 350.00.

This 5½″ vase with Limoges style background, decorated with dragonflies in bamboo and tall grasses and gold highlights, was done by N.J. Hirschfeld. The bottom is marked C.A.P.Co. die stamped, and the hand-incised N.J.H. This is an exceptional example of this work's products. $500.00 – 600.00

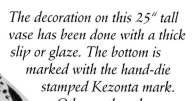

Ewers of this same shape and 11½" size have been identified as products of the Cincinnati Art Pottery Company
by several auction houses and authors. However, this
example is signed only with "Clara-Christmas 1889."
When there is confusion as to the origin of a vessel, if the
artist was an amateur, it matters little. The impor-
tance of an amateur decoration is in the talent
demonstrated in execution of the subject. The
ewer shown here was obviously done by
someone with talent. $250.00 – 300.00.

The decoration on this 25" tall
vase has been done with a thick
slip or glaze. The bottom is
marked with the hand-die
stamped Kezonta mark.
Other authors have sug-
gested that this line of products have
in-mold raised patterns. While parts
of the decorations I have examined
defy conclusion, other raised decorations show absolute thick slip or
glaze application. Because of my
examinations, and the fact that no
"two alike" objects have yet
appeared, I'm discounting the molded
pattern statement. $400.00 – 500.00.

Charles Walter Clewell of Canton, Ohio, started experimenting with copper, brass, bronze, and silver products in about 1899. He made cast, hand-wrought, and riveted items. Some were made of more than one metal, then riveted together. Some of the items made were ashtrays of brass or copper with molded bronze feet and teapots of copper with tin linings "for actual use." Later he made copper-covered ceramic items that had the appearance of having been riveted. Some resembled hammered metal. These ceramic base items were sold in the form of candlesticks, vases, ashtrays, bookends, wall sconces, bowls, and tankard and mug sets. The ceramic bodies were purchased from several Ohio potteries. Clewell's process for the copper covering of these products was somewhat of a secret. However, they appear to be another example the electroplating process that was utilized at other ceramic and glass manufacturers of the period. The early wares had tarnished finishes, as an old penny. Later, products appeared with green patinas. About 1923 he developed a blue-green patina. Clewell's process for

aging his products to appear as ancient with green and blue/green patinas was his real secret. These items were somehow chemically treated to produce the desired effect.

Production of Clewell continued throughout his lifetime, except for a period of about 10 years beginning in 1942, until his death in 1966. All of Clewell's products were done by him. He employed very little help.

Small vases are presently selling for about $400.00, with prices escalating to $3,500.00 for a molded design covered 13" reticulated vase. Products which have had the patina or tarnish removed are considered damaged.

Clewell products are marked with a hand-incised "Clewell," an impressed Clewell Metal Art, Canton, O.," "Clewell Coppers," "Clewell Canton, O.," or a W within a larger C.

A Holland Stein and Tankard Set would add to the elegance of your sideboard. A perfect reproduction of an old-fashioned hammered and riveted drinking set. Made of silver, copper or brass, old tarnished finish, and lined with finely glazed white porcelain. An acceptable wedding present and one not likely to be duplicated as our output is, by necessity, closely limited. Furnished plain or quaintly lettered as ordered with inscription, monogram or initial for trophy or gift purposes. Our work is distinctive—out of the ordinary and appreciated by the really artistic. Prices and our Stein Booklet will be sent if requested.

THE CLEWELL STUDIO
1953 E. 9th St.   CANTON, O.

Country Life in America,
March 1908.

Country Life in America, April 1908.

Old English Tankard and Steins   **"Clewell"**

A drinking set of tarnished copper, brass or silver, hand-made riveted effect. Handsome and quietly elegant, with the attractive quaintness of the better class of old craftsmanship. Serviceable also, the interior being lined with nicely glazed porcelain, to keep the contents away from the metal and to aid in cleaning. An appropriate wedding gift or trophy. *Send for booklet and prices.*

THE CLEWELL STUDIO   1953 E. 9th Street   CANTON, OHIO

Artistic Metal Productions

Well-executed work in copper and brass, hand-made entirely, rivets and all. Made carefully and in good taste to harmonize with tasteful, artistic surroundings. The designs are original and each piece is finished with regard to its character—tarnished, verde antique, or new appearing metal as age or use or both would cause it to appear. No catalogue of this work is issued as only a few of each kind are made, they being followed by other designs. Remit when ordering—if the productions do not appeal to you they will be repurchased at the price paid. If you prefer brass, mention it, otherwise copper will be sent. Orders will be accepted for special work—punch-bowls, tankards, salvers, etc.

C. W. Clewell
1923 E. Tus. Street
Canton, Ohio

ASH TRAY.—Bowl 5½ in. diameter; copper or brass; supports, cast bronze; tarnished finish; price $4.75.
TEAPOT.—5 in. diameter; brews one quart of tea; tinned within for actual use; dull, sand-scoured finish; price $9.75.
CANDLESTICK.—9½ in. tall; copper or brass; tarnished; $5.00 each, $9.50 per pair.

International Studio,
June 1909.

Cowan Pottery

R. Guy Cowan's studio was located in Lakewood, Ohio, on Nicholson Avenue in 1912. Three kilns were used to produce art pottery and tiles. The following year, the Cleveland Pottery and Tile Company, Inc. was organized with Cowan as president and treasure, W.G. Wilcox as vice-president, and Bertha Cowan as secretary. Bertha was the wife of Guy.

In 1917, Cowan enlisted in the Army and production ceased. When Cowan left the Army in 1919, he immediately reopened the Lakewood studio business.

When his gas well at Lakewood ran empty in 1921, Cowan relocated the operation to Lake Road in Rocky River, Ohio. By this time, product demand was steadily increasing and marketing was expanded, and included many of the finer and well known retailers of the time, like Marshall Fields and Ovingtons.

R. Guy Cowan and the talented and famous artists in his employment were among the most award-winning potters of their day. Guy L. Rixford, Arthur Baggs, Alexander Blazys, Thelma Frazier, Jose Martin, Waylande Gregory, and Victor Schreckengost were all on Cowan's team.

In 1927, the company name was changed to the Cowan Pottery Studio. The Lakeware line was introduced as an inexpensive product, intended mainly for

Most Cowan products were signed, and a variety of marks were used. All marked Cowan is identified by the use of either the Cowan or Lakeware names, or a variation of a monogram using the letters RG.

COWAN

LAKEWARE

florists. Sculptured figures continued to gain popularity.

Financial difficulties in 1929 forced a reorganization, and the business name was changed to Cowan Potters, Inc.

The Great Depression continued, and the company declared bankruptcy by the end of 1930. Operating under supervision of the court, the pottery closed in 1931.

An item of special interest is this unsigned candy dish with a figural handle of a draped dancer. The dish is 6¼" tall and 8¼" wide. The figural is an apparent modification of the Cowan figure #709. The trailing gown has been lifted upward and attached to the dancers right hand to provide strength to the otherwise very delicate arm that would have been susceptible to breaking when the dish was lifted. The figure is leaning a little more backward, and has her foot positioned to the rear to keep from losing her balance. The dish and handle were molded as separate pieces, then fused and glazed as one. The decoration around the edge of the plate, the clay, and the glaze are consistent with the design and materials of Cowan ceramics. $150.00 – 200.00.

Make the Dinner Table a Continuous and Delightful Picture

GRACE AND LIGHTNESS through the use of low sticks with tall tapers⸺ A truly correct treatment of the center of the table seen in the shallow fluted bowl and superb porcelain figure with its unusual and delicate flower arrangement⸺And above all, an effect of flower-like beauty from the color contrast with china and linen. A warm ivory color outside, the inside of the bowl and compotes is finished in various rare pastel colorings of correct color value. Four color combinations are available.

The porcelains are modeled by R. Guy Cowan⸺the color treatment is by Arthur E. Baggs⸺both notable creative artists.

Many decorative treatments are illustrated in our new booklet "Charming and Unusual Flower Arrangements", which we will be glad to mail you. The Cowan retailer will be pleased to show this and other table treatments.

THE COWAN POTTERY STUDIO
ROCKY RIVER, OHIO

House and Garden, *November 1926.*

PERSEPHONE, the graceful figure in the center photogra
is another example of the work of a modern American pott
Executed by Waylande Gregory, it has been reproduced by
Cowan Potters, Incorporated, in a limited edition of one hunc
signed copies. Its purpose, of course, is purely decorative, an
was with the idea of making fine sculpture available to the mo
income that it was created. This too comes under the headin;
"reuniting art with every-day life," and the fact that there
market for such things is a cheering commentary on the tren
public taste. The days when art was like the oldtime "parl
rarely open to view and used only as a repository for totally use
and usually hopelessly ugly things, are happily over.

International Studio published this photo and article on "Persephone." The 15" sculpture was a limited edition. She appears in the 1930 Cowan catalog as item No. D-6.

Courtesy Cowan Potters, Inc

"PERSEPHONE"

House and Garden,
May 1927.

An Added Touch of Charm for Every Home

THE exquisite beauty and color of these delightful creations of Cowan Pottery impart that subtle touch of charm frequently lacking in an otherwise attractively furnished room. Masterfully modelled to grace the most pretentious room, yet so simple in line and treatment as not to look out of place in the modest home.

Many new and original designs are now on display in the better stores. The illustration shows a distinctly different conception of candlestick or candelabra—faithfully embodying some of the characteristics of Byzantine art.

The candelabra in the attractive new crackle glazes retails at $12.50. In other Cowan colors $8.50. It is 9" high.

"Charming and Unusual Flower Arrangements," is an interesting booklet which we will gladly mail upon request, with names of local retailers.

THE **COWAN POTTERY** STUDIO
"An added touch of charm for every home"
ROCKY RIVER, OHIO

Faience Manufacturing Co.

The Faience Manufacturing Company of New York and Brooklyn established an art pottery at Greenpoint, Long Island, in 1880. Earlier products made here were majolica and barbotine wares.

After establishing his own successful ceramic business in New York, Mr. Edward Lycett joined the Greenpoint plant in 1884. About 25 skilled decorators were employed under Lycett's direction. They painted ornamental ware which surpassed everything previously produced in this country. He experimented in compounding bodies and glazes, and some of the most artistic vases produced are entirely the work of his hands. He designed, modeled, and decorated with glazes and bodies of his own design and making. Some of the later products are made of a true hard paste porcelain, many of which possess perforated covers, necks, and handles. Lycett severed his connection with the company in 1890. The factory closed in 1892.

Mr. Lycett was considered by E.A. Barber to be the father of china painting in America.

The earlier majolica and barbotine wares are marked with the companies initials, die impressed by hand. When the company switched from making coarse faience to producing finer china bodies, the mark was changed to a capitol R within a circle with a crown on top, and was printed under the glaze. The name of the product using this mark was "Royal Crown." This mark was short lived and was put on very few pieces. The mark used after 1886 was the company monogram penciled above the glaze.

An example of the barbotine ware, this ewer is 9" tall. The applied colored rose and grape decoration are under the glaze. The grape leaves background and gold trim are painted over the glaze. The bottom is marked with the block letter initials, die stamped, and a stamp impressed 232. Great examples with applied decoration in this excellent condition are difficult to find. $350.00 – 500.00.

Only 3½" tall, this simplified example of barbotine was probably made as a souvenir or a commercial piece. The decoration was made as a unit, probably in a mold, then applied and decorated. The molding and application process is similar to Wedgwood, and the yet-to-be produced Peters & Reed sprigged on decorations. This vase has the same mark of the larger ewer, and the numbers 180. These die-stamped numbers probably designate the shape. $50.00 – 75.00.

Ford Ceramic Arts

Walter D. Ford began Ford Ceramic Arts in Columbus, Ohio, in 1936. This firm provided design and engineering services for the ceramics industry. Walter's great grandfather, John Conard, had established a brick factory in Columbus where both Walter and his father had worked as youngsters. Walter graduated from Ohio State University in 1930 with a degree in chemical engineering and a year later with a master's of science.

Together with Paul Bogatay, a well-known designer and sculptor, he perfected a process for placing photographic images on ceramics in relief and intaglio. In 1940, a year before Ford Ceramic Arts succumbed to the prewar recession, Ford disclosed the details of his methods and procedures in ceramic photography to the American Ceramic Society. Some explanation of this process was printed in an article, "Ohio Features Ceramic Genius," in the April – June issue of *Flash Points,* a quarterly bulletin of the Tile Heritage Foundation.

Ford retired in 1971 from the Pittsburgh Corning Corporation as the senior ceramic engineer after 30 years of service. He died in 1988 at the age of 82.

It is frequently stated that some portrait tiles of exceptional detail and likeness, sculptured by the English artist George Cartlidge from 1898 till 1924, are of a photographic process. Terence A. Lockett, in his book, *Collecting Victorian Tiles*, says this is incorrect. Lockett states that in letters written by Cartlidge he explained his methods. No such process is mentioned. This misunderstanding might have originated because

Cartlidge formally recognized the photographers of the photos he copied. Ceramic artists frequently copied photographs, but rarely identified the subjects origin.

I have seen no reference to Ford Ceramics Arts or Ford Ceramic Studio other than those discussed here. Photographic process items may have been their only products, for they were in the services business, not in manufacturing.

The portrait of Chic Harley is on a tray signed "Ford Ceramic Studio, Columbus, Ohio." The 4¾" x 3½" tray also shows a monogram of an F within an O. $40.00 – 60.00.

Frackelton Pottery

Susan Stuart Goodrich Frackelton worked with ceramics from the mid-1870s until about 1910. Her decorated stoneware work won many medals at both national and international expositions. In 1885 she copyrighted her book on china painting, *Tried by Fire.* She organized the National League of Mineral Painters in 1892. The following year she established the Frackelton China Decorating Works in Milwaukee, Wisconsin, to train those eager to improve and expand their skills.

Frackelton pottery is stoneware decorated under the glaze in a delft-like blue, or it has applied and sometimes incised decoration sprayed or painted with blue and covered with a clear glaze.

Salt Glazed Stoneware by Edwin Atlee Barber, copyright in 1906, best describes Mrs. Frackeltons accomplishments with stoneware as an expression of art:

It was reserved for a woman, however, to breathe the breath of artistic life into the body of American stoneware, and under her deft touch, guided by refined instinct and inventive genius, the old utilitarian forms were converted into new and graceful shapes, and the crude blue colouring, which served for ornamentation, gave place to artistic designs in relief, always signifi-cant, harmonious and thoroughly appropriate. The honour of raising the humble manufacture of salt glazed ware in this country to a place beside the finer ceramic arts belongs to Mrs. S. S. Frackelton, formerly of Milwaukee, but now of Chicago. A fine example of her work is a large jar, now in the Museum collection, which was purchased at the Chicago Exposition in 1893. It is over two and a half feet in height, of the ordinary gray colour, supported by winged feline feet and ornamented with fruited olive branches in high relief and rich blue colouring.

Lectures on Arts and Crafts

¶Engagements for single lec-tures or courses on the follow-ing subjects may be made by direct cor-respondence or by application to any Lyceum Bureau.

Mrs. S. S. Frackelton.
1025 Fine Arts Building.

SUBJECTS

Pottery. Demonstrated by use of wheel, casting in molds or modelling.
Glassmaking. History, Stained Glass, Tiffany Favrile Glass.
Crafts and Textiles. Leather, Weaving, Printing from Blocks or Stencils, Brass, Copper, Gems, Indiana Art, Basketry, Weaving, Beadwork.

This ad appeared in the June 1906 issue of Sketch Book. Mrs. Frackelton spent most of her career teaching about ceramic and other arts.

This Frackelton vase is 4" tall and 6" wide. The leaves have been applied, then stems and veins incised. The blue color-ing appears to have been sprayed on, then lightly wiped to expose the high areas of clay. The bottom clearly shows the artist's hand-incised monogram and Roman numeral 9, probably for the year 1909. The monogram and number incis-ing were painted in with blue, and the circled numbers 97.7. painted on the clay prior to being covered with a clear glaze. Frackelton is extreme-ly rare, a piece appears on the open market every three to five years. $4,000.00 – 6,000.00.

Fulper Pottery Co.

The pottery of Samuel Hill was started in Flemington, New Jersey, in 1815. Hill manufactured drain tile. Abraham Fulper, an employee, became a partner in 1847, and in 1860 he purchased the firm. Fulper produced utilitarian items of stoneware. After 1881 the business was operated as the Fulper Brothers. In 1899 they incorporated as the Fulper Pottery Company.

Fulper hired the best designers/modelers and chemists he could find, including designer John O.W. Kugler and ceramic engineer J. Martin Stangl. Fulper himself, also contributed to designs and glaze effects. John Kunsman, hired in 1899, was the master potter.

The first art pottery was produced in 1909 when the firm was under the direction of William H. Fulper II, the grandson of Abraham. They named this art pottery line "Vasekraft." Art pottery production continued for 20 years.

About 1918, Fulper started producing bisque doll heads, and later, complete ceramic doll forms. The doll market fell, and Fulper stopped production in 1922. The bisque facilities turned to manufacturing figural boudoir lamps, perfume burners and other items. Many were designed by Tony Sarg, the artist and puppeteer. Someone who signed their work "Fish" was also a designer. Pavlova posed for the ballerina on one of the boudoir lamps. Mrs. Fulper posed for another one entitled "Finale." An ad from a 1919 issue of *Country Life in America* pictures a humidor in the form of a World War I tank.

A fire destroyed the Fulper Pottery buildings at Flemington in 1929. Most of the operation was moved to their Trenton plant, but a small amount of art pottery was produced in Flemington until 1935. Stangl acquired the firm in 1930 and produced dinnerware. The corporate name was changed to Stangl Pottery in 1955.

At the Panama-Pacific International Exposition of 1915, the Fulper Pottery Exhibit shared space with part of the Gustav Stickley Craftsman Workshops. The Renaissance Wall Light shown here can be seen in the center of a photograph of the exhibit shown in Pottery and Glass, *July 1915. The photo is reproduced in* Art Pottery of the United States *by Paul Evans, and in The Jordan-Volpe Gallery exhibit book referred to later in this chapter. The Fulper factory catalogs list this as item No. 2006, and it is priced at $6.00 complete with socket. The 13" light fixture is covered with a Verte Antique Splash glaze. It is signed with the first vertical ink-stamp mark, and has remnants of a Vasekraft paper label. Complete with original brass socket and iron mounting bracket, $500.00 – 700.00.*

The Fulper Pottery Company is most admired for developing a wide variety of striking glazes and desirable forms. The glazes fall into six categories.

Mirrored: highly polished

Flambés: multiple coloration in dripping and streaking effects

Lustre: iridescence similar to the reflection of oil on water

Matte: the mat texture as it relates to vegetable skins and other organic surfaces

Wisteria: pastel colors in various tones

Crystal: encrusted crystals of varying degree, isolated to concentrated, crystalline

Fulper produced a significant amount of musical liquor decanters with music boxes mounted in the hollow bases. These items are not signed, but are usually recognized by their glazes.

Dating Fulper art pottery is difficult. There are many publications whose combined data is contradictory, confusing, and unclear. Thankfully, Mr. Robert Blasberg, in his articles in *Spinning Wheel*, October '73, and again with co-author Mr. Todd M. Volpe in *American Art & Antiques*, July – August '78, provide the most believable information. The articles were written after personal interviews with Martin Stangl and William Fulper III, and with the extensive research information provided by the New Jersey State Museum.

October '73 *Spinning Wheel*, "Twenty Years of Fulper" — see "Marks."

Fulper pieces are usually marked with the name run vertically, in characters of a vaguely Oriental style, inside a flattened oval. Mr. Stangl said the mark was probably a holdover from the tin glazed Parmelee line done before 1910. Ceramic color mixed with glycerin was used with the stamping — the same technique by which gold is applied to ceramics.

At the risk of disappointing orderly-minded collectors and dealers, it must be reported that the New Jersey State Museum and this writer agreed, following research done independently, that the use of any stamp in any Fulper piece is entirely arbitrary — the kind of variation used proves nothing. Some pieces may still be found with the original paper label bearing the devise of a potter at his wheel and, in some cases, a reference to the 1915 medal. Occasionally, three-dimensional marks were used.

July – August '78 *American Art & Antiques*, "Fulper Art Pottery," — see "Identification."

While rarely dated, Fulper ware was always signed. A piece marked "Vasekraft" was made before 1912. This trademark — the artware's first — was discontinued after three years. To ensure authenticity, the company used a variety of marks, raised, incised, ink stamped, or paper label. The Fulper mark ran vertically, in a slightly Oriental style. These marks were used at random, so it is difficult to date a specific piece unless they match a reference in a catalogue or can be identified by a particular stylistic characteristic. For example, a hexagonal vase or one purely art deco in shape was probably made around 1925. In any case, it could not have been an early piece.

For exhibitions, Fulper potters frequently designed special one-of-a-kind pieces which are signed and dated. One piece is a triple vase dated June 20, 1920, with a flambé glaze in red, black, white and blue. It was signed by John Kunsman, who had been Fulper's chief potter for years.

Fulper Art Pottery: An Aesthetic Appreciation 1909 – 1929, an exhibition of Fulper, along with furniture and accessories of the period, was held at The Jordan-Volpe Gallery in New York in 1979. The exhibition booklet text was done by Robert W. Blasberg with Carol L. Bohdan. The text within includes Blasberg's knowledge shared in his previous publications, with additional input, and learning through more studies of examples. To complicate matters, marks were used at random between 1912 and 1920. While most folks are interested in when a specific piece was manufactured, with Fulper, the glaze and form are by far the most important characteristics. The conclusions of all this data are:

The Mark	*The Production Period*
Vasekraft label	1909 to around 1913 (name discontinued in 1915)
First vertical ink-stamp (block letters in a vertical rectangle)	1909 to around 1913 (some later random use)
Vasekraft ink-stamp	1909 to around 1913 (rare, and only on early pieces)
Panama-Pacific Expo. label	after 1915, for a year or two
Oriental letters in vertical flat oval	most often before 1915, but up to 1920
Nearly square, vertical frame	most often before 1915, but up to 1920
Incised or raised letters in a vertical flat oval	after 1915, especially in late teens to early 20s
Horizontal impressed Fulper	from between 1920 & 1925 to 1929

Other Fulper products are signed Flemington, Prang, or Rafco.

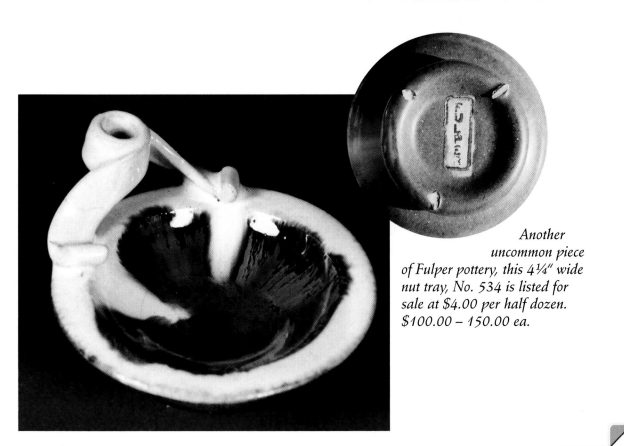

Another uncommon piece of Fulper pottery, this 4¼" wide nut tray, No. 534 is listed for sale at $4.00 per half dozen. $100.00 – 150.00 ea.

Craftsman Electric Table Lamps

No. 57. One-light Electric Lamp with Fulper pottery standard in dull green. Willow shade stained and lined with Habutai silk in any desired colors. Diameter of shade 10½ in.; height over all 15½ in. Price $5.00.

No. 18. Two-light Electric Lamp with reed standard, copper trim, and reed shade stained brown, green or gray; shade lined with figured silk in appropriate tones. Especially suitable for living room or library. Diameter of shade 20 in.; height over all 19 in. Price $15.00.

No. 15. One-light Electric Lamp with fumed oak standard, copper trim and willow shade stained and lined with Habutai silk in any colors preferred. Diameter of shade 10½ in.; height over all 15½ in. Price $3.50.

No. 2635. One-light Electric Lamp with fumed oak standard, brass trim and silk shade in any colors desired. Diameter of shade 12 in.; height over all 20 in. Price complete $8.75; without shade $4.00.

No. 17. One-light Electric Lamp with Lenox pottery standard in white, blue, mauve, gray, soft green, rose, orange or brown, with brass trim. Shade of figured silk in various colors, under silver net, with wooden beads. A charming lamp for bedroom or boudoir. Diameter of shade 10½ in.; height over all 17½ in. Price $15.00.

Any of these lamps will be shipped to you, parcel post prepaid, promptly on receipt of order, at prices named.

 GUSTAV STICKLEY, THE CRAFTSMAN

Craftsman Building NEW YORK   468 Boylston St. BOSTON   1512 H St., N. W. WASHINGTON

The Craftsman, *February 1915.*

The shapes, shown in this ad from the December '09 issue of *The Craftsman,* are quite different than what appears in today's market. Notice the Vase-Kraft logo conjoined with an old Fulper stoneware logo.

The Craftsman,
December 1909.

Theatre Magazine,
December 1917.

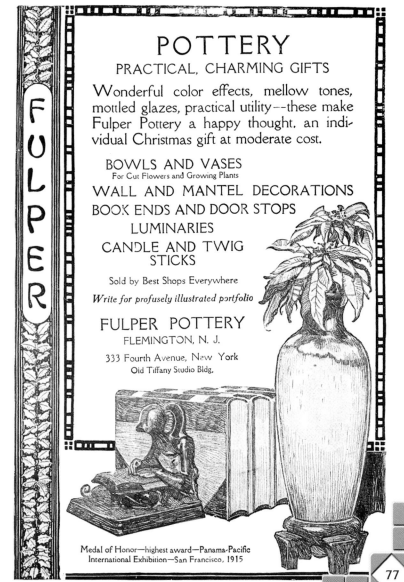

FUNNEL

(Electric)

LAMP

$45.00

(Height 21½ in.)

One of the most beautiful of the

FULPER VASEKRAFT LAMPS

In Matte, mirror or *flambe* and equipped with Fulper pin switch and two lights.

A Fulper lamp adds beauty to any home. It is the "latest thing" in interior decoration.

Illustrated Art Catalogue FREE.

It will help you in the selection of your Christmas gifts—our Clocks, Vases, Tobacco Jars, Toddy Sets, etc., will make presents that will be appreciated—and at most reasonable prices.

Fulper Pottery Company
FOUNDED 1805
11 Fulper Place, FLEMINGTON, N. J.
New York Exhibit: 333 Fourth Avenue
Formerly Tiffany Studios

Country Life,
December 1911.

Give Your Boy when he comes Home a BRITISH TANK Tobacco Jar $12.50

A practical ornamental and altogether acceptable present for a man.

FULPER

Founded 1805

America's Most Distinguished

POTTERY

Delightful and Artistic Pieces in
RARE and BEAUTIFUL GLAZES
VASES and FLOWER HOLDERS
For EASTER

FULPER POTTERY COMPANY
104 Fulper Place   Flemington, New Jersey

NEW YORK
Permanent Branch Exhibition 200 Fifth Ave.

Send for profusely illustrated Book

GRECIAN VASE
A Mirror Black
Glaze—12 in. high
$9.50

HIGHEST AWARDS WHEREVER SHOWN.

Country Life,
March 1919.

FLOWER ARRANGEMENT BY CONSTANCE SPRY

No. 3229 Bowl, 9" wide   No. 3405 Cockatoo, 6" high

Gay Birds...
Bright New Note in Decoration

No. 3443 Flying Duck 9" high

Newest, smartest of gifts... bright pottery birds for focal points of color in your rooms, exciting accessories to accent your flower arrangements. A whole aviary to choose from!

Lovely birds like these once came only as costly imports, now are made in America... exquisite reproductions of nature, expertly hand-painted and glazed. In full natural color, white crackle, or turquoise blue.

These Stangl masterpieces, by artists and skilled potters, climax the creative achievement of nearly a century and a half's training and experience in the ceramic art.

No. 3404 Double Lovebird 5" high

No. 3402 Oriole 3¼" high

If these birds are not obtainable locally, mail coupon for FREE Folder, illustrated in full color.

THE FULPER POTTERY CO.
Established 1805
THE OLDEST POTTERY COMPANY IN AMERICA
TRENTON, NEW JERSEY

THE FULPER POTTERY CO., TRENTON, NEW JERSEY
Please send me without cost, beautiful full-color booklet "GAY BIRDS" together with price list. 27 birds illustrated in nature's own lovely colors.

NAME

ADDRESS

House and Garden, *December 1940.*

Porcelains — Adorable — Unusual
Perfume Burners, Powder Jars, Tea Table Bells, etc. delivered safely, anywhere—send for booklet—

Fulper Pottery   Flemington, N. J.

House and Garden, *January 1923.*

THE MAID
A brilliant hand decorated porcelain
ASH TRAY
Designed by "FISH" famed in Vogue and Vanity Fair

A Charming Gift
$2.00 Safely Delivered
anywhere in the U. S. A. proper

FULPER POTTERY
Founded 1805
Flemington   New Jersey

Country Life, *December 1927.*

Galloway Terra Cotta Co.

Founded as Galloway & Graff in Philadelphia in 1810, this firm produced terra-cotta. Barber, in *Marks of American Potters,* said that the Galloway & Graff firm was founded in 1810, as does much of the company's advertising in trade and retail publications and their own factory catalogs.

This company manufactured an extensive variety of products for the garden and for interior decoration. Sundials, benches, tables, fountains, statues, flower boxes, urns, pedestals, and vases were produced in many styles.

Barber, in his 1893 publication, lists the company as Galloway & Graff, but in his 1904 publication he said it was being operated by William Galloway. I have in my collection of advertising an ad from the July 1904 issue of *International Studio,* showing the firm as William Galloway. So sometime between 1893 and 1904, the firm name was changed to William Galloway. The company operated under this name until 1909, when it was renamed the Galloway Terra-Cotta Co. Advertising as late as 1915 says, "Formerly, William Galloway."

As early as 1913, advertising started emphasizing Galloway Pottery by putting those words in bold print at the top, while de-emphasizing the Galloway Terra-Cotta Co. by putting it in small letters as the mailing address. This continued until sometime between May 1929 and May 1930, when the company name was dropped altogether. Advertising continued from this point to list the company as Galloway Pottery, at the same old address of Walnut and 32nd Streets. I don't know if the company name was ever officially changed.

House Beautiful,
May 1929.

GALLOWAY POTTERY *Gives the Essential Touch*

TO one who loves a garden Galloway Pottery appeals with its grace of line and pleasing color, giving striking contrasts midst flowers and sunshine and the shadows of the trees. Shapely jars, glazed or unglazed and other delightful pieces for the garden, sunroom and porch, including

Bird Baths, Vases, Gazing Globes, Sun Dials, Benches and Flower Pots

High fired Terra Cotta has stood the test of time assuring you of enduring beauty whether used in the garden or indoors.

Send ten cents in stamps for catalogue of 300 numbers

GALLOWAY TERRA-COTTA CO.
3218 WALNUT ST. PHILADELPHIA

GARDEN POTTERY

Sun Dials
Vases
Statuary
Fountains

❧

WM. GALLOWAY
3224 Walnut St.,
PHILADELPHIA
Catalogue on request

ITALIAN FLOWER POT

International Studio,
July 1904.

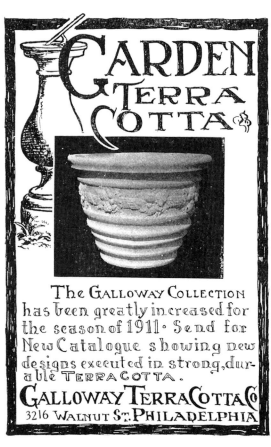

Country Life in America, *February 1911.*

GALLOWAY
TERRA·COTTA
AND POTTERY FOR GARDEN AND ... INTERIOR·DECORATION

YOUR Garden and Home will be beautified by the correct use of flower pots, jardinieres, vases, benches, replicas of classic art, and other furniture.

The Galloway Productions are ideal for both Garden and Indoor use. The extensive collection executed in terra cotta shows delicacy and refinement of detail impossible in other materials, and all the products have the essential qualities of strength and durability.

Highest award has been given the work at several of the International Expositions and the demands of the most exacting for goods of high artistic merit are fully satisfied.

Send for Catalogue, replete with beautiful, original and antique designs.

FLOWER POTS, VASES, PEDESTALS, URNS, FLOWER BOXES, JARDINIERES, SUNDIALS, BENCHES, TABLES, STATUARY, HERMES, FOUNTAINS, ETC.

GALLOWAY TERRA COTTA CO.
3210 WALNUT ST., PHILADELPHIA

International Studio, *April 1910.*

BIRD BATHS
Jars, Vases Sun Dials, Gazing Globes Benches etc.

THE lovely garden or restful sun room becomes even more attractive by the skillful use of GALLOWAY Pottery. High-fired, enduring Terra Cottas; graceful in line, Jars in colorful iridescent glazes.

Ask for illustrated catalogue.

GALLOWAY POTTERY

3214 *Walnut St.,* PHILADELPHIA
Also on display 509 Madison Ave., New York

ESTABLISHED 1810

House Beautiful,
May 1930.

Country Life in America,
March 1915.

GALLOWAY POTTERY
DOUBLES *the* GARDEN'S CHARM

Though your Garden be small, a Sun-Dial, Bird Font or Gazing Globe adds the essential touch. Terraces, Porches, and Cozy Nooks will invite you to linger if Artistically Furnished with Terra Cotta Tables and Benches, while your Plants will have New Beauty in GALLOWAY Pots, Boxes and Vases.

We are the Oldest and Largest Manufacturers of Garden Pottery in America. Our long Experience is Embodied in a Comprehensive Catalogue containing a Wealth of Suggestions for making Your Garden Attractive. This Catalogue will be sent upon request.

GALLOWAY TERRA COTTA CO.
3216 WALNUT STREET, PHILADELPHIA.

NEW YORK SHOWROOM
CRAFTSMAN BUILDING
39TH ST., EAST *of* 5TH AVE.

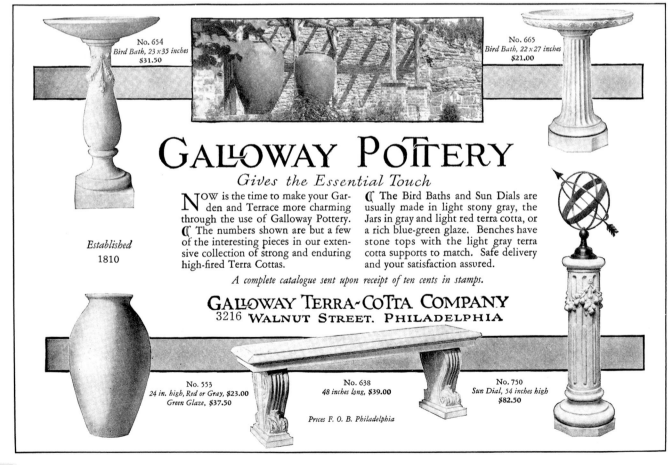

No. 654
Bird Bath, 23 x 35 inches
$31.50

No. 665
Bird Bath, 22 x 27 inches
$21.00

GALLOWAY POTTERY
Gives the Essential Touch

Established 1810

NOW is the time to make your Garden and Terrace more charming through the use of Galloway Pottery. The numbers shown are but a few of the interesting pieces in our extensive collection of strong and enduring high-fired Terra Cottas.

The Bird Baths and Sun Dials are usually made in light stony gray, the Jars in gray and light red terra cotta, or a rich blue-green glaze. Benches have stone tops with the light gray terra cotta supports to match. Safe delivery and your satisfaction assured.

A complete catalogue sent upon receipt of ten cents in stamps.

GALLOWAY TERRA-COTTA COMPANY
3216 WALNUT STREET, PHILADELPHIA

No. 553
*24 in. high, Red or Gray, $23.00
Green Glaze, $37.50*

No. 638
48 inches long, $39.00

No. 750
Sun Dial, 54 inches high
$82.50

Prices F. O. B. Philadelphia

Country Life in America, *April 1928.*

Factory Catalog No. 15 *(page 84)* is titled *Terra-Cotta and Pottery,* with the company as Galloway Terra-Cotta Company. Catalog No. 24 *(below)* is titled *Galloway Pottery,* with the company as the Galloway Terra-Cotta Company. The catalogs have the same basic offering, with deletions of the older, low numbered items and the poor sellers, and the addition of new items. Stock ordering numbers rose from 591 in catalog No. 15 to 734 in catalog No. 24. Prices on like items increased from between 10% to 65%. Although neither catalog is dated, when comparing the items offered and the title or cover pages to those in dated advertising, I believe the catalog numbers are for the years that they were published ie; catalog No. 24 was published for 1924.

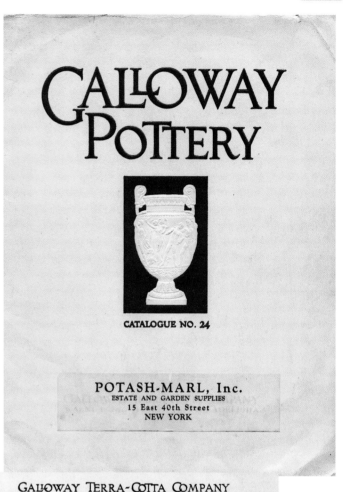

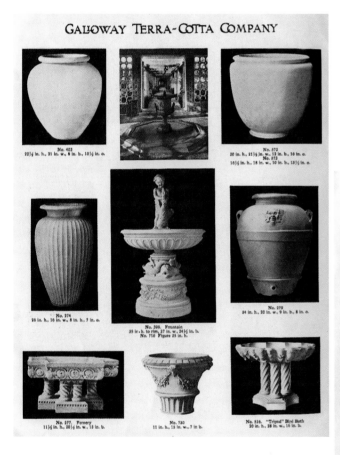

Galloway Terra Cotta Co.

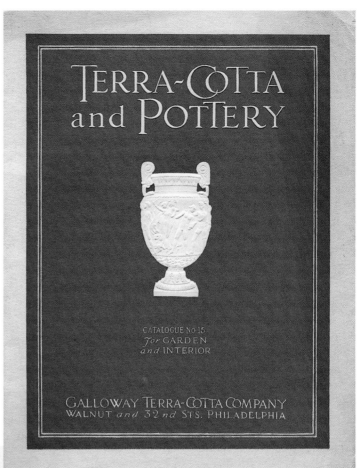

TERRA-COTTA and POTTERY

CATALOGUE No 15
For GARDEN
and INTERIOR

GALLOWAY TERRA-COTTA COMPANY
WALNUT *and* 32nd STS. PHILADELPHIA

GALLOWAY TERRA-COTTA COMPANY

No. 242. Vase (Antique)
30 in. h.

No. 533. Pedestal. Vase No. 2
63 in. total h.

No. 183. Vase (Antique) 35 in. h.
No. 257. 19 in. h.
Original in British Museum

No. 535. Fruit Basket
18 in. h., 10 in. w., 7½ in. b.

No. 250. Vase (Antique)
35 in. h., 25 in. w., 13 in. b.

No. 534. Fruit Basket
42 in. h., 25 in. w., 15 in. b.

GALLOWAY TERRA-COTTA COMPANY

No. 266. Bowl
40 in. w., 12 in. h.

No. 181. Pedestal
43 in. h., 15½ in. t.
No. 405. Pedestal
34 in. h., 12 in. t.

No. 407. Pedestal
45 in. h.

No. 590. Cupid and Goose
25 in. h., 9½ x 10 in. b.

No. 21. Vase (Antique)
16 in. h., 32 in. w., (Bowl, 27 in.), 9 in. b.
No. 17. Pedestal
32 in. h., 11½ in. t., 15½ in. b.
No. 18. Pedestal
35 in. h., 14 in. t., 19 in. b.

No. 590. Cupid and Goose
25 in. h., 9½ x 10 in. b.

Nos. 111 to 115   No. 27

PEDESTALS

No. 117   No. 118

GALLOWAY TERRA-COTTA COMPANY

No. 588
61 in. h., 13½ x 14½ in. b.

No. 303
5 ft. 8 in. h.   No. 302
5 ft. h.
HERMES

No. 589. Hermes-Nymph
61 in. h., 13½ x 14½ in. b.

No. 67. Dancing Girl (by Canova)
69 in. h., 18 in. f.

No. 182. Hebe (by Thorwaldsen)
59 in. h., 12 x 15½ in. b.

No. 64. Diana (de Gabii)
66 in. h., 16 in. b.

GALLOWAY TERRA-COTTA COMPANY

No. 7. "The Fishers" (Group for Fountain)
48 in. h., 28 in. b.

No. 273. Font with
Figure No. 304

No. 6. "Mermaid" Fountain
48 in. h., 28 in. b.

No. 171. Venus de Milo
37 in. h.

No. 273. Vase
48 in. h., 26 in. w., 14 in. b.

No. 301. Venus at Bath
(by Glodion). 33 in. h.

William H. Grueby, a boy of 13, started work at the Low Art Tile Works in Chelsea, Massachusetts, in 1880. He remained at Low until 1890, when he established an architectural faience firm in Revere, Massachusetts. Starting in 1891, he and Eugene R. Atwood worked as Atwood & Grueby. In 1894, Grueby founded the Grueby Faience Company in Boston. The business was incorporated in 1897. That same year, designer and craftsman George P. Kendrick was hired. William H. Graves, an architect, became the firm's business manager. In 1901, Addison B. LeBoutillier, a French architect, succeeded Kendrick as the director of design.

In 1907, the Grueby Pottery Company was incorporated, a move to separate the two distinct divisions of architectural products and decorative pottery products. Grueby became president of the pottery. At about the same time, Augustus A. Carpenter of Chicago, took over as the president of the Grueby Faience Co., probably because he provided financial support to the firm. In 1908, Karl Langenbeck joined the Grueby Faience Co. as superintendent.

Grueby returned to the architectural faience firm in 1909. That same year the Grueby Faience Co. went bankrupt. Grueby secured the release of his name and processes, and established the Grueby Faience and Tile Company.

Graves had replaced Grueby as president of the Grueby Pottery, and Karl Langenbeck moved from the faience firm to become superintendent and technician of the Grueby Pottery. The combined, long experiences and skills of Graves and Langenbeck in this business did not stop the Grueby Pottery from closing early in 1911. The March issue of *Keramic Studio* announced the regretful event.

Grueby Faience and Tile continued to operate until the factory burned in 1913. The factory was rebuilt with more capitol, provided again by Carpenter. In 1919 the firm was purchased by the C. Pardee Works of Perth Amboy, New Jersey. Pardee moved the operations to New Jersey in 1921.

Grueby developed his own superior mat glazes. Although other firms had developed their own mat glazes prior to Grueby, he was the first to successfully produce and market a product that was to be admired by so many. Most pots were hand thrown and hand decorated, modeled, and painted by skilled artists. Only a few were offered with molded bodies and/or sprigged on blossoms, and these were done skillfully and artistically. Some objects, pottery, and tiles are artist signed with ink, glaze, or incising. Grueby won many exhibition awards including two Gold Medals at Paris in 1900, a Gold Medal at Buffalo and at St. Petersburg in 1901, and a Grand Prize at St. Louis in 1904.

This 6" square water lily decorated tile is signed with a small die impressed Grueby, with Boston below. It is also marked with a large number 63 on one edge. Similar marks appear with just Grueby, Grueby over Boston, Mass, or Grueby Pottery over Boston, U.S.A. $400.00 – 500.00.

It was reported in the March – April 1996 issue of the *Journal of the American Art Pottery Association,* that fake tiles of Grueby designs and glazes, with this mark, were appearing from New England to Florida. The mark on the fakes is convincing, but the lotus is narrow and less detailed, looking more like a slightly open bud then a blossom.

Decorated with a galleon, this tile is 4" square, and is signed with the impressed die mark of the Grueby lotus encircled with "Grueby Tile, Boston." $350.00 – 450.00.

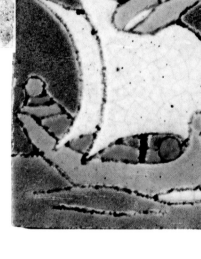

The Monk with Book decoration was done with a curdled matt mustard glaze on a terra cotta clay body. The tile is 6" square and has the number 654 impressed on one edge. $300.00 – 400.00.

These 4¼" square tiles are unsigned, but are of Grueby design. Identifying the origin and date of manufacture of unsigned bisque or unglazed Grueby designs is not possible. The tile shown here with a monk and others were produced at Grueby prior to the purchase by Pardee while still in Boston and through 1930, and maybe till Pardee closed in 1938. See Pardee. $50.00 – 65.00 ea.

Scarab paper-weights, like the one shown here, were introduced at the 1904 St. Louis Exposition. It measures 2½" wide and 4" long and is signed with the die-impressed circular Faience mark. $350.00 – 450.00. Grueby used another mark like this, with the word Pottery used in the place of Faience. With the exception of the circular tile mark, all the marks mentioned above and paper labels were used on both pottery and tiles.

In 1913 this Hauteville mark and in 1921 the large G design were added to Grueby logos.

HAUTEVILLE

GRUEBY·POTTERY·BOSTON·U·S·A·

GRUEBY POTTERY
BOSTON.U.S.A.

GRUEBY

GRUEBY FAIENCE Co. BOSTON.U.S.A.

GRUEBY
BOSTON.MASS

The International Studio, August 1905.

GRUEBY POTTERY

The Grueby Pottery has won the interest of ceramists and connoisseurs throughout the world ❧ ❧ ❧ *Gold medals at Paris, St Petersburg & Buffalo.* Marshall Field & Co sole agents for Chicago.

GRUEBY POTTERY

Christmas Exhibitions at the following places

S. BING,	Paris.
THEODORE B. STARR,	New York.
TAFT & BELKNAP CO.,	New York.
BIGELOW, KENNARD & CO.,	Boston.
POTTER & CO.,	Providence.
J. E. CALDWELL & CO.,	Philadelphia.
DULIN & MARTIN,	Washington.
W. H. GLENNY & CO.,	Rochester.
McCLELLAND & BECKER,	Syracuse.
GEO. W. BENSON,	Buffalo.
CHARLES W. WARREN & CO.,	Detroit.
C. A. SELZER,	Cleveland.
LORING ANDREWS & CO.,	Cincinnati.
MARSHALL FIELD & CO.,	Chicago.
H. KLINGENFELD & CO.,	Milwaukee.
WM. A. FRENCH,	St. Paul.
JOHN S. BRADSTREET & CO.,	Minneapolis.
J. D. SWAN ART CO.	Kansas City.
R. L. BOUTWELL & CO.,	Denver.
J. KENNARD & SONS,	St. Louis.
SHREVE & COMPANY,	San Francisco.

Gold medals won in France, Russia Italy and America

The art work shown in these two early ads is signed by LeBoutillier. House Beautiful, *December 1901 (above);* Century, *December 1903 (right).*

FIREPLACES in Grueby faience and other tiles, marble, stone, cement, caen-stone and brick. Andirons and Firetools, antique and modern, in all metals and finishes. Fenders, English Kerbs, Spark Guards, Dome and Flat Dampers. Foreign and Domestic Tiles for Bathroom and Kitchen Walls. Ceramics and Cut Mosaics and Grueby floor tiles. Grueby Non-slip tiles for Church Entrances, Vestibules, Porches, Loggias, in all designs and colors. Exclusive owners **of the celebrated Grueby Pottery,** all sizes, designs and colors. Choice examples in Shef-field on Copper. Colonial and other period mirrors in gold and mahogany. Candlesticks in pewter, brass, bronze and Sheffield. Pottery for Porches and Formal Gardens in cement and stone. **Art Objects from every part of the world, personally selected, and hence not commercial.**

Write us. Consultation and estimates by mail, or personally by an expert

WILLIAM H. HOOPS & COMPANY
····William H. Hoops Building·····
531 Wabash Avenue, Chicago, U.S.A.

The ad from the January 1912, issue of The American Monthly Magazine *is interesting. While advertising Grueby faience tiles for fireplaces, William H. Hoops & Co. claim to be "Exclusive owners of the celebrated Grueby Pottery." Did they just mean to say they were the exclusive Chicago area dealer for Grueby products, or were they somehow connected to Mr. A. A. Carpenter of Chicago, and therefore beneficiaries under the receiverships entered for the pottery or faience business?*

Adolph Metzner had been working in his backyard facility for a long time, trying to perfect tile. In 1884 he purchased the Royal Pottery Company of Hamilton, Ohio.

During his first year in business, Metzner took in two partners and went through two name changes. Mr. J. L. Bieler joined Metzner after the purchase, and the firm became Adolph Metzner & Bieler. A tile man, Robert Minton Taylor, who had been employed at the U.S.E.T. Works from 1881 to 1883, joined the firm and it became Taylor Ceramic Company. Taylor soon left. Through all this change, Metzner and his sons, Otto and Max, kept working, and eventually perfected enameled tile with a very good clay body, hand-some designs, and glazes of beauty and color. Before the year was over, the firm name was changed to the Hamilton Tile Works Company. By 1887 31 people were employed. They manufactured floor and wall tile, and tiles for decorating fireplaces and mantels. The company failed about 1900, and Adolph and his son Max went to work for the C. Pardee Works. In 1908 they obtained financing and built their own plant in Perth Amboy, New Jersey.

After the failure of the Hamilton Tile Works, some residents of Hamilton organized a new company and called it the Ohio Tile Company. This company failed in 1909.

An advertising paperweight, this 2¼″ x 4¼″ tile has a convex surface. The back mark is "Hamilton, O," in raised letters. I wonder if the Beeler on this paperweight and the Bieler who was probably an investing partner are the same person? $50.00 – 75.00.

The seven putti who are pushing and pulling the goat are in very high relief. The 6″ x 12″ tile is marked with "The-Hamilton-Tile Works Co-Hamilton-Ohio," in raised letters, on five horizontal lines within a large circle. Very high relief tiles are usually of early production and very desirable. $450.00 – 550.00.

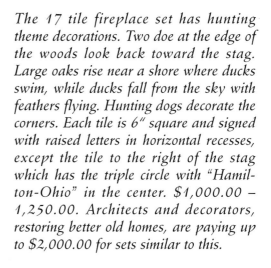

The 17 tile fireplace set has hunting theme decorations. Two doe at the edge of the woods look back toward the stag. Large oaks rise near a shore where ducks swim, while ducks fall from the sky with feathers flying. Hunting dogs decorate the corners. Each tile is 6" square and signed with raised letters in horizontal recesses, except the tile to the right of the stag which has the triple circle with "Hamilton-Ohio" in the center. $1,000.00 – 1,250.00. Architects and decorators, restoring better old homes, are paying up to $2,000.00 for sets similar to this.

Twelve classical figures, playing musical instruments and dancing, decorate this 6″ x 12″ tile. This tile has the same mark as the putti and goat decorated tile. $350.00 – 450.00.

The cast-iron brackets holding this pair of 6″ square tiles were designed to decorate, while supporting a mantel. These tiles are signed with the triple circle mark with the raised words "Hamilton-Ohio." $350.00 – 450.00.

*Both of these 6"
square tiles have the
triple circle mark. The
tile with a lion has the
OM monogram for
Otto Metzner in the
upper left corner. Artist
signed tiles are very
scarce. $300.00 –
350.00. The portrait
of the young lady,
$150.00 – 200.00.*

*This
pair of
ladies'
portrait
tiles are
4⅜" square. Both are marked
with a double circle with the
raised letter words "Hamilton-
Ohio," in the small circle.
$200.00 – 250.00 pr.*

*This 4¼" square
tile is marked with
an ink stamped
"Hamilton Tile
Co." under a thin
protective
coat of glaze.
$20.00 –
25.00.*

Although they were designed as a pair, these 4⅜" square tiles have different colored glazes because they were not purchased together. I purchased the tile with the man several years ago. When I recently purchased the tile with the woman, the dealer had the pair but had them priced individually at the same top of the scale price. The tile I didn't buy was damaged, besides, the tile I did buy is artist signed. The AM monogram of Adolph Metzner, the founder, appears at the lower right corner. Neither tile has a mark on the back. $75.00 – 100.00 for the male, $175.00 – 200.00 for the artist-signed female portrait.

Compare the work of the tiles above to that of the tiles in the cast-iron mantel supports shown on page 93. There are strong similarities in the eyes and noses of both male and female subjects, and the ears of the females. One might easily attribute the tiles in the mantel supports to Adolph Metzner.

These 3" square tiles were used to decorate a hearth. The backs are marked with raised letters in horizontal recesses saying "H.T.Wks.Co-Hamilton-Ohio" on three lines. $2.00 – 3.00 ea.

Hartford Faience Co.

Eugene R. Atwood founded the Hartford Faience Company in Hartford, Connecticut, sometime after 1894. Atwood had been a partner of William Grueby at the firm of Atwood & Grueby in Revere, Massachusetts. Atwood left when the business became the Grueby Faience Co. in 1894.

The Hartford firm manufactured architectural faience and other faience products in the form of tiles, plaques, mantels, and pottery. They also started producing electrical porcelains near the turn of the century. All of their products were of exceptional quality. They won Gold Medals at the St Louis Exposition of 1904 for an artistic faience mantel with a large panel titled "The Sun Worshippers" and for their electrical porcelains.

This photo of the panel "Eventide," signed by the Hartford artist Francis G. Plant, appeared in E. W. Robinson's article in the November 1908 issue of International Studio.

In an article "A Word on Faience" by Edward Wanton Robinson, in the November 1908 issue of *International Studio*, Mr. Robinson used pictures of products of Hartford Faience. One photo in the article credits Hartford Faience for the tile installation at the South Ferry Station of the New York Subway System. The architects for the subway, Heins and LaFarge, are identified as the designers. This installation was completed in 1905. In a Hartford Faience catalog titled *Illustrated Catalog No. 1,* the sailboat plaque of the South Ferry Station installation is pictured and identified. I have several booklets and articles that discuss the tile installations of the New York Subway System. None, but the article in the November 1908 issue of *International Studio* credit Hartford Faience with the installation. Some identify the tiles as Rookwood. Hartford Faience is long overdue the credit deserved for this subway installation. Lee Stookey said it best, though probably unknowingly, when in his publication, *Subway Ceramics,* he stated "Many have said that the South Ferry plaque — is the most splendid of all the ceramic works."

The electrical porcelain products, introduced at the beginning of the century, evolved to become the main products when the business stopped deliveries to utility companies in 1947.

The availability of Hartford products to collectors outside the northeast area is minimal. I have had but one opportunity to purchase a signed piece of Hartford Faience.

In addition to the trademark shown on every page of the catalog, a die-impressed "Hartford Faience" mark was used.

Country Life, October 1907.

EMBELLISHMENTS
FOR
CONCRETE
BUILDINGS
INTERIOR AND EXTERIOR

The problem of making artistic concrete buildings, both private and public, is most satisfactorily solved by the use of

HARTFORD FAIENCE

The Hartford Faience Company will be pleased to correspond with everyone contemplating the erection of concrete residences and other buildings as to the uses of Hartford Faience, and will furnish suggestions and sketches upon request. Kindly address Department E, for CONCRETE BUILDINGS, Medallions, Friezes, Mantels, Mouldings, Caps and Tiles.

THE HARTFORD FAIENCE COMPANY,
HARTFORD, CONN.

ILLUSTRATED CATALOG.

No. 1.

SHOWING

Faience Mantels   Architectural Faience

Faience Tile   Terra Vitrae Tile

Faience Pottery

The Hartford Faience Co.,

HARTFORD, CONN.

The reprinted pages shown here and on the following pages are from The Hartford Faience Company catalog.

TRADE

MARK

BOSTON OFFICE,
294 Washington Street.

NEW YORK OFFICE,
24 Park Place.

Faience Panel and Frieze for South Ferry Station of N. Y. Subway.
All dulls glazed used.   Top course in RED.

Mantel No. 6.

Height, 5 ft. 6 1-2 in.
Width at Base, 5 ft. 10 in.
Width at Top, 6 ft. 10 in.
Opening, 3 ft. 0 in. x 2 ft. 6 in. high.
Hearth, 6 ft. x 1 ft. 8 in.
Shelf, 11 in. Wide.

The most ambitious and and artistic Faience Mantel ever made. After Della Robbia. Done in dull finish greens and yellows.

"The Sun Worshippers."

Base 10′ wide, 5′ high.   Subject: "The Sun Worshippers"
Panel 10′ wide, 5′ high.   awarded a Gold Medal at St. Louis Exposition.

Facing No. 1.

Dutch Facing.
Size of Tile, 9″ x 9″.

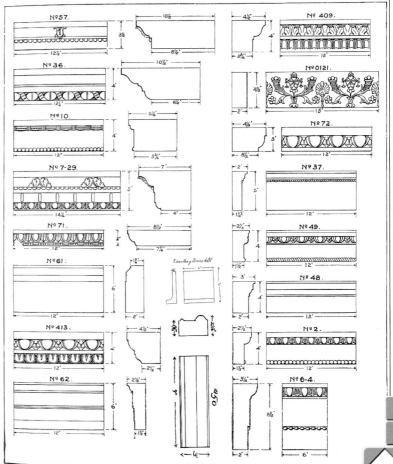

WE take pleasure in introducing to our friends FAIENCE POTTERY, a few examples of which are shown in the above cuts. This line of pottery we have recently put upon the market and in connection with it we shall endeavor NOT to make it the largest line, but shall strive to have it ALWAYS artistic and pleasing.

You can buy this pottery either direct from us at the factory or from our agents. The pottery is made in a bright glaze of a soft apple green color.

In calling your attention to this pottery we feel confident that you will not be disappointed if when you desire to purchase something in pottery you select a piece from this line. You will find a list below giving the number of the piece, name, size, and the list price and in ordering would kindly ask you to use the number as well as the name.

No.	Name	Height	Price
1	Umbrella Stand	22″	$24.00 ea.
2	Wide Mouthed Vase	6″	3.60 ea.
3	Tall Pitcher	10″	6.00 ea.
4	Pitcher Mug	6″	2.70 ea.
5	Basket Pitcher Vase	10″	7.50 ea.
6	Two-handled Vase	8″	6.60 ea.
7	Dutch Jardiniere	6″	10.00 ea.
8	Cocked-hat Pitcher	6″	2.25 ea.
9	Lamp Base	10 1-2″	10.00 ea.
10	Hooded Candlestick	7″	6.00 ea.
11	Wall Vase	8″	7.50 ea.
12	Greek Pitcher	12″	6.00 ea.
13	Wide-mouthed Pitcher	10″	4.50 ea.
14	Candlestick	11″	3.50 ea.
15	Small Vase	3″	1.00 ea.
16	Jardiniere	11″	9.00 ea.
17	Small Pitcher	4″	1.50 ea.
18	Vase	6″	2.00 ea.
19	Duck Pitcher	8″	4.50 ea.
20	Pitcher	11″	5.50 ea.
21	Ring-top Vase	8″	3.00 ea.
22	Low Pitcher	6″	4.50 ea.
23	Vase	7″	3.00 ea.
24	Jardiniere	10″	8.00 ea.
25	Dutch Vase	7″	3.00 ea.
26	Fernery	6″	4.00 ea.
26	Vase	9″	3.00 ea.

A FAIENCE MANTLE

The Readers of "Country Life in America"
will do well to study the Faience Mantels
of the Hartford Faience Company

This illustration shows a most pleasing example — the lines are simple and chaste — the dark green tile of rough texture harmonizes admirably with the tinted unfinished plaster of the room while the beamed ceiling and dark Mission furniture make it into a beautiful picture.

Catalog F illustrates many other pleasing examples in mantels.   It will be sent to anyone interested, and if you will send us a description of your room we will be pleased to suggest a good mantel for you. Address

THE HARTFORD FAIENCE COMPANY
Hartford, Conn.

Country Life,
May 1907.

Ivory White Ware

Ivory white ware is a once fired ceramic body made for the very large amateur art pottery decorating trade. Amateur decorating started growing about 1870 and exploded in the '80s and '90s. There were several American white ware manufacturers in the 1880s, along with many importers who supplied the demand for this art form. Many of the artists, both amateur and professional, and instructors involved in this period of rapid growth of china decorating are now popular names to collectors of pottery and other decorative art.

Mr. D. M. Bedell of New York, New York, was an importer and wholesaler of Minton tiles and English and French plaques and panels suitable for mineral oil and underglaze decoration. He was also the manufacturer of Ivory White Ware. He marked his product with the letters "I.V.W." within a diamond. The mark

The Art Amateur, *May 1883.*

was applied with a rubber ink stamp. Since he was in the wholesale business only, his advertising for ivory white ware advised those interested that his product was "For Sale by Dealers," meaning retailers. A Mr. D. B. Bedell, also of New York, advertised as the "sole agent" in New York for ivory white ware. No doubt the Bedells were related.

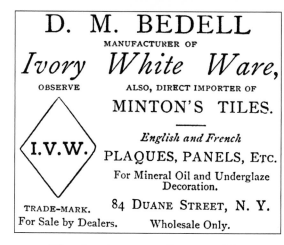

The Art Amateur, *January 1885.*

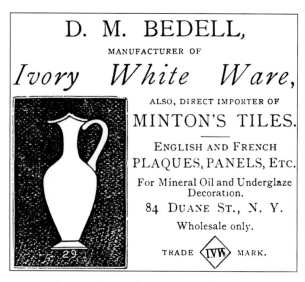

The Art Interchange, *October 1884.*

Shown are ads by both Bedells, attesting to their respective proprietorship. Also shown is an ad for "Lycett's Art Schools and China Decorating Works." The Lycetts had schools in both New York and Atlanta that were recognized as reputable institutions. In their ad they claim to be the sole agents in the state of Georgia for "Bedell's Ivory White Ware." This not only

attests to Bedell's ownership of the brand, but also to the product's quality.

Edwin Atlee Barber states in his book, *Marks of American Potters,* under the section covering the Jersey City Pottery, Jersey City, New Jersey: "About 1880 the firm began to use a new mark on their ivory white ware for decorators. This mark consisted of the letters I.V.W. It was evidently prepared hurriedly, as the middle letter should have been a W, but, since the error had appeared on the ware, it was never corrected."

The Art Interchange, *July 1885.*

I have serious doubts about Mr. Barber's statement of the mark being an uncorrected error. The I.V.W. mark is done with an inexpensive rubber stamp, readily available even in 1880. I think Barber was totally confused about this product, its origin, and the mark.

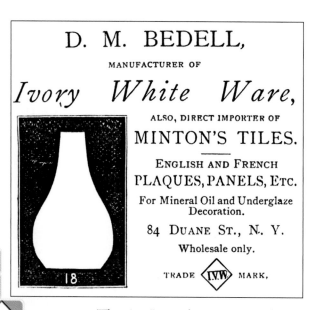

The Art Interchange, *December*

The Art Interchange, *1884 and 1885.*

If in fact the Jersey City Pottery did introduce this product and mark, they soon sold their rights to them to Mr. D.M. Bedell who manufactured and sold the line for several years, in fact 10 years before Barber published his book in 1893.

The tiger lily and gold sponge decoration has been done over the glaze on this I.V.W. shape #18, 9" x 5" vase. $100.00 – 150.00.

This 8½" I.V.W. ewer is artist signed and dated 1887. This decoration is also over the glaze. Over the glaze decorated pieces are not difficult to find. However, they are scarce in good condition and with quality art work. $100.00 – 150.00

Kensington Art Tile Co.

The Kensington Art Tile Company of Newport, Kentucky, has been obscure, the result of very little recorded history, a scarcity of examples of the products, and a trademark sometimes identified as an import.

The five written references I have, although very short and sometimes confusing, provide a general time frame and information for the founding, manufacturing, and failure of Kensington.

The *Bulletin of The American Ceramics Society,* a ceramics history, May 15, 1943, states: "Two brothers, Arthur and Otto Hatt, built a small tile factory sometime before 1886, for it is recorded that they failed during this year. The name of the company was Hatt and Hatt, and they made glazed tile.

After this failure, the Hatt brothers interested Colonel R.W. Wilson, John Meyerberg, Otto Metzner, and John Sheehy in organizing a new company, the Kensington Tile Company, which made enamel glass tile. This company failed in 1892."

In the Cincinnati and northern Kentucky area directory of 1888 – 89, it lists the firm at Lowell and Elm, with R.W. Nelson, president; J.A.H. Hatt, secretary and treasurer; O.W. Hatt, superintendent and manager.

The Newport City Directory of 1890 – 91 has no listing of this company. However, the 1891 publication, *Illustrated Cincinnati: the Queen City of the West,* provides this brief description: "Kensington Art Tile Co., Corner Elm and Lowell Streets. This company was duly organized and incorporated in 1881, and has achieved an international reputation. The works are conveniently located at the corner of Elm and Lowell Streets and extend to Seventh Street. The main building is a substantial brick structure, three stories and basement

in height and 40 by 200 feet in dimensions. The equipment for art tile making purposes is of the most elaborate, complete and modern description, and includes four large kilns, which bake to the extent of 14,000 feet of tile at one filling. The process of preparation of the crude clay are as elaborate as they are complicated. The clay is first puddled and forced through great sieves by steam power. It is then dried, and ground to a fine powder, and then molded and pressed into the tile shapes, which are carefully baked then removed and coated with the enamel and glazing liquids. They are then finally placed in the kilns and thoroughly glazed, when they are finally removed to the sorting and packing room, and forthwith shipped to destination. The most extreme care is taken to have all the materials pure and accurately prepared, and the result is a perfection of quality, an elaborateness of finish, and a beauty and delicacy of colors and tints, nowhere else attempted, much less duplicated. An average force of 100 hands is employed, and ten teams are kept busy constantly. The officers of the company are as follows; Mr. R.W. Nelson, president, and prominently connected with the German National Bank; Mr. James T. Berry, the vice-president and principal stockholder; Mr. Frank M. Brown, secretary and treasurer; and Mr. Samuel W. Berry, superintendent and manager. The Messrs. Berry are brothers, natives of this city. Mr. J.T. Berry has charge of the office, shipping etc., while Mr. S.W. Berry is the superintendent and manager. They ably conduct this immense industry, enforce a thorough system of organization, and maintain for these beautiful art tiles the highest standard of excellence."

Edwin Atlee Barber, the foremost historian of Ameri-

These 3″ diameter stove tiles and all the Kensington trim tiles in my collection are marked Kensington Art Tile in block letters. $75.00 – 100.00 ea.

can ceramics, failed to include anything about Kensington in either of his major publications, *The Pottery and Porcelain of the United States* in 1893, or *Marks of American Potters* in 1904. He included the other failed and successful potteries of the era in Cincinnati. He also credited Herman Mueller, a Kensington contributor, as a source of information for his books, but still no reference of Kensington!

The catalog for the public exhibition of architectural ceramics and sculptural contributions of Herman Carl Mueller at the New Jersey State Museum, January 13 through March 18, 1979, lists two Kensington tiles and describes the Kensington mark. This exhibition was the result of the extensive research project of Lisa Factor Taft. In her writing of Mr. Mueller's life and contributions she states: "Sometime in 1885, Mueller began modeling for the Kensington Art Tile Company that operated for two years in Newport, Kentucky. Little information exists on this small company that seems primarily to have bought individual designs or molds from artists and sculptors on a commission basis.

Sculptured relief portraits and geometric and organic plant forms were the motifs employed on these rare tiles that are generally not found outside the Cincinnati area."

The book, *The Ladies, God Bless' Em,* prepared for an exhibition at the Cincinnati Art Museum in 1979, in its Selected Biographies, says: "The dismissal of The Pottery Club from Rookwood forced Miss McLaughlin (Miss Mary Louise McLaughlin) to expand her artist energies. She began to work in metal and experimented with metallic effects on ceramics painted over the glaze. For a brief period in the 1880's, she decorated tiles at the Kensington Art Tile Company in Newport, Kentucky."

Don't be misled by the large number of Kensington tiles shown here. Tiles from this works are somewhat scarce. I just happened to find someone who had salvaged most of those shown here from a home with six Kensington mantel facings.

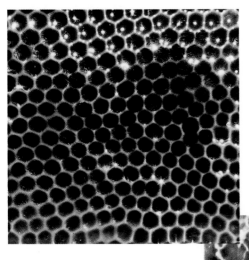

The two patterns shown here are each part of a complete set of 17 removed from fireplace mantel facings. $25.00 – 30.00 each, or $400.00 – 600.00 set

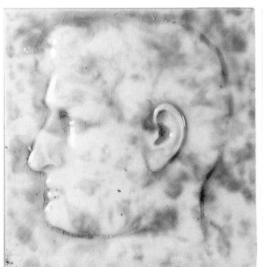

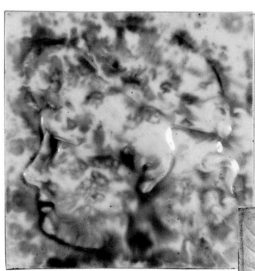

This pair of 6" square Kensington tiles (top) was designed and executed by Herman Mueller. The tile on the right has his monogram (top inset) on the right side edge a little more than an inch above the lower corner. These tiles, and those done by him pictured in the A.E.T.Co. chapter, show Mueller's personal style in his representation of nude juveniles and plants. His tree leaves in particular are like no other tile sculptor. This pair of tiles and the two portraits with mottled colors glazes have the backstamp trademark shown above. The Mueller signed pair, $500.00 – 750.00. Other 6" square portrait tiles, $300.00 – 450.00 pair, or $150.00 – 200.00 ea.

All other 6" square Kensingtons shown have the mark shown above. The two tiles with portraits of females show a striking resemblance to the portrait chargers produced at the Matt Morgan Art Pottery, and are probably also the work of Herman Mueller. $300.00 – 450.00 pair, or $150.00 – 200.00 ea.

These two 6″ square mottled glaze Kensington tiles were probably removed from a mantel facing. The stylized floral design is continuous in that the stem or branch joins the preceding and following tile. $25.00 – 30.00 ea.

Also of a continuous design, these tiles were made to frame or to border. The 2⅛″ x 4¼″ trim tiles are signed with small raised letters, "Kensington Art Tile Co." $3.00 – 5.00 ea.

Low Art Tile Works

The Low Art Tile Works of Chelsea, Massachusetts, fired the first kiln in May of 1879. John Gardner Low, who had worked at the Chelsea Keramic Art Works, established his own business with his father, John Low. The firm was called the J. & J.G. Low Art Tile Works. George Robertson, brother of the founder and employee of the Chelsea Keramic Art Works, and the England-trained artist and sculptor Arthur Osborne, had already joined the Low firm. Within five months they had won a Silver Medal at the Cincinnati Industrial Exposition, the first of many awards.

By 1881 the business was a huge success. A large catalog was published offering an extensive list of hand-modeled products in high and low relief. Fireplace and mantel facings, decorative panels for permanent installation or uniquely framed, floor, wall, and trim tiles were all pictured in the catalog. Before the year was over, about 20 of the very famous Low Plastic Sketches, designed and modeled by Arthur Osborne, were on the market.

All this success at Low was no accident or surprise. J.G. Low, with an artistic background and ceramics experience at the Chelsea Works, had spent two years in planning, constructing, and organizing the pottery. The Low glazes were more than just similar to those at the Chelsea Works, G. Robertson had years of experience at his brother's

"Vox Stellarum" and "Industria" are two of a series of six 6" square tiles copyright in 1881. All are marked on the front with the monogram of Osborne, an

A within an O. Note the "Industria" tile has smoothly ground, small radius corners. Probably an attempt to improve the appearance of a chipped corner. $200.00 – 250.00 ea. in excellent condition. The most desirable tile in this series, the boy reading a book under the words "Hic, Haec, Hoc," could bring closer to $300.00.

"Liberty," was designed and sculpted by Osborne. His initials appear above her left shoulder. The back die-impressed mark is "J.& J.G. Low" with a date of 1881. $175.00 – 225.00.

works, and was an expert at glazing. Theodore Baur was employed as an artist and sculptor, and the American artist Elihu Vedder made several artistic contributions. The name of Arthur Osborne had become synonymous with Low Art Tile.

Low, in 1882, was producing jugs and vases with hand-modeled relief work, some of which were executed by Osborne.

Done in high relief, this portrait of a child is covered with a green glaze. The 6" square tile is mismarked on the back, "Copyright by J.G. & J.F. Low, 1881." The date should read 1883 or later. $175.00 – 200.00.

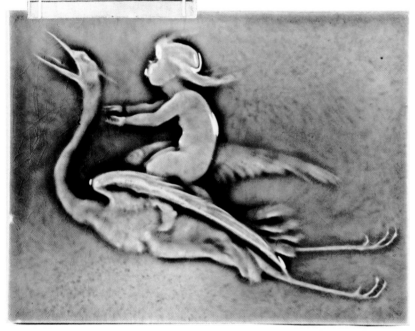

A pale green glaze, speckled with burnt sienna, covers this 4⅝" x 6¼" tile decorated with a young boy on a flying stork. The tile shows a J.G.& J.F. Low copyright date of 1883. The tile is also shown in the catalog, along with the Renaissance No. 3 fireplace, with an 1881 copyright of J. & J.G. Low. In 1883, John F. Low, an expert chemist and son of J.G., joined his father when J. Low retired. The firm then became the J.G. & J.F. Low Art Tile Works. $150.00 – 200.00.

A series of President tiles in low relief was introduced in 1885. The four subjects on 6" x 4½" tiles were Washington, Lincoln, Grant, and Cleveland. "Shylock," from a Shakespearean series of six 8" x 4½" tiles in low relief, was also copyrighted in 1885. $250.00 – 300.00.

Manufacturers of cast-iron stoves had been using Low tiles to decorate their products since 1881. By 1886, the Lows were competing with the fledgling Beaver Falls Art Tile Co. and the experienced Trent Tile Co. for their share of this market. The Low catalogs offered a wide variety of products for the stove manufacturers. The Lows also promoted the sale of their tile by forming the Low Tile and Metal Works for the casting of iron stoves to utilize ceramic tiles and making items of brass and tiles. Products of brass and tile included candlesticks, covered boxes, clock cases, planters, trays, trivets, and lamps. Some items are signed Low Tile & Metal Mfg. Trays $100.00 – 150.00 ea., candlestick $125.00 – 175.00.

This pair of tiles is pictured in a stove in an article by Barbara White Morse, "Buying a Low Art Tile Stove," in the November 1970, issue of Spinning Wheel, and reprinted in the July – December 1991 issue of Flash Point. The tiles are 4¼" in diameter, and dated 1885. $125.00 – 175.00 ea.

In 1889, Low delivered the first tile soda fountain. Having done considerable research and development since 1883, Low started taking orders and applied for a patent for tile soda fountains in 1888. Several installations were completed prior to the patent approval in 1889. A fountain, 16' tall and 20' wide, was on display at the 1893 Chicago Exposition. These fountains were ceramic marvels.

Arthur Osborne left the works in 1893.

The Low Art Tile Works stopped production in 1902, and was liquidated in 1907.

Tiles were marked J. & J.G. Low prior to J. Low retiring in 1883. Tiles were marked J.G. & J.F. Low after his retirement, and the word "Patent" was removed from the backmark. Eventually, about 1890, the name was changed to the Low Art Tile Company. As part of a reorganization in 1899, the name was changed to the Low Tile Co. Factory catalogs are needed to determine when a design was introduced. Copyright dates on Low tiles only tell the last time the copyright was filed prior to the marked tile being made.

The early tiles executed by Arthur Osborne are signed with his initials, an A preceding an O. Later he used the

monogram of an A within an O. The series of 47 plastic sketches are shown in a catalog published in 1887. All of the sketches are signed by Osborne. The first 21 are signed with his initials, the remainder have his monogram. By observing the dates on some sketches, and the sketches referred to in the article "Some American Tiles" by Frank D. Millet, published in the

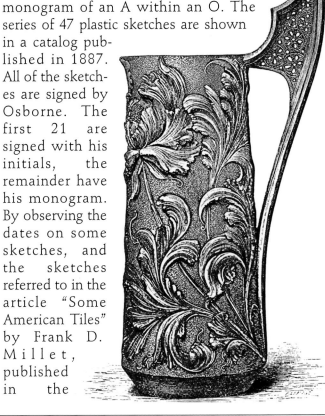

April 1882 issue of *Century Illustrated,* it appears that Osborne changed to his monogram toward the end of 1881. This seems to be confirmed by the fact that other Osborne tiles, with a copyright date of 1881, show he used both marks during that year. Tiles designed and sculpted prior to his changing his mark to an A within an O, continued to be produced with his AO initials mark.

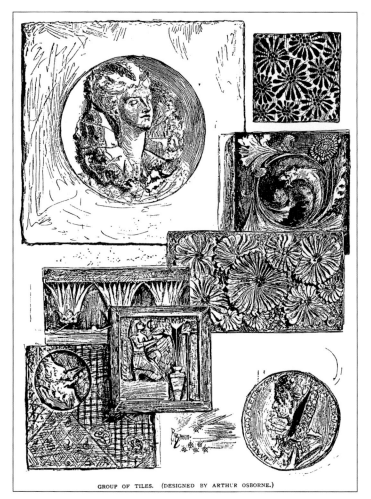

GROUP OF TILES. (DESIGNED BY ARTHUR OSBORNE.)

Century, December 1881.

The Magazine Art, *April 1887.*

Low's Art Tile Soda Fountains.

HOT FOUNTAIN No. 21.

NOT IN THE TRUST.

Our Hot Fountains are perfectly automatic in the supply of both gas and water, and cost only one-quarter as much to run as any other make.

Our Art Tile Soda Fountains are acknowledged by all to be superior in every way to those of any other make.

Write for Catalogue of Hot or Cold Fountains.

THE LOW ART TILE CO.,

Salesrooms:
51 Portland St., BOSTON.
Havemeyer Bldg., 31 Church St., NEW YORK CITY.
908 G St., N. W., WASHINGTON, D. C.

952 BROADWAY,
CHELSEA, MASS.

[S. P. 6.]

The Pharmaceutical Era, *September 1894*

Matt Morgan Art Pottery Co.

Matthew Somerville Morgan, an English artist who had obtained experience in ceramics in Spain, was brought to this country in 1873 by magazine publisher Frank Leslie. In 1878 Morgan moved to Cincinnati to head the lithographic department of Strobridge & Company. In 1882 he worked with Isaac Broome in establishing the Dayton Porcelain Pottery in Dayton, Ohio. Morgan returned to Cincinnati and founded his own works with the assistance of George Ligowsky, inventor of the clay pigeon. They experimented with clay and glazes, and the Matt Morgan Art Pottery was incorporated in January 1883.

This venture was at first quite promising. The wares produced were original in design and treatment. Slip-decorated pottery in the Limoges underglaze style was developed along original lines. Moresque pottery was also produced in rich colorings and lustres, artistically modeled and profusely guilded. Some of the pieces were covered with a brilliant glaze, while others possessed a mat finish. Competent decorators, such as Matthew A. Daley, Nicholas J. Hirschfeld, and other now prominent painters, worked enthusiastically. Shapes were principally designed and modeled by Herman C. Mueller, in conjunction with Mr. Morgan.

The failure of the company in 1885 was caused by the efforts of the stockholders to place the business on a commercial basis, at the expense of the artistic element. Very few art potteries in this country started under as favorable circumstances. Some of the best examples of this pottery reveal a high order of artistic merit.

The above information was given to E. A. Barber by Herman Mueller, except for Morgan's involvement with Broome, which came from Paul Evans, and the failure date of 1885, which is supported by advertisements, one of which is reprinted here.

MATT MORGAN ART POTTERY CO. MATT MORGAN -CIN. O- ART POTTERY CO N.J.H.

The marks used were the title of the company stamped in the bottom, sometimes containing the abbreviated name of the city and state in the center. Artists sometimes incised their initials. The raised, in the back die marks shown on the tiles are exclusive to them.

I purchased these Matt Morgan tiles (shown on the folowing page) from an architectural antiques dealer, who had purchased them at an estate sale in the same Corryville area where the Matt Morgan Art Pottery was located. The lot consisted of over 200 tiles in four patterns. Two stylistic florals were on 6" square tiles, and a "textured" and a "Morning Glory" pattern were made in 6" square, 4" square and 3" x 6" tiles. Many of the examples have one or more manufacturing quality defects of poor embossing, warping, burning, air entrapment, and foreign particles in the clay.

There is no record of art tiles having been manufactured at this establishment. However, considering Matt Morgan had worked with Isaac Broom, and he had in his employment Herman Mueller, tile manufacturing would seem almost natural. Broome and Mueller soon became prominent figures in the designing, sculpting, and manufacture of art tile. The capacity for this establishment to succeed at this endeavor was great. The business prospect would most certainly have been enhanced by all the recent success at other tile works, and tile manufacturing would have fit well with the board of directors desire to operate on a commercial basis.

The rather obvious conclusion to the existence of these unglazed tiles in their present state, and what might have been, suggests that tile development and experimentation was underway when the pottery closed in 1885.

Although most tile collectors don't normally seek out bisque or unglazed products, there is no real alternative for obtaining an example from this short-lived manufacturer. $40.00 – 100.00 ea. for the smaller examples with either the textured or Morning Glory decorations, and $75.00 – 125.00 for the 6" square with the same decoration. $100.00 – 150.00 for the stylized floral (top center). $150.00 – 200.00 for the cross and diagonal stylized floral (top left), the only example in the whole lot.

I had these two, and only these two, glazed tiles glazed by a professional. I value them as defaced or damaged. Having the advantage of having several good examples, I just had to see what might have been.

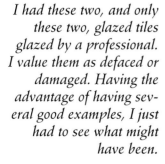

This ad for salesmen appeared in The Art Interchange *from
February 12 through June 18, 1885*

This ad appeared in The Art Interchange *issues of
May 22, 1884, through January 29, 1885.*

Moravian Pottery & Tile Works

There has been more written about the Moravian Pottery and Tile Works of Doylestown, Pennsylvania, and its founder, Henry C. Mercer, than any other American pottery and founder. Mercer's education at Harvard and the University of Pennsylvania, and his career in the fields of archaeology and anthropology, and later, studying and collecting tools as a hobby, covered more than 20 years prior to his initial experiments with clay and glazes in 1897. His vast experiences included trips to Europe and South America. A large part of this background is reflected in his tile products.

"The City of God" tile is 5½" square, and a ca. 1900
design. Unmarked. $100.00 – 125.00.

In 1898, Mercer hired Frank Bartleman, a potter, to assist him. Using local red clay, they continued experimenting and firing tiles in an abandoned kiln. The following year, Mercer constructed a new kiln on his own property. He continued glazing and firing experiments, and in 1899 founded his company, the Moravian Pottery and Tile Works. The Moravian name was used because Mercer had a great interest in the Pennsylvania-German art depicted on antique iron stoveplates from which his first tiles were molded.

Mercer made unglazed, smear glazed, modeled, and slip decorated tiles, with decorations of medieval designs of England and Europe. In 1901, art pottery was added to the tile catalog.

Another tile design of the same period is this "Vicar of Stowe." The Latin epithet meaning, "Pray for the soul of Father Nicholas of Stowe, Vicar." This 4½" square design was offered in two variations. The one shown here was intended to be mounted diagonally, so the potted tree is upright, the other was meant to be mounted in the normal horizontal-vertical manner where the tree would also be upright.

From 1902 till 1904, most of the pottery's output was for Mercer's largest commission, the paving of the Pennsylvania State Capitol in Harrisburg. The project required 53,000 square feet of tile, including 400 panels, some up to five feet in width.

In 1908, Mercer wrote a guidebook for self tours of the installation. The publication has a drawing of each panel, with a narrative for each drawing. The panel, *Frying in Open Fire* (shown at right), has the following narrative: "Reach a long handled wrought iron pan, greased with lard or ham fat, over the glowing oak or hickory embers of the kitchen hearth. In this manner, the farmer's wife fried "saus," ham puddings, mush, scrapple, and pancakes. The pancakes were tossed up the chimney to turn and were caught upside-down. Open fire cooking went into disuse about 1840."

The guidebook, with all its drawings and narratives, offers an excellent view of Mercer and his tiles.

This 5¾" square tile, "The Birds of Tintern Abbey," was pictured in the following 1903 article. It was also shown in a corner fireplace. It is the only decorated tile used, 20 in the fireplace facing and 13 in the hearth, each separated by two horizontal and two vertical rows of 3" square tiles. Unmarked. $130.00 – 160.00.

In the article, "The Mercer Tiles and other Matters," in the July 1903 issue of *The House Beautiful*, Oliver Coleman said:

We can see from the foregoing how the finding of a rude form of pottery and many very interesting designs upon stove-plates may have been brought in such an apposition in Mr. Mercer's mind as to result in the now well-known Mercer tiles. At any rate, he experimented for several years with colors and local clays, until he became an efficient potter, and then began to reproduce in tiles for the fireplace the designs that long-forgotten artists had invented for the similar purpose of stove-plates. Mr. Mercer has long since exhausted the supply of stove-plate designs, and has followed other and broader inspirations, Dutch and German many of them, but not a few from Spain and the Moors. The colors range from somber to gay; the most I have been fortunate to see, however, are subdued in hue — browns, muddy yellows, dull greens, and low-toned reds. They are made for fireplaces, or for walls and floors so as to present a smooth surface for cleansing; but the fireplace tiles are frequently modeled, the lines being raised or depressed. This adds texture to the color, and greatly enhances the decorative effect. They are not of a character to be used in drawing-rooms with French gilt furniture, rather in libraries and living-rooms, billiard-rooms and dens, and such places where strength is more to be desired than fineness. One can scarcely fancy these tiles surrounding a set of small gas logs, but think of them always as appropriate to the crackling, swirling, blaze of a real fire on a full-sized hearth.

Next to the Museum and Mr. Mercer's studio, the place to visit at Doylestown is The Jug in the Wall. This is a very small but unique tavern on one of the principal streets, where the single room is divided into an upper and a lower part. In the latter, the great beams and yawning fireplace repeat the interiors of the eighteenth century, and against the wall one sees the sign of the tavern, the 'jug', partly emerging from the masonry. This jug, half buried in the wall, is the old sign of a completed house so far as the masons are concerned, like the tree that carpenters set up when they get a roof on a new building. It is a gentle hint to the proprietor or builder to supply a keg of beer or a demijohn of whiskey. At The Jug in the Wall, the fireplace is just the spot for an oyster-roast on cold winter evenings at a huge log-fire. All the lower part of the room is decorated with Mercer tiles, set in a flooring of ordinary bricks cut in half; the upper part of the fireplace has inserts of these tiles, and suspended from the walls are iron implements belonging to colonial days. Perhaps the drinks in The Jug in the Wall are no better than one gets in the ordinary village inn, but the surroundings make them taste sweeter. The fame of this inn has already gone abroad.

Not an expensive way, in the long run, to sweeten one's drinks or one's daily life, for that matter. If people would only learn the incalculable, though often indefinable, influence of pleasant surroundings in houses and rooms, there would be much less unhappiness in this world of ours. It is not probable that one out of a hundred patrons of The Jug are conscious of why they prefer to take their night-caps while seated before Mr. Mercer's fireplace than at a bent-wood table in the establishment across the street; but the psychological influence is present and compelling, nevertheless.

It is a true achievement in this world to create something out of nothing, or to save something from oblivion which is worth the saving. Both of these things Mr. Mercer has already accomplished.

More pottery items were added in 1904. They included boxes, inkwells, bowls, cups, and mugs. And about 1908, the Brocade tile line of sculptured people, animals, and birds was introduced. After the original studio was destroyed by fire in 1910, Mercer built a new works.

A 1900 – 1910 design, the "Knight of Margam" tile measures 4¾" x 7⅜". Unmarked. $150.00 – 175.00.

In an article, "Picture Fireplaces; Illustrating Stories for Sitting Room, Library and Nursery," published in the December 1916 issue of *The Craftsman,* there are several Mercer fireplaces shown, including the Bluebeard and His Castle *(shown below).* Others illustrated or described include The Night Before Christmas, Bible Stories, Arkansas Traveler, Pickwick, Rip Van-Winkle, New World, and Mother Goose.

Mercer died in 1930. He had willed the pottery to Frank Swain, who had been his assistant since 1896. After Swains death, and several changes in ownership, the pottery closed in 1956. The tile works was reopened in 1967 under the direction of the Bucks County Commission, and it continues to operate.

There are several references to marks used by the Moravian Pottery and Tile Works. E. A. Barber shows a beehive outline with the word Moravian within the arch and Henry C. Mercer's conjoined initials at the bottom within the hive. Barber also shows a block letter Moravian mark, and says both are impressed. The Kovels

MORAVIAN

repeat Barber's marks, and show a colored photo of a third. The third mark is a die-stamped Moravian in block letters with two small lotus blossoms, one above the O and one above the second A, with Mercer's conjoined initials in front of the word Moravian. Barber's marks were probably used, Kovel's third mark obviously was. However, there is no reference as to where they were used.

The 1979 exposition, *American Decorative Tiles 1870 – 1930,* displayed 13 Moravian tiles, most lent by the Moravian Pottery and Tile Works, the Smithsonian, and The Newark Museum. One tile was signed with the conjoined MOR, and one had a small remnant of a paper label. The other 11 examples were unsigned.

In the 1984 publication, *The Newark Museum Collection of American Art Pottery,* of 20 tiles and a cup shown, all Moravian, only two pieces are signed. Both are signed with the conjoined MOR, one of which was the same one displayed at the previously mentioned exposition. Both were purchased in 1919.

The conclusions of marks on Moravian pottery and tiles are, except for some new tiles that are signed and dated, only about ten percent are signed with either a surviving paper label or the conjoined MOR. The MOR mark was introduced in about 1914. Any other mark is scarce to rare.

The Moravian Pottery and Tile Works was never more than a studio operation, making handmade products. No more than 16 people were employed at one time.

Moravian
Tiles and Mosaics

GRAND PRIZE
ST. LOUIS, 1904

J. H. INGHAM
439 Land Title Building, Philadelphia

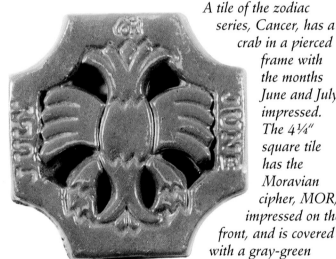

A tile of the zodiac series, Cancer, has a crab in a pierced frame with the months June and July impressed. The 4¼" square tile has the Moravian cipher, MOR, impressed on the front, and is covered with a gray-green glaze. $60.00 – 90.00.

International Studio, *August 1905.*

Another series, these 4" square ship tiles have a natural, burned clay finish, against a dead mat blue slip background, ca. 1920. $75.00 – 100.00 ea.

Karl Langenbeck and Herman Mueller were the major force that resulted in the incorporation of the Mosaic Tile Co. in Zanesville, Ohio, in September, 1894. Langenbeck and Mueller had worked together at the American Encaustic Tile Co. Langenbeck had been A.E.'s chemist since 1890, and Mueller the principal artist and sculptor since 1887. While at A.E., they decided to form their own company, and they left in 1893. This new corporation had as its backers and officers, David Lee, president; William Bateman, vice president; and W.M. Shinnick, secretary and treasurer.

The company started with one kiln and 30 employees. They manufactured all kinds of floor tile, and soon introduced a product of considerable artistic and technical merit. Called "Florentine Mosaic," it was a heavy, vitreous, annealed tile, with a dull finish, inlaid in elaborate designs by an ingenious process, invented and patented by Mueller. The surface of the tile is inlaid to a depth of ⅛" to ¼" with colored clays, by great pressure. A minute mosaic work is produced by forming little squares or blocks, so small that 2600 are inlaid on a six-inch square tile. In 1898 three more kilns were added, and in 1900 six periodic kilns were constructed.

Langenbeck, America's first ceramic chemist, wrote the book, *The Chemistry of Pottery*, which was published in 1895. He dedicated his book to his associate, Herman Mueller.

Mueller and Langenbeck were both superintendents of the works. They alternated between the responsibilities of running the plant and being out on the road with customers. This arrangement evidently worked well, for the business grew rapidly. The company established an office and warehouse in New York City in 1901, and later in other major American cities. But in 1903, both Mueller and Langenbeck resigned from Mosaic.

In 1906, Bateman became president of the company, and W.E. Miller was made vice president. In 1907, Shinnick was made general manager, a position he held until his death in 1923. The company prospered

Postcard, 1909.

1908 photo of Mosaic Tile Co.

under Shinnick's leadership. Faience tiles were added to the company's products in 1918. Plant construction and additions were ongoing, and in 1920, Mosaic purchased the Atlantic Tile Manufacturing Company of Matawan, New Jersey.

Production peaked in 1925 – 1927. Then the Great Depression caused the plant to reduce its output by operating on a part-time basis. Mosaic survived the depression, and in 1935 acquired the Carlyle Tile Co. of Ironton, Ohio, and in 1937 the controlling interest of the General Tile Corporation of El Segundo, Califor-

nia. Mosaic reached its highest production era in 1941 when it employed over 1200 people. The survivors of the depression also survived the war years. In 1959, faience tile production stopped. And in 1967, the once largest American tile manufacturer, ceased operations.

The monogram of the initials M T C, superimposed within a circle, is the only mark for the Mosaic Tile Co. shown in Barber's *Marks of American Potters,* published in 1909. This mark appears raised in the back die on the series of advertising and commemorative portrait paperweights done in a Wedgwood cameo style during the WWI era. These tiles were popular, and the production of the advertising paperweights continued until the 1920s. Sometime in the 1920s a new mark was introduced with the name Mosaic within a race-track shape oval. Early faience tile, first introduced in 1918, has the first mark within a circle, die impressed by hand. For a while, faience tile was marked with the race-track mark, die impressed by hand. The latest faience was impressed by a machine process, with the race-track mark. Tiles other than faience were marked with a raised race track in the back die after introduction. On the latest tiles, "Made In U.S.A." appears below the race track.

This framed Lincoln cameo has, taped to the back, a letter written by the famous Zanesville ceramic historian, Norris Schneider. Mr. Schneider wrote that the Mosaic cameo tiles were produced from 1912 to 1920. $75.00 – 100.00.

Other Lincoln cameos and their backmarks shown here include a Cambridge Tile Co. reproduction, probably from the 1930s. All of the hex paperweights measure 3" across. $40.00 – 50.00 ea.

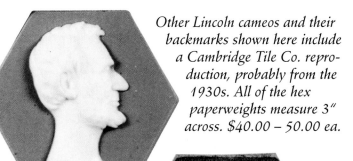

This is a tile commemorating the 250th anniversary of Newark, New Jersey. I presume Robert Treat was the founder. Evidently there was not enough room for the normal raised circle mark, so they impressed the factory information on the foot of the tile. $50.00 – 60.00.

Woodrow Wilson and his running mate, Mr. Marshall. $50.00 – 60.00 ea.

The Pershing tile measures 5¼" x 3⅝". By the raised letter writing on the back, it appears these were made for a fund raiser to erect a new building for the Zanesville American Legion, Post No. 29. $60.00 – 75.00.

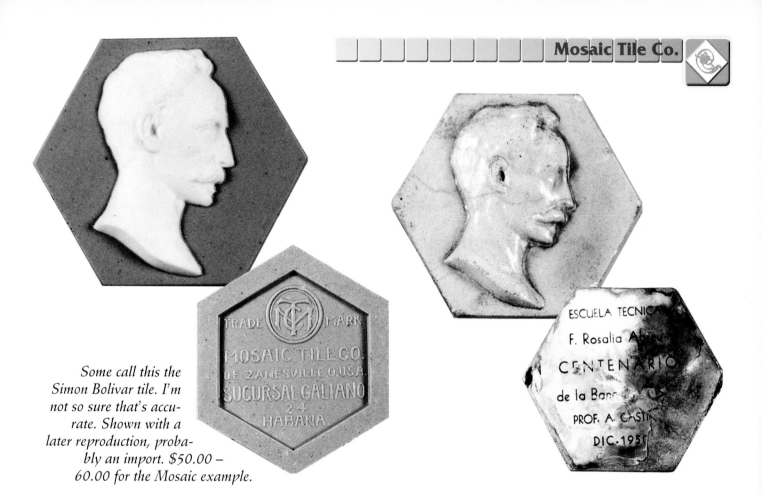

Some call this the Simon Bolivar tile. I'm not so sure that's accurate. Shown with a later reproduction, probably an import. $50.00 – 60.00 for the Mosaic example.

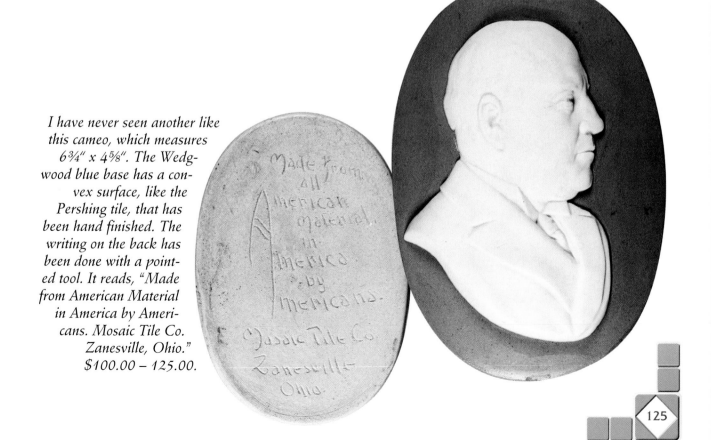

I have never seen another like this cameo, which measures 6¾" x 4⅝". The Wedgwood blue base has a convex surface, like the Pershing tile, that has been hand finished. The writing on the back has been done with a pointed tool. It reads, "Made from American Material in America by Americans. Mosaic Tile Co. Zanesville, Ohio." $100.00 – 125.00.

This Zanesville Rotary disc was meant to be worn around the neck, hanging on a string or ribbon. The disc is 2⅜" in diameter and ¼" thick, and has the raised circle mark. $30.00 – 35.00.

This 6" square faience tile, with the raised line decoration of a sitting rabbit, is from the Evan and Louise Purviance, White Pillars Museum Collection, and is pictured in their publication, Zanesville Art Tile, In Color. A variation of this tile, and one with an elephant, were produced with the circle mark on the front of the tile for advertising purposes. This tile is marked with the die impressed by hand, circle mark, ca. 1920. $200.00 – 250.00.

A "dry line" process was used to decorate this lotus tile. A mixture of oil and manganese was applied to the surface, probably with the assistance of a stencil, prior to applying the colored glazes. When the tile was fired, the glazes would pool within the confines of the lines. This tile is 4¼" square and has the hand-impressed circle mark. $75.00 – 100.00.

Although these nicely glazed embossed geometric tiles are hand stamped with a circle mark, they do appear as offerings in factory catalogs as late as 1932. The tiles are 3" square $20.00 – 25.00 ea.

Mosaic, like other producers of faience, made statues, fountains, and fixtures for the decoration of home and garden. This ceiling light fixture measures 3½" x 9½," and has a die impressed by hand, racetrack mark. $150.00 – 200.00.

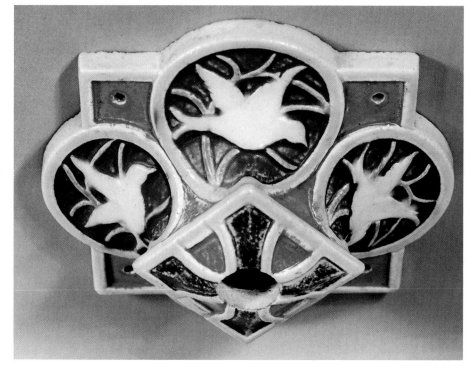

Mosaic took advantage of the fine reputation they had earned for their quality products and design and installation services. For several years after the introduction of the racetrack mark, they continued to use their old, very recognized circular logo for advertising purposes. A faience rabbit tile, with the circular mark on the front, was offered in factory catalogs as late as 1929. This small, 2" hex tile was mounted in some of their installations. The logo on the front of the tile is the old circle mark, but the back has the raised race-track mark. $20.00 – 25.00 ea.

The pelican and owl tiles are part of a series decorated with birds and animals. The faience tiles are 3″ square and have the impressed, hand-stamped race track mark and their respective catalog numbers. $40.00 – 50.00 ea.

There are two pages of colored faience tiles in the 1929 catalog showing glazes similar to the "separating" or "stretch glass" type shown here. This 6″ square tile is marked with 20 lightly impressed racetracks. These marks were probably made while passing under a wheel, with the marks being made by the conveyor or by a die on the wheel. $20.00 – 25.00.

Walter Crane designed transfer-printed tiles were popular for many years. This 6" square example has his monogram on the front, and the raised race track on the back. $150.00 – 175.00.

A later model of paperweights were made in 3" diameter circles with printed advertising. All are marked with the raised race track. The only one dated here is from the 1947 Zanesville, Ohio, Sesquicentennial. $25.00 – 30.00 ea.

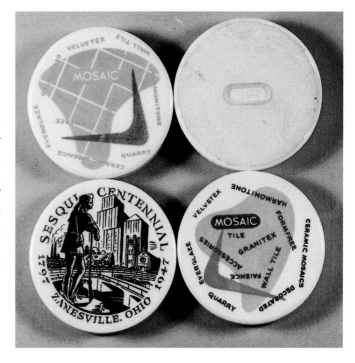

These 4¾" square Pottery Festival tiles are marked with a raised race track with "Made in U.S.A." beneath. The tiles were made for the 1968 and the 1969 Roseville-Crooksville Festivals. They are Mosaic solid color floor and wall tiles, probably decorated elsewhere. $25.00 – 30.00 ea.

DECORATIVE INSERTS AND TRIMS IN MOSAIC FAIENCE

6 x 6
Pattern No. 3008
Decoration No. 2721

6 x 6
Pattern No. 4091
Decoration No. 1882

6 x 6
Pattern No. 3092
Decoration No. 2564

6 x 1   P. 4027   D. 1926

6 x 1   P. 4027   D. 2585

6 x 1   P. 4069   D. 2892

6 x 1   P. 4069   D. 1740

6 x 6
Pattern No. 4050
Decoration No. 2806

6 x 6
Pattern No. 3011
Decoration No. 2653

6 x 6
Pattern No. 3002
Decoration No. 2535

6 x 1   P. 5002   D. 2626

6 x 1   P. 5002   D. 1883

6 x 1¼   P. 4038   D. 2849

6 x 1¼   P. 4038   D. 2893

4¼ x 4¼
Pattern No. 3074
Decoration No. 2810

4¼ x 4¼
Pattern No. 3017
Decoration No. 2688

2 x 2
P. 3184
D. 2682

6 x 4   P. 3099   D. 2890

6 x 1¼   P. 4035   D. 892

6 x 1¼   P. 4035   D. 2763

2 x 2
P. 3046
D. 2843

6 x 3   P. 3108   D. 2392

6 x 1¼   P. 5003   D. 1884

6 x 1¼   P. 5003   D. 2715

4¼ x 4¼
Pattern No. 3093
Decoration No. 2841

4¼ x 4¼
Pattern No. 3082
Decoration No. 2635

2 x 2
P. 3047
D. 2891

6 x 2   P. 4070   D. 2743

6 x 1¼   P. 4060   D. 2275

6 x 1¼   P. 4060   D. 833

6 x 2   P. 4062   D. 1211

6 x 1¼   P. 4058   D. 1444

3 x 3
P. 3031
D. 2700

3 x 3
P. 3081
D. 2865

3 x 3
P. 4093
D. 2889

6 x 2   P. 3091   D. 2894

6 x 1¼   P. 4058   D. 1505

[64]

Page from the 1929 factory catalog.

DECORATIVE INSERTS AND TRIMS IN MOSAIC FAIENCE

6x6 Tiles 4163

4¼x4¼ Tiles 4162

24x12 4160

15" Dia. 4161

40x4¼
4100

24x12 Panel 4164

24x12 Panel 4163

Page from the 1929 factory catalog.

MOSAIC DECORATIVE FAIENCE

6 x 6
Pattern 5015
Decoration 6498

6 x 6
Pattern 5016
Decoration 6499

6 x 6
Pattern 5017
Decoration 6500

6 x 6
Pattern 5018
Decoration 6501

6 x 6
Pattern 5019
Decoration 6502

6 x 6
Pattern 5020
Decoration 6503

6 x 6
Pattern 5021
Decoration 6504

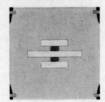
6 x 6
Pattern 5022
Decoration 6505

6 x 6
Pattern 5023
Decoration 6506

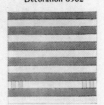
6 x 6
Pattern 5024
Decoration 6507

6 x 6
Pattern 3008
Decoration 6496

6 x 6
Pattern 3009
Decoration 6493

6 x 6
Pattern 3083
Decoration 6524

6 x 6
Pattern 4189
Decoration 3052

6 x 6
Pattern 3096
Decoration 2016

6 x 2
P. 4225
D. 6525

6 x 2
P. 4210
D. 5246

6 x 2
P. 4062
D. 2992

6 x 2
P. 4074
D. 5158

6 x 6
Pattern 3092
Decoration 6415

6 x 3
P. 4040
D.1091

6 x 3
P. 3103
D. 5396

6 x 3
P. 3090
D. 5287

6 x 3
P. 3108
D. 2392

4¼ x 4¼
Patt. 3093
Dec. 2841

4¼ x 4¼
Patt. 3015
Dec. 5043

4¼ x 4¼
Patt. 3028
Dec. 6256

4¼ x 4¼
Patt. 3019
Dec. 6526

4¼ x 4¼
Patt. 3074
Dec. 2810

4¼ x 4¼
Patt. 3082
Dec. 6258

4¼ x 4¼
Patt. 4226
Dec. 6527

6x1   P. 5025 D. 6508

6x1   P. 5026 D. 6509

6x1¼ P. 4038 D. 4679

6x1¼ P. 4035 D. 892

6x1¼ P. 3101 D. 6363

8¾ x 4¼
Patt. 3202
Dec. 4007

8¾ x 8¾
Pattern 3201
Decoration 6428

8¾ x 4¼
Patt. 3203
Dec. 4007

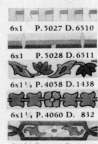
6x1   P. 5027 D. 6510

6x1   P. 5028 D. 6511

6x1¼ P. 4058 D. 1438

6x1¼ P. 4060 D. 832

6x1¼ P. 5005 D. 6426

Reproduced from Tile

Page from the 1930 factory catalog.

ONE of a SERIES of four-color
Advertisements of the Mosaic Tile
Company now appearing in the
following Magazines

House Beautiful
House & Garden
Harper's
Scribner's
Atlantic Monthly
Golden Book
World's Work
Review of Reviews

Specifications for MOSAIC TILES used in Interiors Illustrated in Mosaic Consumer Advertising

Lower Illustration—BATHROOM

FLOOR, Mosaic Faience, 4¼ x 4¼. Color No. 347.
BASE, 6 x 6, No. 2208. Color No. 924-B. CAP, 6 x 2, No. 2004.
Color No. 347.   DECORATED BORDER, 6 x 2½, No. 3106.
WAINSCOTING, Mosaic Faience, 4¼ x 4¼. Colors, Peacock
Blue No. 347 and Cream No. 286.   ACCESSORIES, Mosaic
"All-Tile" in colors to harmonize.

Upper Illustration—

LIVING ROOM and MANTEL in MOSAIC FAIENCE

MANTEL, Mosaic Faience Design, No. F-2803, with 38" fire
opening.   Color, Brown No. 316.

FLOOR, Mosaic Faience, Random Pattern, 6 x 6, 6 x 3 and
3 x 3.   Colors, Buffs, Browns and Reds.

Mosaic Tiles are available in a range of shapes, sizes, colors, designs and types that offer the architect a
wide choice of the most appropriate tiles for every type of building, residential, commercial or industrial.

THE MOSAIC TILE COMPANY   DEPT. A.R.5 ZANESVILLE, OHIO

NEW YORK	SAN FRANCISCO	ST. LOUIS	CHICAGO	LOS ANGELES
327 W. 42nd Street	563 Second Street	Railway Exchange Building	1336 W. Washington Boulevard	2470 Enterprise Street

MOSAIC TILES

FOR BRILLIANT ACHIEVEMENT IN TODAY'S INTERIORS

PERSONALITY in home decoration ... that subtle touch of you yourself ... finds its widest expression through the fine, the enduring, the genuine. Thus it is that real tiles—Mosaic Tiles—are chosen for floors and walls. Good taste insists on them. Good judgment prescribes them. No need to have the standardized. Achieve your own beauty.

Achieve it with hand-wrought, quality-conceived Mosaic Tiles. You know they last from generation to generation ... offering the economy as well as the beauty of the genuine. Considering this, the cost of installation is truly modest ... the first and last ... a life-long investment in home contentment.

Tiles made by The Mosaic Tile Company bear the trade-name, "Mosaic." This name is stamped on all Mosaic Products, which include tiles of an extremely wide range of designs, colors and purposes. The word, "Mosaic," should be used in writing tile specifications.

Write for your copy of the booklet, "Mosaic Tiles in Color." It contains an abundance of color illustrations and suggestions about the use of tile in the home, which you will find valuable if you plan to build or remodel. Your copy is gladly sent on request.

Finely Wrought Keramic Tiles

THE MOSAIC TILE CO., 203 Coopermill Road, Zanesville, O.
NEW YORK   CHICAGO   ST. LOUIS   LOS ANGELES   SAN FRANCISCO

House Beautiful, *March 1930.*

MOSAIC TILES

unmarred by wear
undimmed by time

THIS beauty never fades . . . this beauty that tile alone possesses. Radiant in color . . . rich in distinction . . . gleaming unmarred by wear and undimmed by time as the years come and go. The charm of real tile that the ages have prized is brought to you so completely by Mosaic Tiles. Bathrooms of splendor or simplicity. Living-rooms of lasting delight, whether in mansion or modest home. In them and throughout the dwelling the glory of Mosaic Tiles lives on.

For economy use the genuine

WHEN you use Mosaic Tiles—real tiles— in your home, you apply a material prescribed by good taste through the centuries. They have the charm of the genuine because they *are* genuine. They give values that are lacking in what attempts to look like them. Mosaic Tiles are therefore more satisfying. They are economical. At moderate expenditures you enjoy their enduring advantages. You have the designs, the effects you exactly wish, because of the wide range of types, colors, sizes and shapes offered by this unmatched material, Mosaic Tiles.

The trade name "Mosaic" is applied to all tiles which are made exclusively by The Mosaic Tile Company. The word "Mosaic" should be used in writing tile specifications.

Consult your tile contractor or write for illustrated booklets giving a wealth of suggestions for the use of color tiles.

THE MOSAIC TILE COMPANY 205 Coopermill Road ZANESVILLE, OHIO

NEW YORK · CHICAGO · ST. LOUIS · LOS ANGELES · SAN FRANCISCO

Mueller Mosaic Co.

In May of 1908, the Mueller Mosaic Company began operating in the plant of the former Artistic Porcelain Company in Trenton, New Jersey. In April of the following year, the company was incorporated with the financial backing of Mr. Fischer, a shoe retailer. Herman Mueller was president, George Grigsby treasurer, and James Grigsby was the superintendent.

When Mueller left the Mosaic Tile Co. in 1903, he moved his brother's family, the two young Grigsby brothers and their families, all together in a private railroad coach to Morrisville, Pennsylvania, where he accepted a job with the Robertson Art Branch of the National Tile Company. Prior to the move, the Grigsbys and Mueller had planned on going to New Jersey to operate their own pottery, using New Jersey clay and resources.

The firm manufactured floor, wall, and decorative tiles. Mueller was once more in charge of his own business, and still doing the hands-on work of designing and sculpting. He worked closely with architects, and wrote advertising with them in mind. A variety of commissions for businesses, schools, and government projects made them successful.

Both the Grigsby brothers had died by 1917, and Mueller's sons, Edward and William joined the firm. William eventually became the vice-president. Mueller

Mosaic completed many fine architectural commissions in the twenties and into the thirties. The company failed, like many of their competitors, as a result of the depression, and declining business because of the availability of new building products that were less expensive than tile. Herman Mueller died in 1941, and production ceased. Herman Mueller is among the most talented and respected personalities of our ceramic heritage.

Mueller Mosaic products were marked with this three shields and banner mark, showing the MMCo. initials. This mark is on the catalog pages and advertising shown here.

The ads shown appeared in *Pencil Points,* 1926 to 1932. The Mueller Mosaic Co. catalog pages reprinted here are from an undated issue. The Muellers considered their "frost proof" enameled tiles to be among their best achievements.

Faience Wall Fountain
No. 7. Scale 2" = 1'-0"
MUELLER MOSAIC CO.
FACTORY: TRENTON, N. J.
New York Office: 160 East 56th Street
SEND FOR BOOKLET

Pencil Points, *October 1928.*

FAIENCE EXTERIOR

FROST PROOF TILE

WILLIAM UNCLES TILES

MUELLER MOSAIC CO.,   TRENTON, NEW JERSEY
NEW YORK OFFICE: 156 W. 49th STREET
---- SEND FOR BOOKLET ----

Pencil Points,
July 1926.

Pencil Points, *May 1932.*

Pencil Points, *July 1932.*

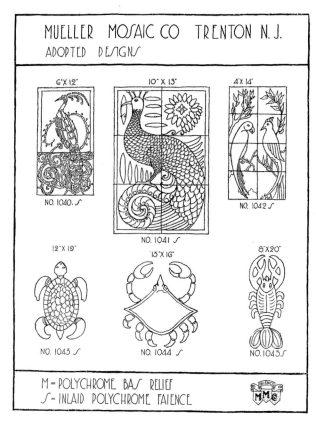

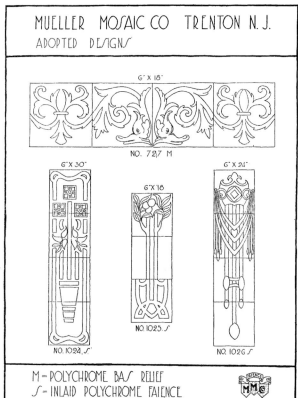

Mueller Mosaic Co. catalog pages.

Mueller Mosaic Co.

MUELLER MOSAIC CO TRENTON N.J. — ADOPTED DESIGNS

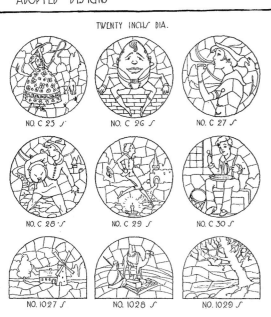

TWENTY INCHS DIA.

NO. C 25 S · NO. C 26 S · NO. C 27 S
NO. C 28 S · NO. C 29 S · NO. C 30 S
NO. 1027 S · NO. 1028 S · NO. 1029 S

M = POLYCHROME BAS RELIEF
S = INLAID POLYCHROME FAIENCE

MUELLER MOSAIC CO TRENTON N.J. — ADOPTED DESIGNS

NO. C. 21 S · NO. C. 22 S · NO. C. 23 S
NO. C. 24 S · C. 32 S · C. 31 S
NO. 1208 INTARSIA · NO. 1050 S · NO. 1019 S

M = POLYCHROME BAS RELIEF
S = INLAID POLYCHROME FAIENCE

MUELLER MOSAIC CO TRENTON N.J. — ADOPTED DESIGNS

EIGHT INCH SQUARES

NO. 846 M · NO. 847 M · NO. 848 M · NO. 849 M
NO. 850 M · NO. 851 M · NO. 852 M · NO. 853 M
NO. 854 M · NO. 855 M · NO. 856 M · NO. 857 M
NO. 866 S · NO. 867 S · NO. 868 S · NO. 869 S

M = POLYCHROME BAS RELIEF
S = INLAID POLYCHROME FAIENCE

MUELLER MOSAIC CO TRENTON N.J. — ADOPTED DESIGNS

EIGHT INCH SQUARES

NO. 886 S · NO. 887 S · NO. 888 S · NO. 889 S
NO. 890 S · NO. 891 M · NO. 892 S · NO. 893 S
NO. 894 S · NO. 895 M · NO. 896 S · NO. 897 S
NO. 8000 S · NO. 8001 S · NO. 8002 S · NO. 8003 S

M = POLYCHROME BAS RELIEF
S = INLAID POLYCHROME FAIENCE

Mueller Mosaic Co. catalog pages.

National Tile Co.

In 1903, the Columbia Encaustic Tiling Company of Anderson, Indiana, the Old Bridge Enameled Brick and Tile Company, and the Robertson Art Tile Company merged to form the National Tile Company. The three original organizations believed that they could operate more economically with a more complete offering of products with but one sales organization and some combined geographical advantages.

After the first year of combined operations, it was evident that the expenses of the project were greater and production less than anticipated. Although two of the companies had paid dividends to investors the year prior to merging, the new organization could pay none. This prompted the Old Bridge people to buy their way out of the merger agreement. They

Factory catalog page.

THE NATIONAL TILE COMPANY, ANDERSON, INDIANA

NATIONAL ARTLINE

A few examples of National's great variety of decorative strips, inserts and panels are shown on this and the following page.

In addition to a wide range of stock patterns of various types, we offer the architect or contractor the services of a staff of artists who can carry out his individual ideas and designs. Our artists can also prepare for architects or contractors, original suggestions and colored sketches for unusual tile treatments.

When confronted by special decorative problems National invites you to use this service. It is gladly given without obligation.

PAGE EIGHT

140

reclaimed their staff, plant, and company name.

By 1906, the Robertson people felt they too had had enough of the merger, and made a financial offer to buy their way out. The offer was accepted, and they left to regroup their old facilities and staff. The Columbia organization continued to operate under the newer name of National Tile.

The company was sold in 1927, and became a publicly owned business. By 1943 the capacity at National Tile was 8,000,000 square feet annually.

The mark used by National Tile was the name National, in block letters, raised on the back.

The factory catalog pages shown here are from an undated publication.

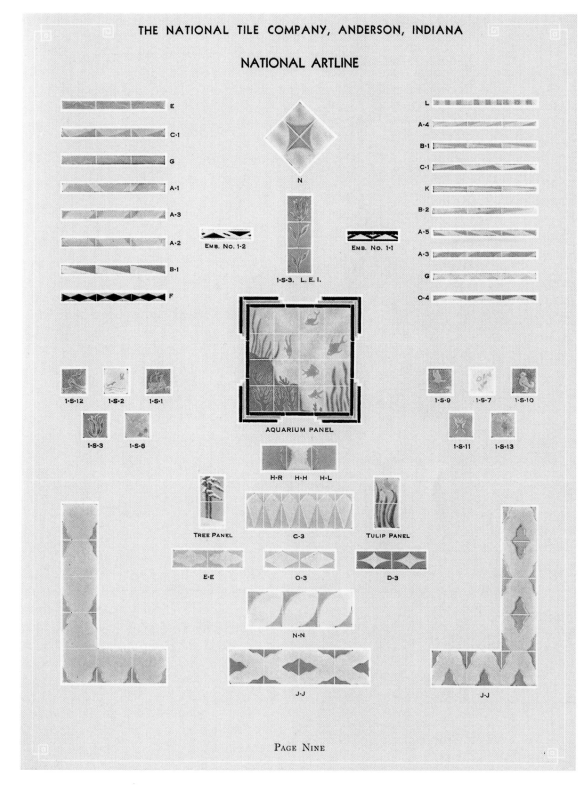

Factory catalog page.

William Woodard had been a professor of art at Tulane University since 1887. His brother, Ellsworth, had supervised fine arts at Sophie Newcomb College, the women's college of Tulane, since its founding in 1886. In 1894, they convinced the college to start a pottery class and sell the products made by the students. Funding was approved, and pottery classes were added to the existing art department's curriculum. Classes began in October of the same year.

The first potter hired was a Frenchman named Gabry, who had been working at his trade in New Orleans. Within a few months, Gabry drowned in the Mississippi River. Another potter, George Wasmuth, was hired. His tenure was also very short.

Newcomb College then hired two potters of the old New Orleans Art Pottery, Joseph Fortune Meyer and George E. Ohr. Meyer and Ohr knew each other well. They not only set up the New Orleans Art Pottery in 1886, they had been playmates in Biloxi, Mississippi, and had been employed by Meyer's father. They were both accomplished potters who had learned their trade through apprenticeship. Ohr was fired in 1898 because he was seen as "not fit" to instruct young ladies. This potter's firing, no pun intended, certainly "fit" with the "Wild PotOhr of Biloxi" reputation he earned. Ohr was probably the most talented potter and glazer ever. Meyer continued his career as the master potter at Newcomb until his retirement in 1927. Although Meyer is usually recognized as a master potter, he also was an artist, as he demonstrated in his work at the New Orleans Art Pottery.

A very early tile, this example is signed only with the conjoined monogram of Joseph Meyer and the identification letter of U, for the white clay body. This white clay and U mark were used with others, throughout the early years, and discontinued in 1902. Since no other marks exist, this tile may have been a test or experiment. The tile measures 12½" x 5½" and is decorated by incising the floral outline then painting the colors in slip and covering with a clear gloss glaze. The incising serves to keep the colors separated, and by not painting the incising, the white clay shows under the clear glaze and outlines the subject. A few other examples of this form of decoration can be seen in Louisiana's Art Nouveau *by Suzanne Ormond and Mary E. Irvine, and in* Newcomb Pottery *by Jessie Poesch. The similar examples shown in the books were made from 1895 to 1898.*
$1,750.00 – 2,250.00.

Mary G. Sheerer, who had studied at the Cincinnati Art Academy and the Art Students League in Cincinnati, was hired in 1894, to teach pottery decoration. The winter of 1894 – 1895 was used to experiment with clays and glazes. Sheerer introduced courses in china painting offered to students enrolled in the Normal Art Course, a program for those who wished to become teachers. In 1895, a course on the complete manufacture of art pottery and ornamentation was introduced. Sheerer is recognized as having played a vital role in the shaping and direction of the design and character of the pottery, especially during the period 1894 – 1910. She retired in 1931.

Experiments with clays, glazes, and decorating techniques continued until about 1900, when the blues and greens were chosen as basic colors. This was a creative period when almost all decoration was based on the local environment. Decorations were covered with a gloss glaze. This period of decoration lasted until 1910, when Paul Cox was employed to apply his technical skills. Among other things, Cox soon developed a mat glaze that was to be used almost exclusively with designs that were increasingly modeled and naturalistic. Designs, modeled in low relief, were carved in the clay when it was still damp. About 1925, a new design called Espanol was introduced, and touches of pink used with the ever-popular blues and greens. Due to the depression, output was limited, and production of the familiar mat ware ceased.

Most pieces of Newcomb are signed with one of the marks shown here.

A detailed listing of contributing Newcomb artists, potters, and ceramists, their ciphers and Newcomb biographies, and the marking system used by the pottery, appears in each of the books listed next to the tile. The students, teachers, and potters; the dates they were at Newcomb; and their marks can be seen in *American Art Pottery* by Kovels.

Northwestern Terra Cotta Co.

John R. True, John Brunkhorst, Henry Rohkam, and Gustav Hottinger of True, Brunkhorst and Company founded the Northwestern Terra Cotta Works in Chicago, Illinois, in 1882. The founders had been employees of the Chicago Terra Cotta Company that failed in 1880. True became the accountant, Brunkhorst and Henry Rohkam potters, and Gustav Hottinger the artist.

A thriving terra-cotta industry existed in Chicago because rebuilding was still underway as a result of the Great Fire of 1871. Additionally, nearby clay deposits and an excellent transportation network made the business more economical.

Brunkhorst died in 1886, and the firm was reorganized as the Northwestern Terra Cotta Company the following year.

Several authors record Henry Rohkam as a founding potter. However, one of the advertising paperweights shown here has the name Henry Plasschaert in raised letters, along with True and Brunkhorst. The other paperweight has had the Plasschaert name intentionally obliterated in the forming die, probably because he left the works. I can't find the name of Plasschaert or Rohkam in any other pottery reference. These advertising pieces were made before 1886 and they measure 5¼" x4". $75.00 – 125.00 ea

The company made architectural terra-cotta designs, including chimney pots, columns, coping, cornices, and medallions. Items were available from stock patterns or custom designs. By 1900 the firm was the largest producer of architectural terra cotta in the United States, employing 750 workers.

Sometime before 1907, for about a 12 year period, they produced an art pottery line called Norweta. Porcelain vases with crystalline glazes and modeled forms with mat glazes were made. Not all are marked. Some were marked with the line name and the company name impressed.

In the Sweet's architectural catalog of 1915, the Northwestern ad claims they are the largest producer of architectural terra cotta in the world.

Northwestern acquired the Chicago Crucible Company who also produced an art pottery. And in 1924, they acquired the St. Louis Terra Cotta Co. and the Denver Terra Cotta Co. Some art pottery products of the Denver works are signed "Northwestern Terra Cotta Co., Denver, Colo."

Operations were discontinued about 1956.

"NORTHWESTERN" FAIENCE

This class of work is particularly adapted for interiors. Any color scheme can be produced either in bright or dull enamel

Sweets, *1917.*

The Architectural Record, *December 1913.*

144

NEW home of the Broadway Motor Sales Co., Chicago; a gem in small-building design; Mr. Percy T. Johnstone, Architect.

The plain and moulded surfaces of the terra cotta are tan and white in a mottled finish with dark mottled terra cotta base course. The ornamental features are emphasized by the use of the tan on backgrounds and in the depths of the ornament, with pure white on the high relief. This arrangement produces a notable and highly satisfactory effect in the frieze.

Attention is called to the placing of signs so as not to mar architectural beauty, and to the delicate detail of the ornamental features, the perfect alignment of courses and the excellent jointing and setting—usual characteristics of Northwestern terra cotta.

NORTHWESTERN is a short form of specification for architectural Terra Cotta of superior quality.

THE NORTHWESTERN TERRA COTTA CO.

CHICAGO

Chicago Theatre, Chicago, Illinois, C. W. & Geo. L. Rapp,
Architects. Attention is called to the crispness and delicate
detail of the ornamental features of this facade—an effect obtained by use of Northwestern terra cotta in old ivory finish.

NORTHWESTERN
is a short form of
specification for archi-
tectural Terra Cotta
of superior quality.

THE NORTHWESTERN TERRA COTTA COMPANY
CHICAGO

NORTHWESTERN TERRA COTTA

The superiority of Northwestern terra cotta as a medium to carry out individual expression in form and color is illustrated in these details of building, State and Elm Streets, Chicago. B. Leo Steif & Company, Architects. Full size building was pictured in the January issue. See color detail June issue Pencil Points.

THE NORTHWESTERN TERRA COTTA COMPANY
DENVER · S⁺ LOUIS · CHICAGO · CHICAGO HEIGHTS

Owens Floor & Wall Tile Co.

J.B. Owens started in the pottery business in Roseville, Ohio, in 1888. He moved his pottery to Zanesville in 1892, and operated under the name of the J.B. Owens Pottery Company. In 1905 he started producing tile and called the business the Zanesville Tile Co. In 1906, it went into the hands of a receiver.

He soon got his factory back. He sold tile for considerably less than other manufacturers, and was always considered an annoyance by members of the Tile Manufacturers Association. The Association tried unsuccessfully to get him to join their organization, and in 1908 made Owens an offer to buy him out. Owens accepted the offer, but within a year he was producing tile at another pottery he had purchased. He named this works the J.B. Owens Floor & Wall Tile

Co. In 1910, Owens changed the name of his tile works to the Empire Floor & Wall Tile Co. Soon after, he joined the Tile Manufacturers Association.

The Empire firm prospered, and in 1915 a new plant in Metuchen, New Jersey, was built. A tunnel kiln was installed that Owens claimed was his own design.

About 1920, Owens started another factory in Greensburg, Pennsylvania, which he called the Domex Floor & Wall Tile Co. This company went into the hands of a receiver in 1927. The Zanesville plant was consumed by fire in 1928. Owens rebuilt, but the plant never started back up due to the effects of the Depression. The Metuchen plant also failed in 1929. J.B. Owens died in 1934.

In the last few years, several large and colorful Owens scenic tiles, done in an arts and crafts style, have appeared at auction.

Both of these 6" square faience tiles are signed with the die-impressed mark "Owens," used by the J.B. Owens Floor & Wall Tile Co. Signed Owens tiles are scarce. $150.00-$250.00 ea.

148

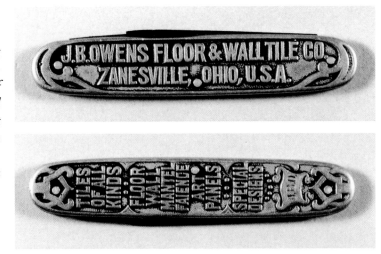

The advertising pocketknife, promoting the sale of floor, wall, mantel faience, and art panels, and the tiles shown above, are from the same 1908 – 1910 era.

Pardee Works

Around 1890, the C. Pardee Works was established in Perth Amboy, New Jersey. The company manufactured front, fire, and paving brick, sewer pipe, and a limited amount of floor and glazed tiles. Within a year or two, after the arrival of Christian Nielson, the Danish ceramic artist, they were producing art tiles for wall decorations. Hand-painted underglaze tiles and tiles with intaglio modeled heads of Emperor William, Ex-President Benjamin Harrison, President Grover Cleveland, and other celebrities were made. In 1893, tests were conducted to produce printed underglaze

and overglaze products, and W.W. Gallimore was commissioned to execute some designs.

From this late 1890s period, until Pardee purchased the Grueby Tile and Faience Co. in about 1919, there is very little recorded history. By 1920, Pardee had an annual production capacity of 6,000,000 square feet. Grueby joined the Pardee staff and brought with him many of the Grueby designs. In 1921, Pardee moved the Grueby operations to Perth Amboy. About 50 Addison B. LeBoutillier designs were eventually produced at the C. Pardee Works.

This 6" square bisque tile is signed on the back "C. Pardee Works, Perth Amboy, N. J." The decoration of a young woman admiring a bouquet was designed and modeled by Nielson, and has his initials, a C superimposed over an N, in the lower right corner. Nielson was hired by the American Encaustic Tiling Co. in 1894, after their loss of Herman Mueller. The Helen B. Henderson article on the C. Pardee Works as it appeared in the June 10, 1996, issue of Antique Week, states that no specific designs have as yet been attributed to Nielson. The example shown here is the only one I'm aware of. Very rare, $250.00 – 300.00.

These tiles were marketed as "Grueby Faience." Determining whether they are products of the Grueby factory or the C. Pardee Works is difficult, unless signed with the marks of one of the factories. $75.00 – 125.00 ea.

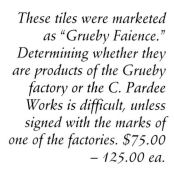

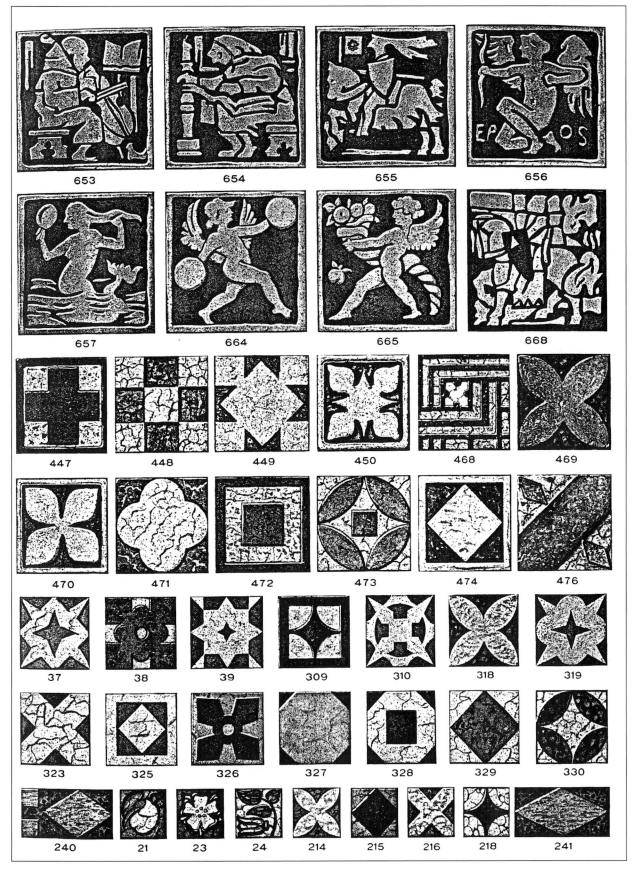

The page reproduced here from an undated C. Pardee catalog shows some of the Grueby designed tiles. Signed Pardee tiles show variations in marks that sometimes include one or all the additions of the first initial C, Works, Perth Amboy, New Jersey, or P.A. N.J

Pauline Pottery

The Pauline Pottery was established in 1883 by Mrs. Pauline Jacobus. The original pottery was founded in Chicago but relocated to Edgerton, Wisconsin, in 1888 because of the convenience of the quality clay located there. The pottery went through bankruptcy proceedings in 1894.

Mrs. Jacobus produced Pauline Pottery and conducted summer schools in pottery art at her residence from 1902 to about 1909.

The two most common types of Pauline decoration are a thick slip and an outlined water-color style, both under the glaze. The thick slip variety can be found on either white or red clay, while the water-color decorating was done on white clay. Almost all of the examples have a very fine crazing. Some of the water-color examples appear to have started the crazing process while the glaze was still molten, creating small glaze filled valleys between plateaus. The red clay used is similar in appearance to that produced at Rookwood.

An article in the June 1906 issue of *The Sketch Book,* "Our American Potteries — The Pauline Pottery," by Bertha Jaques who visited Mrs. Jacobus at her home while the pottery was in operation there describes the products.

It would be difficult to name any one distinguishing feature of the Pauline Pottery, so widely does it vary in color, form, and decoration. In working out a problem for one's self, where no hard and fast rules are followed, there is always a tendency to experiment; to explain or reproduce happy accidents; to try new combinations; and the results must of necessity be varied. But the definite object has been to produce perfect examples of underglaze ware.

It is a bewildering array that looks down upon one from the long shelves of the display room, with no duplicate in color or decoration. Of form there is an infinite variety — vases which seem to express every combination of the curve and straight line; bowls in every state of plumpness and attenuation; pompous jardinieres; squatty pitchers and tall slender ewers; jugs with curious handles; dishes and jars with covers; rose bowls and incense burners in pierced work; candlesticks and wallpockets around which scaly dragons crawl; inviting looking tea-pots with their attendant tea-caddies.

These forms are made by throwing on the wheel, *molding, and casting according to their purpose or design. Neither picture nor description can convey the subtlety of color. There are pieces suggesting old Italian Faience with a background of rich yellow or cream on which appears garlands, scrolls, and griffins in deeper tones. A dragon in old blue seems about to wriggle from a dark olive green bowl. Flowers and fruit in decorative forms appear on soft yellows and greens. Brown bowls there are with cream froth running over the edge and trickling part way down the sides; or the combination may be in pale blues and greens with a cream ground. Another form of decoration suggests 'the breaking waves dashing high,' being the reverse of the running over process with the froth in the shape of curling waves.*

But the eye is apt to rest longest on the peacock colors where the deep blue blends with the dark green so imperceptibly that the transition cannot be marked. These pieces of ware are truly satisfying because of the mystery of color, their only decoration, which varies from every point of view. It constantly invites return of inspection to solve the attraction. One might regard this as the representative achievement of the pottery, were it not for the discovery of an equally agreeable transition of soft Autumn browns into yellow; of yellow into dull green; and both olive and deep blue into a glowing rose pink. After these warm colors, it is a pleasurable surprise to meet a cool gray pitcher with melting lines of deep ultramarine blue.

Of the eight pieces of Pauline Pottery I have owned four were unsigned. Identifying unsigned Pauline is usually not difficult. The predominate factors for identification are as follows.

- ∾ Most examples have a very fine crazing.
- ∾ Most examples show a cream colored clay under the glaze, an ivory clay unglazed.
- ∾ Many outlined water-color style decorations were produced.
- ∾ Many products are trimmed with gold.
- ∾ Some decorations were done in thick slip.
- ∾ Some red clay was used.

This 10″ thrown vase has the water-color style decoration. An outlined floral was painted in with yellow blossoms and green leaves on the lower half. Then a blue sponging was applied. After the glazing, gold was sponged all over, mostly on the upper half. "Trade Mark" above the double-P crown was impressed in the bottom, then glazed over. $500.00 – 750.00.

These marks are reproduced from an article "Pauline Pottery of Edgerton, Wisconsin" by Bertha Kitchell Whyte in the April 1958 issue of Spinning Wheel.

This 8" jug has the decoration of a monk done in thick slip, and is signed with the artist's monogram of DA. The "Trade Mark" above the double-P crown is clearly impressed in the unglazed bottom of the jug. $700.00 – 900.00.

The unsigned creamer and sugar bowl shown here has an ivory clay body that appears cream under the glaze, with very fine crazing, and decorated with an outlined watercolor floral with gold trim. The molded sea shell pattern matches the 5¼" bowl or plate pictured in Kovels' American Art Pottery. Unsigned, $100.00 – 150.00 set.

The impressed double-P crown and "Trade Mark" are on the bottom of this 5½" tall ewer-shaped candle-holder. The shape number 22 is also impressed. This example is an excellent representation of the most common Pauline products. $450.00 – 600.00

The Sketchbook,
June 1906.

Pauline Pottery

NEAR EDGERTON, WIS.

Study and recreation combined. Summer school during July for practical instruction in Art of Pottery. Number of pupils limited. For rates and further particulars,

=== ADDRESS ===

Mrs. Pauline Jacobus
EDGERTON, WISCONSIN

John Peters and Adam Reed were both employed at the Weller Pottery when they decided to establish their own firm. They started their operations in 1898, in a building that had been occupied by the Clark Stoneware Company in Zanesville, Ohio. A year later they moved their operations to South Zanesville, and incorporated.

The major part of their early production consisted of flower pots, jardinieres, and cuspidors. All products were made of a dark red clay. In 1903 they added a line of cooking ware with a white lining. Attempts at producing art wares were made as early as 1901. The first successful art pottery line had a dark brown or "Standard Glaze" background, with a sparse amount of molded and applied decorations of garlands, grapes, lion heads, and portraits. The cooking ware line was discontinued in 1906.

Frank Ferrell, who had been an artist and designer at several potteries, was employed by Peters and Reed in 1912. One of his most successful designs was Moss Aztec. This line was molded of dark red clay in low and in high relief with decorations of garlands, ivy, grapes, oak leaves with acorns, and classical figures. These pieces were sprayed on the outside with a green coloring which was wiped from the high points, leaving an almost natural green moss coloring on the low areas. The interiors were glazed clear to render the objects waterproof. Some examples have the Ferrell signature on the side.

Several other art lines were introduced including Pereco, with a semi-mat glaze in green, cream, tan, or blue colors. Pereco forms had molded decorations with sharp edges that allowed the dark red clay to peek through the glaze.

Landsun is a blended mat colors line where blue, brown, tan, yellow, and green were painted in circular bands with predominate brush strokes. The Chromal line was a variation of Landsun, but with the center or upper portions decorated with a scene usually showing a house, barn, or lake.

In the Brush McCoy Pottery factory catalog of 1920, the Peters and Reed lines of pottery are shown. The old line of cooking ware is identified as "Perfection," Moss Aztec is called "Pompeian," Landsun is named "Oriental," and a modified Chromal is called "Chromart," and some molded products of the Pereco line are shown and simply called "New idea in mat-glazed ware." The Peters and Reed Pottery and the Brush McCoy Pottery obviously had some kind of manufacturing-marketing agreement. In 1919 McCoy had entered the jobbing business with the Hall China Company selling products manufactured by Hall. This was probably an expansion of that concept. These Peters and Reed products can be seen in the publication *The Collector's Encyclopedia of Brush McCoy Pottery* by Sharon and Bob Huxford.

The 13" window box shown here is signed "Ferrell" on one end. $175.00 – 250.00.

In 1921 Peters retired, and Reed changed the name of the business to the Zane Pottery Company. The ad shown here is from the September 1922 issue of *The House Beautiful.* Reed retired in 1922, and was succeeded as president by Harry S. McClelland, who had been an employee since 1903. C.W. Chilcote was put in charge of design. Most of the old lines continued to be produced, along with a few new ones.

The pottery continued to operate until 1941, when it was sold to Gonder Ceramic Arts, Inc.

This very unusual and probably rare Pereco example depicts a Swami gazing into a crystal ball. The bottom is typical of this and other glazed Peters and Reed pottery lines showing the red clay on the foot and a glazed center with no mark. The interior of the 4¾" x 5¾" vase is covered with the same cream colored semi-mat glaze. This item may be better used for supporting a crystal ball. $125.00 – 175.00.

House Beautiful,
September 1922.

In 1926 the clay was changed from the long standing dark red to white. The bowl shown here is a white clay product made from an old Moss Aztec design mold. The dragonfly decorated bowl is 2" tall and 4" wide. Although sometime after the name was changed to Zane some pottery started to be marked Zane Ware, this example is not. The Zane Ware mark was impressed or ink stamped and frequently is covered with, or partially obscured by, the glaze. $25.00 – 40.00.

Pewabic Pottery

In 1879 Mary Chase Perry, already a young artist of twelve, moved with her widowed mother, brother, and sister from Ann Arbor, Michigan, to Detroit. Mrs. Perry had rented the house next to the home of the Horace J. Caulkins family. Mr. Caulkins was the owner of the Detroit Dental Depot, a dental supply business.

About 1891, after spending two years attending the Cincinnati Art Academy developing her formal art education, Miss Perry traveled the eastern United States and earned an admirable reputation by teaching and writing on china decoration. She sold some examples of her wares, and won several awards.

When she returned to Detroit, she began a long-standing association with her friend, Horace Caulkins. Caulkins had, in the early '90s, developed the Revelation Kiln for producing porcelain dental ware. After some experimentation, he recognized some potential for his product for the overglaze decoration on pottery. He asked Perry for her assistance in marketing his kilns by demonstrating and promoting the kilns while touring the art potteries and giving instruction to china painters. The advantages of Caulkin's kilns were numerous, and the venture was successful.

Perry and Caulkins began experimenting with clays and glazes. They set up a studio in a rented carriage house behind a residence. Equipment was installed and a part-time potter was hired. Perry developed glazes and designed shapes while Caulkins became a clay specialist. They called their works the Revelation Pottery, after their still successful association with the Revelation China Kilns business. When they succeeded in making good products, examples were sold through major retailers in Chicago and Detroit. Then they received an order to make a cosmetic container for Frederick B. Sterns Co. in Detroit, and they had to install another kiln. The potter Joseph Heerich was put on full time.

Caulkins produced a 90-page catalog to promote the kilns. The catalog has illustrations, descriptions, and instructions for 18 different kilns. It also contains photographs of Pewabic tiles and vases and written testimonials from some of the most recognizable ceramic and glass artists and manufacturers of the day.

In 1903, when they received their first major commission through the renowned Burley and Co. in Chicago, they changed the pottery name to the Pewabic Pottery.

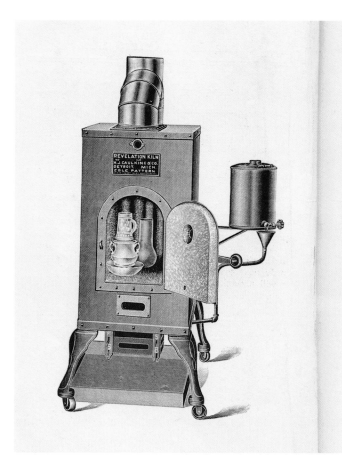

Pages from Caulkins' catalog.

THE REVELATION KILN   15

Number Five

Inside measurements—19 in. long, 15 in. high, 10 in. wide. Door frame, 10 in. wide, 14 in. high.

Price, including tank and connections, lined Tee pipe, and pan to go underneath, $81.50.

This size will admit the 14 in. punch bowl, 21 in. ice cream trays, and 15 in. table tops. It fires in one hour and fifteen minutes, and consumes a gallon and a half of oil. Being of tubular construction, the lining of the oven is a portion of the wall of the kiln itself.

This is a very good size for a teacher with a small class. The outside dimensions are 45 in. high, 25 in. long and 20 in. wide. The approximate weight, when crated for shipment, is about 550 lbs.

THE REVELATION KILN   73

2558 Eden Ave., Mt. Auburn, Cincinnati,
October 2nd, 1905.

The great, especial advantage of the kiln is the avoidance of the necessity for using seggars and the accompanying annoyances connected with wad-clay for sealing them.

If only because the use of seggars and wad clay may be avoided, the Revelation kilns would prove the superiority of this method of firing. There are other advantages, however, in the greater ease with which the fire can be controlled, the possibility of firing without annoyance from the smoke of combustion, the much more conveniently managed fuel, and the greatly shortened time. Yours very truly,
M. Louise McLaughlin.

Moylan, Pa., Oct. 14, 1905.

I have been using one of your Pottery Kilns for about a year and have had much more uniform results from it than I could obtain in any other kiln I have tried. The heat is so absolutely under control that results can be obtained impossible under other conditions. The greater cleanliness and absence of heavy manual labor are also important factors. Yours faithfully, W. P. Jervis.

Hull-House, 335 South Halsted Street, Chicago, Oct. 7, 1905.

Your letter of Sept. 26th is at hand. In reply we can say that we have used your Revelation Kiln for some years. We have found it thoroughly satisfactory and are glad to recommend it. Very truly yours,
Jane Addams,
President Hull-House.

I shall always be pleased to recommend your Kilns, and as to using my name, you are at liberty to do so in connection with Caulkins' Kiln. Yours truly,
Charles B. Upjohn.

Examples of Pewabic pottery showing matt glazes in ivory and browns. This entire product has been developed from the earliest experiments to the present point of artistic and technical interest, entirely by the means of the Revelation Pottery Kilns.

Pages from Caulkins' catalog.

Like other young potteries of the period, Pewabic's earliest glazes were limited largely to green mats. But at the St Louis Exposition of 1904, the Pewabic Pottery displayed yellow, buff, and brown mat glazes. Sales increased, and in 1906 they constructed a new studio and laboratory. By 1909 flowing glazes in orange-yellow, brown or blue, purple, and white had been introduced. In 1910 the building was enlarged and Perry's popular Persian or Egyptian glaze had been perfected. Other glazes were developed including crystalline, volcanic, iridescent, and luster. Clays to compliment their glazes were also developed.

Tile production soon became the major output. Many installations were made throughout America. Tiles were handmade for bathrooms, fireplaces, fountains, swimming pools, and entryways to be installed in residences, schools, churches, and businesses. All installations were custom made and one of a kind. Perry used a 1906 catalog from the Moravian Pottery and Tile Works, and a copy of the *Handbook of Ornament* by Franz S. Meyer as sources for many of her original designs. She admired the work of Henry Mercer and Franz Meyer, but did not copy their creations.

This fire-place shows examples of Pewabic tile with matt glazes. The tile are a foot square, with a soft grey above, green pine trees with dark brown trunks, and golden yellow hills and hearth.

Mary Chase Perry married William Buck Stratton in 1918. Mr. Caulkins died in 1923, and Mrs. Stratton continued running the pottery until her death in 1961 when the pottery was closed. The Pewabic Pottery became the property of the Michigan State University about 1966, and was reopened in 1968. The Pewabic Society, a non-profit organization, was founded in 1981 to resume the production of pottery and educational programs.

The founding of the Pewabic Pottery by Mary Chase Perry, along with her next door neighbor, Horace James Caulkins, is no less strange or less important than when Karl Langenbeck gave his neighbor, Maria Longworth Nichols, a set of paints for decorating china, and she later established the Rookwood Pottery.

Other Pewabic employees who made significant contributions were as follows.

- Joseph Ender, kiln operator, employed 1912 – 1959, nephew of Joseph Heerich.
- Louis Tomas, tile installer, 1910 – 1919 & 1922 – ?, died in 1969.
- John Graziosi, potter and installer, employed 1912 – 1959.
- Gwen Lux, artist and sculptor, from late twenties till 1961.
- Alexis Lapteff, sculptor, employed 1930 – 1961.

Prior to the pottery being named Pewabic in October 1903, small experimental pieces were signed "Perry" by hand in ink or glaze. Later, for a short time, pieces were signed "Revelation Pottery" with the initials M.C.P. below. The first Pewabic mark was circular with Pewabic above Detroit. This mark was either die impressed in the clay or black ink stamped on a tan 1" square paper label. A variation of this circle mark was made later with a large P sheltering a smaller P within the center. These circle marks are the most common. Other marks were an impressed arched Pewabic with maple leaves above, a hand-incised Pewabic with a date, and a printed paper label with the words Pewabic-Pottery-Detroit forming a triangle.

A copper luster glaze was painted over a turquoise glaze to produce this red wine luster on a gray-green background. Unsigned. $300.00 – 350.00.

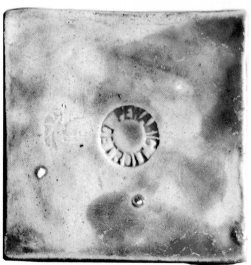

This 3″ square hand-carved relief tile, with the decoration of an owl, is signed with the circular Pewabic-Detroit mark, die impressed. $125.00 – 175.00.

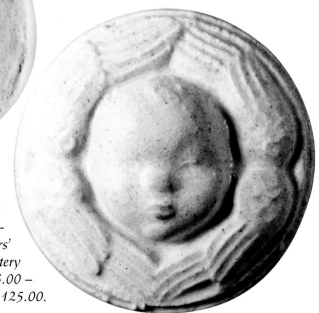

This 3⅜″ diameter tile or paperweight was probably made sometime between 1961 and 1969 when Ella Peters, Mrs. Stratton's secretary of 23 years, and Mrs. Peters' husband Ira were maintaining the pottery after the death of Mrs. Stratton. $75.00 – 125.00.

Providential Tile Works

The Providential Tile Works was founded in Trenton, New Jersey, in 1885 by Joseph L. Kirkham, James H. Robinson, and C. Louis Whitehead. The first products were made in the spring of 1886. Isaac Broome, who had previously been with the Trent Tile Co., was the first designer and modeler. Scott Callowhill was also employed as a modeler, and his sons, Hubert and Ronald, were hired as artists. Kirkham didn't stay long, for he started his own company in 1891.

The products were glazed tiles, plain and in relief. Early on, some relief tiles had the raised designs painted different colors, or tints, with some good results. Underglaze decoration was also produced for a while, but both styles were abandoned as being unsuitable for the American market. Tiles were made for mantels, hearths, and wall decoration, in relief and intaglio. From 1900 until 1910, beautiful relief designs, in white glaze decorated in gold, were very popular.

In about 1900, Robinson left the partnership. Whitehead died in 1912, and the company failed a year later.

The female 12" x 6" panel is pictured in E. A. Barbers' The Pottery and Porcelain of the United States, *published in 1893. "Mignon," by modeler Scott Callowhill, after Lefebvre, is signed on the back with the raised letters, P.T.W., as is the companion tile. The sharpness of the relief, detail, and edge frame are excellent. $750.00 – 850.00 the pair.*

This framed tile of sea creatures is an example of the relief coloring or tinting done at this works. The tile is 4½" x 6", and has the raised initials of the company. $150.00 – 200.00.

163

The back of this 6" tile with a berry bush decoration has an embossed checkerboard pattern with the company name. $30.00 – 35.00.

The black-grape glaze on this pair of 6" square portrait tiles also defines the sharp detail in the modeling by this manufacturer. Although there are no identifying marks on these tiles, the female subject is pictured in an article, "American Art Pottery" by Dave Rago, in the March 9, 1983, issue of the Antique Trader. The example is identified as Providential, and it is signed by Isaac Broome. Broome modeled tiles at the Beaver Falls Art Tile Co. after he left Providential. While at Beaver Falls he modeled this same pair of characters, but dressed them in large lace collars. His second version can be seen in an article by Barbara White Morse, "Tiles Made by Isaac Broome — Sculptor and Genius," in the January/February 1973 issue of Spinning Wheel. $450.00 – 500.00 for the pair.

This 12″ x 6″ two piece panel is signed by the artist with the initials CH in the lower right corner of the bottom tile. Marks on the back are in three recessed valleys. The letters are raised and read "The Providential - Tile Works - Trenton, N. J." $450.00 – 500.00.

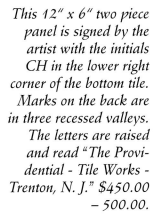

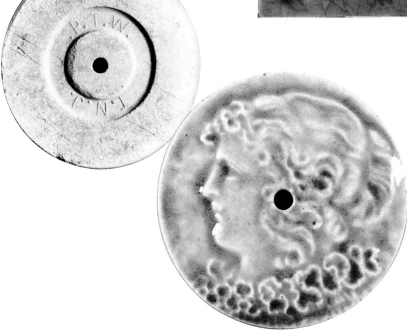

Providential also produced stove tiles. Their output must have been minimal because they are scarce. The molded center hole was designed for attaching the tile with a screw. This stove tile is 3″ in diameter, and signed twice with the company's initials within a recessed circle. $75.00 – 125.00.

In 1873 Maria Longworth Nichols became involved with china painting when she was given a set of china decorating paints by a neighbor boy, Karl Langenbeck. China decorating soon became a mania in America. Nichols became involved in more than just decorating. She started experimenting with glazes and clays. In 1880 Nichols founded the Rookwood Pottery of Cincinnati, Ohio, in an old school house her father, Joseph Longworth, had purchased at a sale.

Nichols hired artists and workers and started producing pottery for sale. Early production included art pottery and utilitarian wares. Some utilitarian items and wares for amateur decorators were undecorated. The pottery was not a profitable venture, so her father, a long-time patron of the arts, provided the financial support necessary to keep the pottery operating.

William Watts Taylor joined the pottery as the administrator and a partner in 1883. Mr. Nichols died in 1885, and in 1886 Mrs. Nichols became the wife of Bellamy Storer. The pottery business continued operating at a loss until 1889. Mrs. Storer retired from the Rookwood Pottery in 1890, and transferred her interests to Taylor. In 1890, the Rookwood Pottery became a stock company, and Taylor became the president.

Rookwood gained international recognition with the winning of a gold medal at the 1889 Exposition Universelle in Paris, and the first prize gold metal at the Exposition of American Art Industry in Philadelphia. Business was growing rapidly, and in 1891 ground was broken for the construction of a new factory on the summit of Mount Adams, a suburb overlooking the Ohio River and the downtown area, and near the Cincinnati Art Museum and the Art Academy. The operations were moved into the new facility in 1892.

Rookwood had several displays at the World Columbian Exposition in Chicago in 1893, and they won a "Highest Award" medal. The publicity resulted in a sales boost, and many foreign museums purchased examples.

Rookwood's earliest financial success was, for a large part, the result of the enthusiastic acceptance of their Standard Glaze line. Investment in developing new clays and glazes helped insure their continuing success. In the 1890s several lines were introduced, and in 1901, after five years of experimenting, mat glazes were introduced. A year later the new architectural department received its first order.

The business continued to thrive, and national and international awards became almost commonplace. The architectural department established in 1902 was, for

The Limoges glaze line was among the first produced at Rookwood. Introduced in 1880 and discontinued about 1885, these usually heavily slip painted items were covered with a gloss glaze. The factory-made Limoges lamp shown here has a 6" tall ceramic body and is signed with a die-impressed Rookwood and the date of 1883 in small block letters. The impressed monogram of William P. McDonald and a small paper label with numbers, also appear on the bottom. Inside the cylinder is a paper label remnant identifying the Hollins & Co. as the lamp manufacturer. The amber glass globe and Rookwood cylinder are decorated with birds and bats in a Japanese style. The globe is signed Baccarat in the mold. $1,500.00 – 2,000.00.

several years, a drain on the company's profits. Just like the establishing of a successful art pottery, where true craft prevails, the architectural profits were slow in coming. By 1912 the architectural products accounted for 35% of the company's total sales, but the department was still operating at a loss while the profits from the sale of art pottery maintained the business.

Late in 1913 Taylor died unexpectedly. Taylor's will gave his controlling interest to a trust whose profits would go to the "benefit and improvement of the said Rookwood Pottery Company." Taylor had already been a major reason for Rookwood's success, now, just as Storer had done, he left the company revealing his character and interest for the pottery's welfare.

Standard glaze products were exceptionally popular after their introduction in 1884. They maintained the public's interest until 1907. This three-piece covered soap dish was decorated by Matthew Daley in 1890. Expertly decorated with spider mums, the set measures 5" wide. The bottom and the inner tray each have small S's impressed. The S was used to designate a piece as "special," when it was observed being made by a visiting dignitary. $450.00 – 600.00.

The Tiger Eye line was an unexpected glaze accident that occurred in 1884. When the kiln was opened, seven pieces had a "shimmering gold" crystalline glaze. The accident happened to a Mahogany glaze item, a variation of the Standard glaze, where the decoration was applied to a red clay form instead of the regular white clay. Although this glaze was repeated successfully, the company never really learned the secret of reproducing it consistently enough to make it practical. The two test pieces shown here are of the red clay, and both are hand turned. The 6¼" shouldered vase has had a dark brown background color applied to a controlled surface of the red clay body. The words incised in the bottom point to the control area, saying "Tigereye-No. 6-C." Hopefully, this area would have shown some flecks of gold. The company name in small block letters and the date 1884 are die impressed in the bottom. $250.00 – 300.00.

Joseph Henry Gest was named president to replace Taylor. Gest had been vice-president and director since 1902, and had an excellent understanding of the business. The pottery had slightly up and slightly down finances during Gest's reign as president, surviving WWI and the Depression, but never having a strong financial period. Gest retired in frustration in 1934, but maintained his relationship with the pottery as chairman of the board.

John D. Wareham, an employee since 1893, replaced Gest. Wareham had been hired as an artist, promoted to head of the decorating department, and had been vice-president since 1914. Rookwood entered a long period of financial re-constructions, layoffs, part-time work, and several owners. This "survival" mode of operation continued through Wareham's reign until his death in 1954, having served Rookwood 61 years.

During the following 13 years Rookwood employees and other Cincinnatians spent more time and money trying to preserve Rookwood's heritage than they did in operating to supply a nearly extinct demand. Rookwood's operation ended in 1967.

In 1983 Dr. Arthur J. Townley purchased the Rookwood Pottery Company molds and name. Production of new Rookwood started soon thereafter. The items made have been limited mostly to paperweights. Products are signed and dated. No attempt has been made to manufacture articles with the old Rookwood marks.

The 7¾" vase with the extended neck has some result that looks like flecks of foil. This is a positive result, but not exactly what was desired. Impressed in the bottom are the company name, shape no. 167, and 1885. $250.00 – 300.00.

Standard glaze products are most commonly seen with background colors in shades of dark brown to orange, sometimes yellow or green. However, other colors were used, sometimes shading into a second color, or a lone color was shaded or solid. This green or teal candleholder was decorated with lily of the valley in 1894 by Lenore Asbury. $450.00 – 550.00.

This blue-green Standard glaze has a background shading from dark at the top to lighter toward the bottom. Decorated with a rare full length portrait, this 14½" vase was painted by Bruce Horsfal in 1894. The title Spirit of the Summit *and* "B-," Horsfal's monogram were hand incised in the bottom with a sharp object. The yellow tinted glaze, a hallmark of the Standard line, is very evident over the subject and snow covered mountain peaks in the background. $7,500.00 – 9,000.00.

Although these Queen City Club menus, one for an honored guest or member, are not signed Rookwood, they are from the factory. Stanley Burt and Joseph Gest were Rookwood employees and officers, and were members of the club. They frequently lunched there together. William Taylor, the president, was likely a member as was his best friend Pitts Harrison Burt, father of Stanley. These menus were probably made by volunteer artists that assisted in providing whatever number was needed for the occasion. The Standard glaze line is evident in the slip painted art work of one and the yellow glaze of the other. $600.00 – 800.00 pr.

Rookwood Pottery

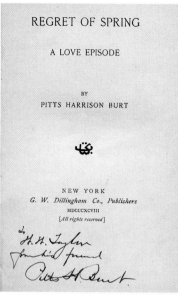

Pitts Harrison Burt was a pioneer stockbroker and a director of the Rookwood Pottery. He designed over 40 shapes of pottery. In 1898 he published Regret of Spring, *a love episode. This copy belonged to his friend, William Watts Taylor. The cover and inside decorations were done by Artus Van Briggle. The vases illustrated were made at the pottery and are after designs by Burt.*

Copyrighted, 1901, by The U. S. Playing Card Co., Cincinnati.

SITTING BULL CARD BACK.

An authentic likeness of this most noted of Indian chiefs. A companion to the famous Rookwood Indian design—printed in the rich, mellow colors which have helped to make the Rookwood back so popular. Found only in our

Congress
Playing Cards

(Gold edges.) Thin, crisp, elastic. Preferred by wise entertainers, who know that handsome cards do much to make the party a success. Booklet, "Entertaining with Cards," illustrates all the popular backs, such as Rookwood Indian, Spinning Wheel, Good Night, George Washington, Mill, Rube, Delft and many others Sold by dealers.

Adjudged "perfect," and accorded highest possible award, Pan-American Exposition, Buffalo, 1901, and World's Fair, Chicago, 1893.

Awarded "Grand Prix" against all nations, Paris, 1900; the only Playing Cards ever deemed worthy a "Grand Prix."

Rookwood artists decorated Standard glaze wares with portraits of Native Americans from about 1898 till 1902. By 1899 Rookwood was so well recognized for its high quality products, others wanted to capitalize on its name. During this year the United States Playing Card Company of Cincinnati introduced a copyright Rookwood Indian deck of cards. The deck must have been a good seller, for in 1901 they introduced another Native American portrait deck. Ad appeared in Munsey's Magazine in 1901.

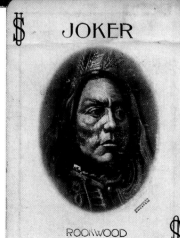

CUT THIS OUT and send with 2c. stamp and we will mail you sample Sitting Bull card and above booklet, describing an Indian and many other novel card parties.

Our Goddess of Liberty Trade Mark Ace.   THE U. S. PLAYING CARD CO.
Department 14,   Cincinnati, Ohio.

170

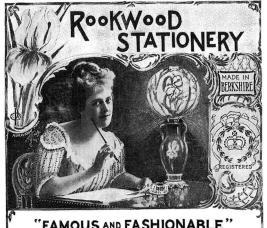

"FAMOUS AND FASHIONABLE"

AMERICAN manufacturers have not for years produced such a new and original paper of distinction as found in "Rookwood." It originated from the merits and popularity of "Rookwood Pottery," which it resembles, and appears in four distinct variations of effective and delicate tints : Sea Green, Aerial Blue, Tiger Eye and Iris, producing a line of papers which has never been approached in completeness of artistic effects. Its marked individuality, aside from the superiority of stock, is that no two sheets are alike. Although each harmonize perfectly with the other, the waves of color are not identical in each, which produces an unusual and charming effect.

It is made up in the latest and most fashionable shapes and sizes for society use, and is absolutely correct in every detail.

Samples sent to any address for a leading stationer's name, who does not have it.

EATON-HURLBUT PAPER COMPANY, Pittsfield, Mass.
Makers of High-Grade Papers and Society Stationery

The Swift & Company wrote the Rookwood Pottery in 1901, asking for permission to use the company name for a new brand of soap. The request was denied. However, the Eaton-Hurlbut Paper Company of Pittsfield, Massachusetts, advertised "Rookwood Stationery" and also sold brands under the names "Iris," "Sea Green," "Tiger Eye," and "Aerial Blue." Eaton-Hurlbut was asked to discontinue the use of the Rookwood names. Stationery box (above); Ladies' Home Journal ad, November 1900 (left).

This vase, decorated with diving swallows, is another Standard line product. Josephine Zettel painted the 11" vessel in 1900. $800.00 – 1,000.00.

An experimental mat glaze bowl, done in 1900 by W. P. MacDonald, has the colors similar to the most popular Van Briggle products. The surface area has been divided into three equal sections, each showing a different level of opaqueness. The bowl has been hand turned. The bottom has the die-impressed company logo, date, and shape number 90 Z. An impressed Z following a shape number was used from 1900 to 1904 to denote the shape was made for the mat glaze line. Other bottom marks include test section numbers 1, 2, and 3, item 5, and the artist's monogram, all in the same ink or slip used to divide the surface sections. $300.00 – 350.00.

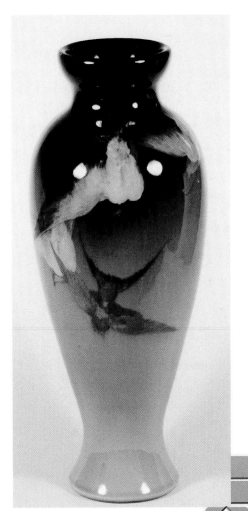

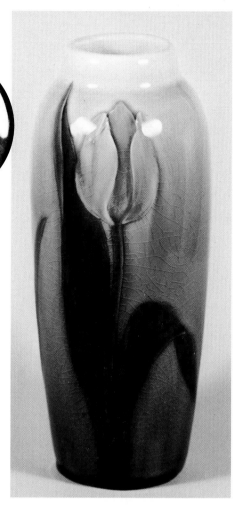

The Sea Green glaze line was introduced in 1894, and production continued for 10 years. The slip painting process was the same as that of the Standard line, but the predominant colors of green, blue, and yellow were covered with a green tinted glaze. The 8½" example shown here was decorated by Sturgis Lawrence in 1901. A small impressed G on the bottom instructed the glazer to apply this glaze. This example has an "X" ground on the bottom, identifying it as a factory second available at a reduced price. The vase was probably determined to be a second because of the underglaze separation in the slip at the top of the tulip. The line was never a good seller and examples are scarce. $1,750.00 – 2,250.00.

Decorated in 1902 by Caroline Steinle, this 7" vase has a colorful iris with blue and yellow petals on a background shading from dark brown to bright yellow. $450.00 – 550.00.

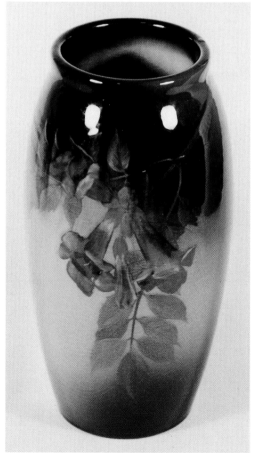

Mary Nourse painted this Standard glaze decoration of trumpet vine. The 9" vase was made in 1903. $500.00 – 600.00.

The Iris glaze line was officially introduced in 1894,
more of a convenient publicity
event, for Iris line of products
were made in quantity in
1893. This line continued
until 1912. The decorating
process was similar to that of
Standard and Sea Green, but
Iris had a larger palette of
colors for both atomized
backgrounds and slip painting. The decoration was then
covered with a crystal clear
glaze. The poppy decoration
on the 9½" vase shown here
was done by Sallie Coyne in
1906. $1,500.00 –
1,800.00.

Also dated 1906 and 9½" tall, this
Iris line vase was decorated with daf-
fodils by Sara Sax. $1,750.00 –
2,000.00.

Decorated with
cyclamen by Sallie
Coyne, this 9¾"
Iris vase is dated
1907. $1,500.00
– 1,800.00.

The Vellum glaze line was introduced at the Louisiana Purchase Exposition in St. Louis in 1904. It won the Grand Prize for its sensational translucent, yet mat, non-reflecting glaze. Vellum production ran through 1948. All Vellums were marked on the bottom with a die-impressed V to instruct the glazer. Vellum glazes tinted green or yellow were also made, but are much less common. Made in 1915, this 8" pine-cone decorated Vellum was done by Lorinda Epply. $700.00 – 900.00.

Scenic Vellums were introduced in 1905. This 13" example was decorated with trees surrounding a pond by Elizabeth McDermott in 1920. $2,400.00 – 2,800.00.

This Scenic Vellum plaque, probably from a sketch or photo of the nearby Ohio River, was painted by Sallie Coyne and titled "Winter." The date on this 7" x 9" plaque is covered by a backing. Although Scenic Vellum plaque production continued until 1948, output had diminished considerably by the late '20s. Coyne left the company in 1931. The frame is original, but has been repainted. $1,800.00 – 2,300.00.

Lenore Asbury named this Scenic Vellum plaque "The Pines." The date of the 8" x 6" plaque is covered by a backing. Asbury left the pottery in 1931. The repainted frame is original. $1,800.00 – 2,300.00.

The peacock decoration was in vogue, and Sara Sax loved to use it. This 5⅝" experimental Vellum has, within a small 1" circular recess in the bottom, the impressed marks of the factory, the date of 1913, the V for Vellum, the shape number and size 821 F, the Sax monogram, and the Rookwood experimental designation 3942HH. The decoration appears to be lightly carved, but the purpose of the test is not evident. $500.00 – 600.00.

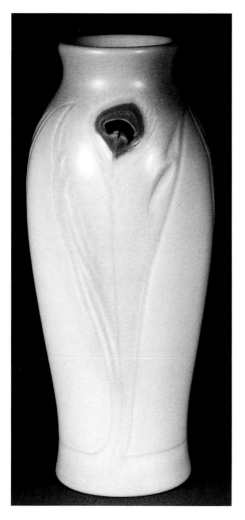

This 10" carved Vellum vase was also done by Sara Sax in 1913. The feather decoration was carved in the clay while it was still wet. Very fine carving was done around the "eye" prior to painting the thick slip colors of blue, gold, and cobalt. The background appears to be lightly tinted green and blue glazes, rather than the normal sprayed on colors. Examples of carved Vellums are scarce to rare. $1,750.00 – 2,250.00.

The Decorated Mat line was introduced in 1905, and continued until about 1920. The relief carved peacock decoration on this thrown vase was done by Charles Todd in 1914. Four peacocks appear confined behind a fence or wall on this 11" vase. $1,800.00 – 2,200.00.

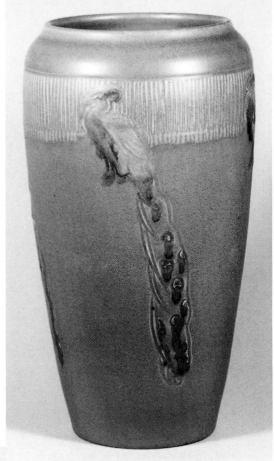

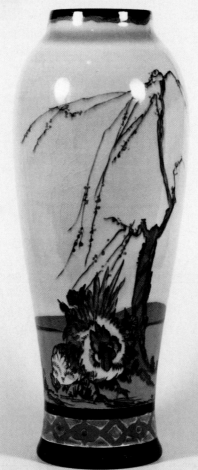

The earliest known example of the Turquoise Blue line is dated 1916. Production continued till the Depression with most pieces dated in the '20s. The exceptional example shown here was executed in 1917 by Arthur Conant. The high gloss Oriental scenic has four colorful chickens pecking for food around the base of two trees. The colors are unusual because they are lighter than most of this line. The 10¼" vase has the impressed P of a the soft porcelain body introduced in 1914. $3,200.00 – 3,700.00.

Lorinda Epply decorated this Turquoise Blue vase in 1920. The myriad of tiny bubbles embedded in the glaze of this line gives the decoration a hazy appearance, similar to the Vellums, but the glaze of Turquoise Blue is glossy rather than mat. The bubbles are especially evident over the dark decoration of foliage on this 17¼" example. $2,250.00 – 2,750.00.

The French Red line can be identified by the glossy rose glaze used in the decoration and the interior lining of the vessel. The rose glaze was used with other gloss enamels and mat colors, and is most frequently seen with mat or gloss black backgrounds. The line was made from 1919 to 1927, with most examples dated in the 1921 to 1924 time period. This line was not produced long because the oxide used in the red glaze was expensive. The line was never officially named by the company, but the artists called it French Red because the oxide was obtained in France. Several years ago, when I purchased the covered candy shown here, I thought the piece was just different or unusual. I cataloged it as "Old Cloisonné," a style where the decoration was raised above a black background. The description fits with many of this line, which has recently been properly identified.

In 1927, following Charles Lindbergh's historic flight, "The Women of Cincinnati" presented him with a large Oriental covered jar of the French Red line. The jar is pictured in *The Book of Rookwood Pottery* by Herbert Peck, and it also looks like old cloisonné.

Lindbergh's jar was decorated by Sara Sax, who did most of the French Reds.

The French Red covered candy shown here is 5½" tall and 6¾" wide. Elizabeth Lincoln did the decoration in 1922. Only a few examples of French Red have appeared, and all except this one have been stylistic florals. French Reds are rare, those with butterflies or other embellishments almost unknown. $3,250.00 – 3,850.00.

Anita Ellis, curator of decorative arts at the Cincinnati Art Museum, in her publication *Rookwood Pottery — The Glaze Lines,* calls this the Double Vellum line. For as long as I can remember, everyone has incorrectly called this Wax Mat. Rookwood, in one of their catalogs, called it a Decorated Mat, and there is another line the company called Wax Mat. To end the confusion, Ellis calls this Double Vellum because of the process used to decorate it. A vessel is fired, covered with a Vellum glaze, decorated, covered with a Vellum glaze, and fired again, hence, Double Vellum.

Katherine Jones decorated this Double Vellum vase (right) in 1927. The 7½" form has a turquoise shaded background with a floral draped around its shoulder. $550.00 – 700.00. The larger form Double Vellum (left) measures 8½" x 6½", and was done by Jens Jenson in 1930. Both vases have artists' monograms painted on the bottom in ink or thin slip, a characteristic of Double Vellums. $1,000.00 – 1,200.00.

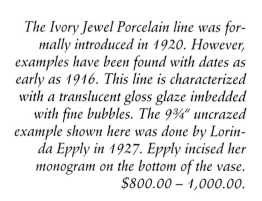

The Ivory Jewel Porcelain line was formally introduced in 1920. However, examples have been found with dates as early as 1916. This line is characterized with a translucent gloss glaze imbedded with fine bubbles. The 9¾" uncrazed example shown here was done by Lorinda Epply in 1927. Epply incised her monogram on the bottom of the vase. $800.00 – 1,000.00.

This 1943 Ivory Jewel Porcelain was painted by Lorinda Epply. The vase has unusual reversible decorations. One side is painted with a soft lavender and green floral. The opposite side is decorated with an exotic flying bird. $550.00 – 700.00.

Twin sisters, Flora and Ora King painted these smoker sets in 1946. The sets are covered with the glaze of the Ivory Jewel Porcelain line. Flora painted the goats and Ora did the squirrels. These items, and the previous vase, have the artists' marks painted on the bottoms in ink or black slip. $500.00 – 700.00 pr. set.

Clotilda Zanetta was hired at Rookwood to sculpt religious items in about 1943. The 5" medallion of "Our Lady of Cincinnati," shown here, is dated 1953, and has her incised initials to the right, below center. Two other similar medallions were designed by Zanetta in 1947. She left the pottery in 1948. $150.00 – 200.00.

The 9" square faience plaque shown here was painted by the pottery artist Albert Ponds. The plaque has been painted in the technique of the Painted Mat Inlay line. This process has the artist apply the mat colors decoration, then outline the work and sign the artists monogram with the same black glaze. The Ponds monogram appears in the lower left corner. The Painted Mat Inlay line was produced from 1900 to 1906, and Ponds was a decorator from 1904 until 1911. This plaque was probably made about 1904 to 1906. I purchased this plaque at an Ohio auction about a dozen years ago. After the bidding had started the auctioneer stopped to relate the consignor's story of this being the artist's rendering of the Rookwood Pottery, as it appears from across the river in Kentucky. I thought the comment was typical of an auctioneer trying to extract more money. However, after years of looking at this, one might say its the view of Rookwood, rendered in a medieval arts and crafts style. $1,250.00 – 1,500.00.

Decorated in the style of the Incised Mat line, this framed tile or plaque depicts an ocean steamer under a large puffy cloud. Incised Mat objects were made from 1900 until 1915. The process required the decoration to be deeply incised in the wet clay form which was then fired, covered with a mat glaze, then fired again. This 3¾" x 5" faience example is signed on both the back and an edge, but only with the common Rookwood four digit experimental number, preceded and followed with X's, all in black ink or slip. The incised decoration is covered with a burnt sienna mat glaze. Rarely will you see unmarked examples of Rookwood, even in test or experimental objects. I have absolutely no reservations about the origin of this unsigned Rookwood faience. $200.00 – 300.00.

This 4¾" x 1" white clay test tile was made to test mat glazes in shades of pink for the art pottery department. The test was conducted under the direction or with the assistance of the artist Amelia B. Sprague, and her monogram appears on the back along with the test control information. Sprague was employed as an artist from 1887 to 1903. An early mat glaze test. $125.00 – 175.00.

These two faience tiles are part of a larger set. The poppies in high relief decoration was designed about 1910. The tiles are each 6" square. $350.00 – 450.00 the pair.

Introduced about 1910, this Dutch boat design is shown in the reprint of a factory catalog in The Book of Rookwood Pottery by Peck. The raised line decoration was given the catalog number 3355YE. Like all Rookwood faience tile, this 6" square example is clearly marked. $350.00 – 500.00.

This 12" diameter faience tile appeared in an ad in a 1924 issue of The House Beautiful. Identified as Ship Panel A 1485, it is shown with a border made of eight tile segments. The same ship design was also pictured in an issue of The Architectural Record in 1927. The design was also advertised as one of a set of four 12" square tiles. This piece, while the clay was still wet, had a recess carved in the back, at the top, so a wire or twine could be attached for hanging on a wall. The tile is also glazed on the side or edge, something that wouldn't have been done were it intended to be permanently mounted in cement. The mold and decoration numbers and the reversed R and P factory mark are deeply impressed in the back.
$1,750.00 – 2,250.00.

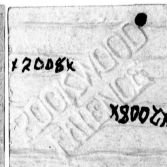

A grouping of 4" square test tiles shows a variety of factory marks used over an extended time. A difference in the faience clay is also evident. The mat green over turquoise on the broken-in-half tile is an exceptional test example. $20.00 – 200.00 each.

A sampling of commercial wares. Left to right, front to back. Female paperweight signed Able, 1926, $300.00. Rabbit paperweight, 1937, $350.00. Reclining kitten, 1945, $450.00. Vase, 4½", #6064, 1931, daisy border, $160.00. Vase, 4½", #6108, 1931, deco, $160.00. Vase, 4½", #1681, 1911, pea pods, $275.00. Vase, 7½", #6516, 1936, herons, $400.00. Vase, 6½", #1889, 1928, pine cones, $250.00. Vase, 9¼", #2420, 1922, arts & crafts, $400.00. Vase, 8½", #1358, 1924, $275.00.

Rookwood marks are reproduced here from a company brochure published about 1920.

ROOKWOOD
1882

Impressed in the clay. The regular mark from 1882, the date changing each year until 1886.

This mark was adopted in 1886. The flame at the top indicates 1887, and a flame is added for every year thereafter, so that the mark for 1900 shows fourteen. For the next century the mark of 1900 is continued with the Roman numerals to designate the year. The mark for 1901 is given in the margin.

It is also customary for purposes of record, to stamp on the bottom of each piece a shape number with a letter indicating size, and another letter referring to the color of the clay used in the body of the piece, W for white, etc.

DECORATORS' MARKS

THE decorators have always cut their initials in the clay on the bottom of pieces painted by them. The complete list of monograms is too long to be given here, but the following list contains the marks of all the present decorators and also the marks of most of the older artists whose pieces are most often seen.

A.R.V	A. R. Valentien	JDW	John D. Wareham		W. E. Hentschel
WᴹD	Wm. P. McDonald	LA	Leonore Asbury		
	Matt. A. Daly	SL	Sturgis Laurence	C.S.T.	Charles S. Todd
AᵐV	Anna M. Valentien	R.	Fred. Rothenbusch	EM	Elizabeth F. McDermott
ϒ	Grace Young	EᴳD	Edward G. Diers	MᴴD	Margaret Helen McDonald
AℰW	Harriet E. Wilcox	ETH	E. T. Hurley		Mary Grace Denzler
	K. Shirayamadani	A·F·	Rose Fechheimer	HᴹL	Helen M. Lyons
	Amelia B. Sprague	S	Sara Sax	CJM	Chas. J. McLaughlin
	Sallie Toohey		Carl Schmidt	PC	Patti M. Conant
O.G.R.	O. Geneva Reed Pinney	M	Marianne Mitchell	C	Arthur P. Conant
mn	Mary Nourse	EN	Edith Noonan		
S	Carrie Steinle	LE	Lorinda Epply	VT	Vera Tischler
CAB	Constance A. Baker	A	Albert F. Pons	A	Louise Abel
Z	Josephine E. Zettel	CAD	Cecil A. Duell		
LNL	Elizabeth Lincoln	KM	Katherine Van Horne		
HRS·	Harriet R. Strafer				
SC	Sallie E. Coyne				

"IRIS"

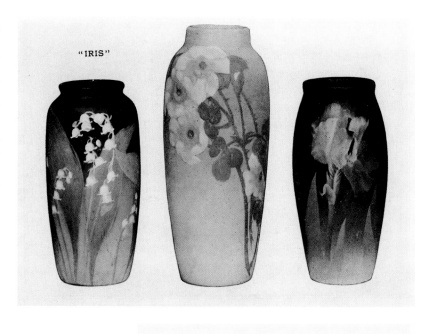

"IRIS"

"CONVENTIONAL
AND INCISED
MAT GLAZES"

''STANDARD'

Some pages reproduced from a 1904 catalog.

Early postcards. Post-marked 1899 (top); note signed by artist (left).

Rookwood Residence of Nicholas Longworth   24. - CINCINNATI (Ohio).

Handcolored

7381 THE ROOKWOOD POTTERY, CINCINNATI, O.

Early postcards. Postmarked 1904, note the handwritten comments (left); 1904 addition nearing completion (below).

Cincinnati, O. The Rookwood Pottery Mt. Adams.

Rookwood Pottery, Cincinnati, U. S. A.

Early postcards. The original 1891 building above left, the 1899 addition center, and 1904 addition at right.

Early postcards. Used 1910 – 1920 (right); used 1915 – 1940 (below).

ROOKWOOD POTTERY, CINCINNATI, OHIO.

Mt. Adams Incline and Rockwood Pottery on left.
Cincinnati, Ohio

Beauty of Form

Is the first essential in Pottery, and of this the chief elements are simplicity of line and adaptation to use. The constant effort of the Rookwood designers is to apply these principles to every model which receives the stamp of the pottery.

ROOKWOOD POTTERY, Cincinnati.

Century, *March 1887.*

A PRIZE WINNER.

AT THE POTTERY AND PORCELAIN EXHIBITION of the Pennsylvania Museum, held at Memorial Hall, Philadelphia, November, 1888, the ROOKWOOD POTTERY was awarded the FIRST PRIZE for "POTTERY MODELED AND DECORATED," and the FIRST PRIZE for "PAINTING UNDERGLAZE," and was the only ware in competition whose QUALITIES OF FORM WERE SPECIALLY COMMENDED by the Judges, Messrs. JOSEPH T. BAILEY, W. P. P. LONGFELLOW, HENRY STEELE.

Century, *January 1889.*

The Magazine of Art, *May 1889.*

THE ❧ ROOKWOOD ❧ POTTERY.

(OF CINCINNATI.)

The ROOKWOOD POTTERY, whose productions are without a rival among American wares, was established at Cincinnati in 1880, by Mrs. Maria Longworth Storer. It is devoted exclusively to artistic work. No printing is done, but the decorations, which are never duplicated, are entirely freehand work under the glaze, while the shapes are formed mainly upon the potter's wheel, without the seam, so objectionable in common ware. The result of these methods of manufacture is seen in the delicacy of the form, the soft lustre of the coloring (such as is unattainable in overglaze work), and, above all, in the remarkably individual character of the pieces. The production comprises a wide variety of both useful and ornamental ware.

DAVIS COLLAMORE & CO.
LIMITED,

921 BROADWAY.   151 FIFTH AVENUE,
CONNECTING.

Sole Agents for New York and Brooklyn.

Rookwood
Pottery

Grand Prix

Paris 1900

The
World's Highest
Honors

ℜP

This mark
is incised on
each piece. The
ware is for sale by a
dealer in every large
city. A book about
it is sent on
request.
**Rookwood Pottery
Cincinnati**

Scribner's, *December 1900.*

Century,
October 1890.

ROOKWOOD
POTTERY

*This monogram
is on the bot-
tom of every*
*piece, and there
is no Rookwood
without it.*

GRAND PRIX

PARIS 1900

Rookwood ware is for sale by a dealer in
each of the larger cities and at the Pottery.

ROOKWOOD POTTERY, CINCINNATI

A book about this ware, and showing its distinguishing marks, will be sent to any address.

Century, *1891.*

The only award to American Pottery at the
Paris Exposition, 1889, was
A GOLD MEDAL TO ROOKWOOD POTTERY.
This ware may be found with a leading
dealer in each large city, or inquiries
may be addressed to
ROOKWOOD POTTERY, Cincinnati, Ohio.

McClure's, *1904.*

Country Life
in America,
October 1904.

Country Life in America, December 1905.

"Mat"   "Iris"   "Vellum" "Sea Green" "Standard"   "Iris"   "Mat"   "Mat"
                       "Mat"   "Mat"

Rookwood Pottery

Such mastery has been shown in bringing about new color effects and glazes that in addition to the widely-known brown Rookwood there is now a practically unlimited variety of designs and decorations, each, however, unmistakably "Rookwood."

A Rookwood vase brings to the owner the knowledge that there is no other like it. Composed, painted and signed by the artist just as a fine painting is The same idea *is never repeated.*

Country Life, November 1906.

ROOKWOOD
FAIENCE
MANTEL

Executed in rich Mat Glaze Colors

ROOKWOOD
POTTERY COMPANY

CINCINNATI, U. S. A.

Architects Building
N. E. Cor. 40th and Park Ave.
New York

The Craftsman,
February 1915.

ROOKWOOD FAIENCE
UNGLAZED URN *for*
SUN ROOM *or* GARDEN

THE
ROOKWOOD
POTTERY CO.
CINCINNATI

The House Beautiful,
May 1917.

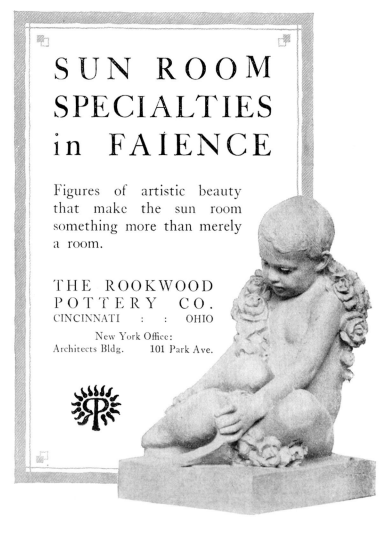

SUN ROOM
SPECIALTIES
in FAIENCE

Figures of artistic beauty
that make the sun room
something more than merely
a room.

THE ROOKWOOD
POTTERY CO.
CINCINNATI : : OHIO
New York Office:
Architects Bldg.   101 Park Ave.

House & Garden,
September 1917.

The House
Beautiful,
April 1919.

House & Garden, *May 1920.*

House &
Garden,
November 1920.

THE ROOKWOOD POTTERY CO.
CINCINNATI, OHIO
Makers of Fine Pottery and Tiles
A summer dining room in which all wall and floor sur aces were executed in Rookwood Mat Glaze Faience. Write for literature.

House & Garden, *January 1921.*

R O O K W O O D

adds a new and living expression to the venerable handicraft of the potter as it has existed from the most romantic and primitive times.

Call upon our representative in your locality or write to us

THE ROOKWOOD POTTERY COMPANY
Rookwood Place, Cincinnati, Ohio

House & Garden, *June 1924.*

ROOKWOOD

This mark on all Rookwood

Gifts for Christmas

THE age-old appreciation of pottery still persists. Rookwood is a gift that is always appropriate, and never more so than at the holiday season.

The great variety of form, color, type and price in which Rookwood is made, makes selection easy and interesting. Even the smallest pieces, in a single color, satisfy one's sense of what is beautiful, just as do, in their way, the larger more elaborate hand painted vases and lamps.

For the convenience of those who value the opportunity to purchase Rookwood as Christmas gifts, we have agents in most cities, but orders sent direct to us will be filled carefully.

We describe and price below the various articles shown in this advertisement. Make your selection and send us a check or money order for the amount given. We will supply either the exact piece you select or one substantially similar.

Folders illustrating a large number of other articles will be mailed on request.

1 — Vase 7½ inches high, mat glaze, pink, blue, buff, and other colors, $5.00 each.

2 — Elephant book ends, two sizes 4¾ inches high, $10.00; 5½ inches high, $15.00 per pair. Blue, green, ivory, and many other colors.

3 — Bowl, 6½ or 10 inch diameter $8 and $15. Outside and lining different colors; green and yellow, ivory and blue, black and red.

4 — Bowl, mat glaze outside, high glaze inside; 10 inch diameter, $15.00; 13 inch diameter, $20.00; ivory-lined turquoise, black-jade, and other color combinations. Flower holder separate, $15.00.

5 — Two candlesticks, each 7½ inches high mat glaze, rose, blue, yellow, and other colors, $5.00 for either shape.

6 — Vase, mat glaze, 9½ inches high, green, blue, rose and yellow, and other colors, $8.00.

7 — Vase, height 7 inches; bowl, diameter 6 inches, mat glaze, pink, blue, yellow, various colors, $3.50 either piece.

THE
ROOKWOOD POTTERY CO.
Rookwood Place, Cincinnati, Ohio

House & Garden, *December 1923.*

ROOKWOOD

PRE-EMINENCE ESTABLISHED BY WORLD'S HIGHEST HONORS

In selecting Rookwood for yourself or as a gift, your own good judgment is confirmed by the highest awards in International Exhibitions throughout the last half century.

Every piece of Rookwood is a masterpiece—a triumph of the potter's skill, decorated and signed by a renowned artist.

Study a piece of Rookwood. You cannot fail to recognize the perfect harmony of form, color, decoration, and glaze which makes it supreme.

Exclusive distributors in most cities have Rookwood. If you do not know the name of your Rookwood dealer, write us direct.

THE ROOKWOOD POTTERY COMPANY
Celestial Place, Cincinnati, Ohio

House & Garden, *February 1928.*

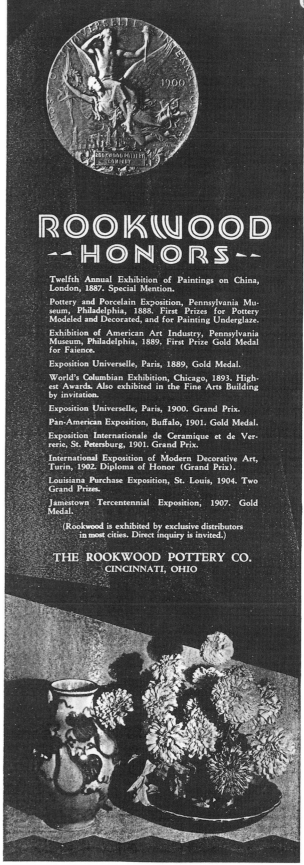

ROOKWOOD
~•~ HONORS ~•~

Twelfth Annual Exhibition of Paintings on China, London, 1887. Special Mention.

Pottery and Porcelain Exposition, Pennsylvania Museum, Philadelphia, 1888. First Prizes for Pottery Modeled and Decorated, and for Painting Underglaze.

Exhibition of American Art Industry, Pennsylvania Museum, Philadelphia, 1889. First Prize Gold Medal for Faience.

Exposition Universelle, Paris, 1889, Gold Medal.

World's Columbian Exhibition, Chicago, 1893. Highest Awards. Also exhibited in the Fine Arts Building by invitation.

Exposition Universelle, Paris, 1900. Grand Prix.

Pan-American Exposition, Buffalo, 1901. Gold Medal.

Exposition Internationale de Ceramique et de Verrerie, St. Petersburg, 1901. Grand Prix.

International Exposition of Modern Decorative Art, Turin, 1902. Diploma of Honor (Grand Prix).

Louisiana Purchase Exposition, St. Louis, 1904. Two Grand Prizes.

Jamestown Tercentennial Exposition, 1907. Gold Medal.

(Rookwood is exhibited by exclusive distributors in most cities. Direct inquiry is invited.)

THE ROOKWOOD POTTERY CO.
CINCINNATI, OHIO

House & Garden, *April 1928.*

ROOKWOOD

sails on the new and wide sea of unexplored discovery. Yet it respects the discoveries and traditions of a hallowed past in this porcelain flower boat, symbolic of one of the caravels of Columbus and in these pieces of garden pottery of Spanish influence.

Pieces harmonious with other periods are to be found with our exclusive distributor in your locality.

THE ROOKWOOD POTTERY CO.
Celestial Place, Mt. Adams
Cincinnati, Ohio

ROOKWOOD LAMPS

The Rookwood lamp is not alone an individual and distinguished lighting fixture -- it embodies also a rare Rookwood vase. Many of our agents show Rookwood lamps made up from pieces taken from their stock, and all of our dealers carry Rookwood vases which can be assembled to meet particular requirements.

Tiffany and Company, Jewelers, New York City; Marshall Field and Company, Chicago; Shervee Studios, Inc., Boston; Frederick and Nelson, Seattle; are Rookwood distributors. A store of similar quality, (whose name will be sent on request) represents the Pottery exclusively in your city. Or your direct inquiry, specifying what you want, will receive our very careful attention.

THE ROOKWOOD POTTERY CO.
CINCINNATI, OHIO

House & Garden, *October 1928.*

House Beautiful, *May 1929.*

Celadon and Peach

The very newest of Rookwood's creations are in exquisitely delicate colors -- celadon and peach. From the simplest pieces to the most elaborate, Rookwood stands supreme in design, texture and color. The range in sizes and prices makes provision for every gift requirement.

Rookwood pieces of enduring quality will be found at the following stores:

Tiffany and Company, Jewelers, New York City; Marshall Field and Company, Chicago; Schervee Studios, Inc., Boston; L. B. King and Company, Detroit; Frederick and Nelson, Seattle; Brock and Company, Los Angeles; C. A. Seltzer, Cleveland.

A store of similar quality represents the pottery exclusively in your city. We invite your direct inquiry.

ROOKWOOD POTTERY
CINCINNATI

THIS MARK IS ON EVERY PIECE

House Beautiful, *December 1929.*

Garden Pottery

Rookwood garden pottery . . . like Rookwood vase products . . . combines complete sympathy for setting with distinctive individuality.

This oil jar, decorated in unglazed colored clays, embodies the symbolic forms of plants and animals . . . yet holds them in a unity of balance and harmony that only art can bring to the forms of Nature.

Individually decorated and signed by the artist, this piece is priced at one hundred dollars; finished in colored glaze drip it is sixty dollars; in plain unglazed finish, twenty-five dollars.

Rookwood makes a wide variety of garden vases, figures and other decorative accessories. Tell us of your particular needs. We will send you complete information about the pieces especially adapted to meet your requirements.

Rookwood Pottery
Cincinnati, Ohio

THIS MARK IS ON EVERY PIECE

Country Life in America, *March 1930.*

ROOKWOOD'S SUPREME TEXTURES

Texture . . . the important part of the great art of all time, is today paramount at Rookwood, color and form following in close harmony. These lovely pieces in Ivory Wax Mat are but one type showing Rookwood's fulfillment of this ideal.

Rookwood pieces of supreme texture may be had at moderate price through Tiffany and Company, B. Altman and Company and Frederick Loeser and Company, Inc., in the Metropolitan New York area. A store of similar quality represents the pottery exclusively in your city. We invite your direct inquiry.

ROOKWOOD POTTERY   **CINCINNATI**

International Studio, October 1930.

THE GLORIOUS PRIVILEGE

Christmas giving may not be ignored but precious pieces of Rookwood from one dollar and a half up will help solve the problem economically.

Rookwood gifts to meet your requirements in quality and price will be found at the following stores:

Tiffany and Company, Jewelers, New York City; B. Altman and Company, New York City; Frederick Loeser and Company, Inc., Brooklyn; Strawbridge & Clothier, Philadelphia; Marshall Field and Company, Chicago; Joseph Horne Co., Pittsburgh; Schervee Studios, Inc., Boston; L. B. King and Company, Detroit; Brock and Company, Los Angeles; Dulin and Martin, Washington, D. C.; Frederick and Nelson, Seattle. A store of similar quality represents the pottery exclusively in your city. We invite your direct inquiry.

Rookwood Pottery
Cincinnati

THIS MARK IS ON EVERY PIECE

House Beautiful, December 1930.

3232Y-C   3230Y-C

3231Y-C   3229Y-C

Decorative Tiles, 12x12″

ROOKWOOD

is preeminent in the field of decorative tiles. Designs conforming to all periods are at your disposal for use with marble, brick, stucco and with any plain tile. We invite inquiries.

THE ROOKWOOD POTTERY CO.

Tile Department   Cincinnati, Ohio

Architectural Record, January 1927.

Roseville Pottery

The Roseville Pottery was founded in Roseville, Ohio, by George F. Young in 1890.

Mr. Young purchased the property of the J. B. Owens Pottery, and the Owens operation moved to Zanesville. Young made stoneware jars, flowerpots, and cuspidors. The Roseville Pottery Company was incorporated in 1892.

In 1897 Young purchased the Midland Pottery in Roseville. The additional capacity of this second plant was also utilized to manufacture stoneware.

The following year Young purchased the Clark Stoneware Co. on Linden Avenue in Zanesville. The operations of both Roseville plants were moved to Zanesville. The *Zanesville Courier* reported that the facilities were to be enlarged, and was expected to employ up to 100 workers.

Roseville continued to manufacture stoneware and started making printed ware. In 1900, Young decided he wanted some of the booming art ware business that the Weller, Owens, and Rookwood factories were competing for. He hired artist Ross C. Purdy to prepare Roseville to enter the well established art pottery market. Within the year Roseville introduced the Rozane line to compete with the Louwelsa, Utopian, and Standard Line products. The Rozane line of slip-painted decorations over a brown shaded background was very similar to the competition. The demand for Rozane provided Roseville the piece of the market Young was looking for.

Roseville had successfully entered the art pottery market, but utility ware continued to be the company's main source of revenue. During the next few years the company evolved into a major art pottery producer. The Muskingum Stoneware plant in Zanesville was purchased to manufacture only the utility products lines, while the Linden Ave. plant became more and more an art pottery producer. Well qualified artists and ceramic technicians were hired. John J. Herold developed Rozane Mongol, which won first prize at the Louisiana Purchase Centennial Exposition in 1904. Gazo Fudji made Rozane Woodland and the Fudji line. Christian Nielson designed Rozane Egypto and Frederick Hurten Rhead introduced the unusual carving and squeeze-bag techniques in the Della Robbia and Aztec lines. The original Rozane name had become famous, so the Rozane prefix was added to new lines to provide a marketing advantage. The original Rozane line was then called Rozane Royal. Shortly after the original Rozane had been introduced, light-colored backgrounds were being made. Today these lines are referred to as Rozane dark and Rozane light.

Utilitarian wares continued to provide significant financial revenue. Blue and white stoneware, brown stoneware, brown cooking ware with white glazed linings, and toilet sets with sponged colors and lots of gold decoration sold well. In 1905 Roseville employed 300 workers and was producing up to 5,000 pieces a day.

This German Farmware line fruit jar is 7½" tall. This early Roseville stoneware product has molded and applied handles and is an attribution shown in Roseville Pottery, for Love or Money, *by Virginia Hillway Buxton. Early Roseville stoneware is not signed Roseville. However, a later line of bowls named Venetian, sold in blue and white or unglazed on the outside with a brown glaze lining, were usually signed Venetian on the bottom. $45.00 – 65.00.*

Cornelian Ware was introduced near the turn of the century. Usually finished in a carmel color, sponged all over and brushed on the handles. It was then glazed and fired, then sponged with gold. Shapes include complete toilet sets, cracker jars, oatmeal bowls, and creamers. 8" pitcher, $80.00 – 120.00. 3¾" mug, $50.00 – 75.00.

By 1908, designers F. H. Rhead, Neilson, and Fudji had left the pottery. Harry Rhead replaced his brother Frederick as art director. Later, Harry developed the Donatello line that gave Roseville some financial security.

The demand for artist-decorated products started declining by 1910. The buying public wanted less glossy items. Embossed and transfer-printed lines were introduced with mat and semi-mat glazes.

The Muskingum plant burned in 1917, and the operation was moved to the Linden Ave. plant. Russel T. Young replaced his father as secretary-treasurer and general manager. A year later George Krause became the technical supervisor, and Frank Ferrell replaced Harry Rhead as the art director.

All artist decorating had been discontinued by 1920, in favor of forms with embossed or molded designs. The twenties were productive, with a flood of new lines appearing with Art Deco and Art Nouveau designs.

Roseville survived the Depression, but not without the problems felt by the rest of the competition. The company needed a boost, and they found it in a long-ago rejected Ferrell design. The introduction of the Pinecone line in 1931 was a lifesaver for the pottery. The bestseller since Donatello brought the company back to life. Russel Young died in 1931, and was succeeded by his moth-

er, Mrs. Anna M. Young. Mrs. Young and Frank Ferrell not only brought the company through the Depression, they produced the designs cherished by collectors today. The art department continued to supply what the buyers wanted. Mrs. Young maintained the operating principals of her husband, and pursued an aggressive advertising campaign to keep the business alive.

Anna was succeeded by her son-in-law F. S. Clement in 1938. Business was good and the public wanted more. Ferrell met the challenge of the early forties by introducing more successful lines. The success however, was short lived. After the war ended, other materials developed as a result of the war, along with foreign competition, all but eliminated the demand for Roseville products.

Clement was succeeded by his son-in-law, Robert P. Windisch, in 1945. The company had high expectations for several lines introduced over the next several years, including dinnerware, but none were accepted by the public. In November of 1954 the Roseville Pottery Inc. was sold to the Mosaic Tile Company. The following month Mosaic sold all the Roseville molds, dies, and trademarks to the New England Ceramics Company.

The vast majority of Roseville left the pottery with the factory name on it. Most are marked with the name in full, RPCo., or a large R enveloping a small v stamped in ink. A few items can be found with only their line or pattern name like Azurean, Fujiyama, Rozane, Pauleo Pottery, Hyde Park (used on late ashtrays), and some Lotus. Some small items made after 1930 only have room on the bottom for an R in script.

Unsigned Roseville is usually the result of a factory paper label having been removed. Products without marks are not difficult to identify given a few references for Roseville shapes and decorations.

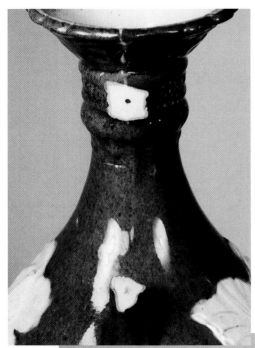

An early Roseville catalog shows this vase and 11 similar Victorian forms, all with handles. The vases are simply called "Vase Assortment No.60." The Wedgwood-style vases were made with background colors of blue, gray, brown, orange, or red. Gold overglaze trim is extensive. The process for manufacturing this line of ware is unlike any other used at Roseville. The example shown here with a broken handle reveals that the clay body was made in a two-piece mold. Each half was painted with a layer of blue clay, avoiding the floral area. The molds were then assembled and filled with liquid white clay, the excess being poured out after a drying time. The glazing and firing were followed by the overglaze gold decorations and another firing. Some of the 12 shapes shown in this vase assortment have appeared as Rozane dark glaze pieces without the floral in relief. $250.00 – 350.00 if perfect.

This Rozane dark tankard was decorated with three different colored grape bunches by Harry Larzelere. The tankard is 14" tall and has the artist's monogram just above the base. The bottom has the marks "Rozane - 856 - RPCo" die impressed. $450.00 – 550.00.

The clover decoration on this Rozane light candlestick was done by Mae Timberlake. The full name of the artist appears just above the base at the back. Unsigned. $300.00 – 400.00.

Keramic Studio, *December 1911.*

When Roseville introduced the Chloron line in 1907, I expect they had a different or new glaze to put on some new forms. However, over time the line has become indistinguishable from the Rozane Egypto line. Shapes from each line were glazed with that of the other line. Roseville advertised Chloron showing some of the 1904 Egypto forms.

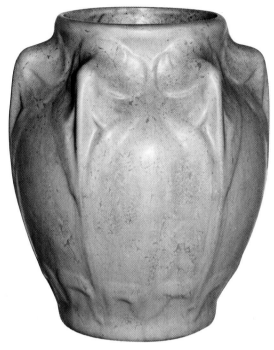

The 8½" vase shown above is pictured as part of the Chloron line in a factory catalog (below), and is designated as No. C 101 8½. It's also pictured in the 1905 catalog (right) as Rozane Egypto No. E-10. If you want Egypto, or if you want Chloron, then buy one so marked, but don't be surprised when you find one just like yours with the other mark. Unmarked. $300.00 – 500.00.

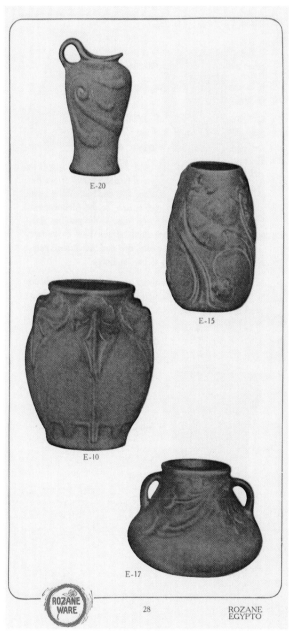

E-20

E-15

E-10

E-17

ROZANE WARE

28

ROZANE EGYPTO

This Donatello-like pattern has occasionally appeared in books and auction catalogs and is attributed to Weller, Roseville, or Brush-McCoy. Sometimes the prefix "Experimental" is included. Examples of this line are scarce or uncommon, but by no means scarce enough to have been an experiment.

Brush-McCoy made tinted color patterns of Ivory, Ivotint, and Sylvan. The molded forms in each of these lines were also used in several other lines, a prevailing practice at the Brush works. If this were a Brush product I'd expect to see it in other patterns or with other glazes. This manufacturer's products lacked the sharpness of detail shown on this example. Although some of the early Brush work is very artistic and skillfully made, sharp detailed molding was not an attribute of this company.

Weller also produced several lines where brushed or atomized tints were wiped or removed with steel wool to expose the clay or underglaze. However, Weller creamware clay and clear overglazes are quite different than those on the product shown here. Weller also lacked the sharpness in their molded forms. Weller's Fairfield line is similar to this example, but the sharpness of detail and definition is even less than that of the Brush-McCoy lines.

An examination of this 9½" wide bowl reveals a creamware clay and clear glaze common to the many creamware lines produced at the Roseville Pottery. The lines of Old Ivory, Ivory Tint, Green Tint, Fern Trail, and Cameo were decorated in this wiped colors style. Also, the cherub faces have a strong resemblance to those on Donatello.

So why are there no signed examples, no catalog pages, and such a limited supply?

Most of the many Roseville creamware lines of products were not marked. A very small number of pieces were marked with a red ink stamp. Late line Juvenile items were sometimes marked with an ink stamped Rv.

I believe the line was either manufactured for a retailer's exclusive dealership, or more likely, the line was discontinued for economic reasons before a catalog was published.

Close examination reveals a labor intensive manufacturing process. The clay design was difficult to mold due to air entrapment that resulted in voids in the details of the finished form. This flaw is evident in the finished products. The decorating process started with a covering of blue tinted glaze, with the decorator being careful not to get any blue on the cameos. Then the stylistic leaves under the six cameos and the edge of the neck were sprayed with a beige tint. A green tinted color was then brushed or sprayed on the cameos. The six pillars and six cameos then had to be wiped, or rubbed with steel wool, to remove the colors and expose the clay. The piece was covered with a clear glaze and fired. The process may have required two or even three firings, for there are nine stilt marks on the bottom of this example. If someone finds a marked piece of this pattern, I expect it will say "Roseville."

Donatello-like 9½" wide bowl. $100.00 – 150.00.

The Cremona line was introduced in 1927. A 10″ Cremona vase was used to make this lamp that measurers 23″ to the top of the shade. The fittings are solid brass and original, the shade is not. Unsigned. $150.00 – 250.00.

The Futura line was introduced in 1928. This example is 7″ tall. $450.00 – 500.00.

Blackberry, a favorite today, was introduced in 1933. The bowl shown here is 7½″ wide. The companion flower frog is 3½″ wide. Unsigned. $400.00 – 500.00 the set.

The first piece of American art pottery I ever purchased is this Cosmos vase. Introduced in 1940, this 5" example is signed with recessed, in the mold marks, "Roseville-945-5." $75.00 – 90.00.

 AZUREAN

 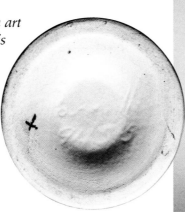

Most Roseville that has a factory mark is identified with the Roseville or Rozane names, or with the Rv mark. Other marks include the line names of Fujiama, Azurine, Pauleo, or Donatello.

Harper's, April 1904.

"FOR THE HOUSE BEAUTIFUL"

ROZANE WARE

Most truly decorative of modern art products.

It lends itself ideally to the interior ornamentation of the most luxuriously appointed home, breathing an atmosphere of art and refinement.

Exquisitely modeled in hundreds of artistic shapes for scores of purposes; superbly colored and decorated—the chosen ware of the art lover.

There is a piece for every nook, to harmonize with every room and every scheme of decoration.

Ask to see ROZANE WARE at your art dealer's.

The genuine bears this Trade Mark.

Our handsomely illustrated booklet, *"The Story of Rozane Ware,"* tells how the ware is produced and offers helpful hints on home decoration. *Mailed free on request.*

THE ROSEVILLE POTTERY COMPANY   ZANESVILLE OHIO

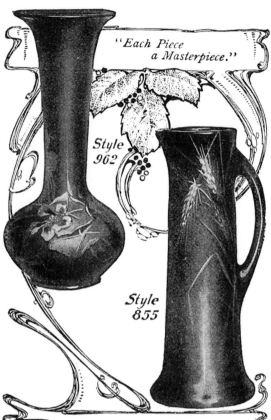

"Each Piece a Masterpiece."

Style 962

Style 855

Rozane Ware

Above are shown two Rozane pieces which for delicacy, artistic quality and warmth of coloring especially commend themselves for gift purposes.

The Vase *962* is gracefully patterned; hand decorated in simple floral design. Done in red, green and yellow, shading off from golden- to deep-brown. Very lustrous.

The Tankard *855* is also of rich brown with wheat sprig in yellow and green. Has beautiful gloss.

Rozane Ware is made in vases, jardinieres, and art pieces for nooks and corners. For many purposes of utility and decoration.

The genuine bears this mark.

Write for our beautiful booklet, "*The Story of Rozane Ware.*" It is full of appropriate gift suggestions. Sent free on request.

THE ROSEVILLE POTTERY COMPANY
ZANESVILLE, OHIO

Booklovers, *1904.*

"THE WARE OF BEAUTY"

ROZANE WARE

for charm, richness, graceful design and exquisite coloring surpasses all other art pottery.

It imparts the crowning touch of ornamentation—gives added "tone" and "atmosphere" to the most beautifully furnished apartment—lends itself ideally to any scheme of decoration.

It is made in many pieces for many purposes.

This trade mark proves the genuine. Our booklet, "The Story of Rozane Ware," tells how this beautiful ware is produced. Handsomely illustrated. Mailed free.

THE ROSEVILLE POTTERY COMPANY
ZANESVILLE, OHIO

Booklovers, *1904.*

"Art Ware Beyond Compare"

Rozane Ware

has set a new standard in the decorative furnishing of the home.

Its distinctive grace of modeling, rare beauty of design and delicate and harmonious blending of colors make it the chosen ware of the connoisseur, the collector and the furnisher of the house beautiful.

Made in hundreds of tasteful and effective pieces for many purposes.

The genuine is distinguished by this trade mark.

"The Story of Rozane Ware"—a beautifully illustrated brochure describes how Rozane Ware is made and illustrates in colors a large number of pieces. Mailed free on request.

THE ROSEVILLE POTTERY CO.
ZANESVILLE, OHIO.

Country Life, *October 1904.*

Style K-14

Style R-865

Always a wise Selection

For wedding gifts there is nothing more appropriate than

Rozane

It is a permanent, useful reminder of the giver. Rozane comes in many designs and is a genuine art product, strong and substantial.

The Jug, *K-14,* is Rozane Mara, a new ware, resembling most beautiful sea shells. This is a reproduction of an old Italian ware, the iridescence of which is the result of time's action upon it's chemical composition.

The Vase, *R-865,* is an exquisite design, hand painted. The blended brown and gold tints make a rich background. This variety, known as Rozane Royal, is one of the choicest art potteries now obtainable.

Other Rozanes are: Rozane Mongol, a most beautiful red, very lustrous; Rozane Egypto, in artistic green, very popular; Rozane Woodland, new and unique, with enameled designs on mat background, in wood shades.

Original colorings of these decorations are shown in our new and valuable pottery booklet, "*Rozane.*" Every connoisseur should read it All genuine Rozanes bear this mark.

THE ROSEVILLE POTTERY COMPANY
Sales Department, No. 59
ZANESVILLE, OHIO

McClure's, *1904.*

Style K-14

Style R-865

Always a wise Selection

For wedding gifts there is nothing more appropriate than

Rozane

It is a permanent, useful reminder of the giver. Rozane comes in many designs and is a genuine art product, strong and substantial.

The Jug, *K-14*, is Rozane Mara, a new ware, resembling most beautiful sea shells. This is a reproduction of an old Italian ware, the iridescence of which is the result of time's action upon it's chemical composition.

The Vase, *R-865*, is an exquisite design, hand painted. The blended brown and gold tints make a rich background. This variety, known as Rozane Royal, is one of the choicest art potteries now obtainable.

Other Rozanes are: Rozane Mongol, a most beautiful red, very lustrous; Rozane Egypto, in artistic green, very popular; Rozane Woodland, new and unique, with enameled designs on mat background, in wood shades.

Original colorings of these decorations are shown in our new and valuable pottery booklet, *"Rozane."* Every connoisseur should read it. All genuine Rozanes bear this mark.

THE ROSEVILLE POTTERY COMPANY
Sales Dept. No. 60.
ZANESVILLE   OHIO

Colliers, *May 1905.*

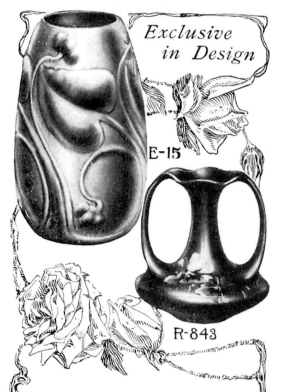

Exclusive in Design

E-15

R-843

Permanence in art has been achieved in

Rozane

a beautiful, strong, art pottery, reproducing perfect oil painting effects. Its presence in the home is a refining influence.

E-15 is Rozane Egypto, in popular shades of green. This "mat" finish is one of the richest effects ever obtained in pottery. All flowers look well in this vase.

R-843 is a useful and highly decorative vase in Rozane Royal with rich background in soft shades of lustrous browns and yellows.

Rozane Mara is another variety, shading from rose to deep magenta, with exquisite iridescent effects. *Rozane Woodland* is in browns, mat finish, with enameled designs. *Rozane Mongol*, glazed, is a luxurious red.

All genuine Rozanes bear this mark.
Rozane decorations are described and illustrated in original colors, in our new booklet-- ROZANE. It will interest every collector.

THE ROSEVILLE POTTERY COMPANY
Sales Department 60
Zanesville, Ohio

Colliers, *May 1905.*

All Sorts of Beautiful and Useful Gift Suggestions
For Weddings, Birthdays, Bridge Favors and Christmas
50 PIECE ASSORTMENT

Retail for $2.50 Ea.

Your Cost $1.25 Ea.

No Two Alike

Every Piece Different

AMERICAN ART POTTERY
Beautiful gift pieces of hard faience body ware in a variety of colors including ivory, walnut brown, dull soft green, etc., all hand decorated, high relief embossed, allover satin finish glazing.

E3— 50 pieces carefully packed in crate. Weight 160 lbs.
$1.25 EACH PIECE
(Total for Assortment [50 pcs] $62.50).

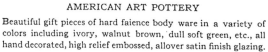

Butler Brothers catalog, November 1926.

210

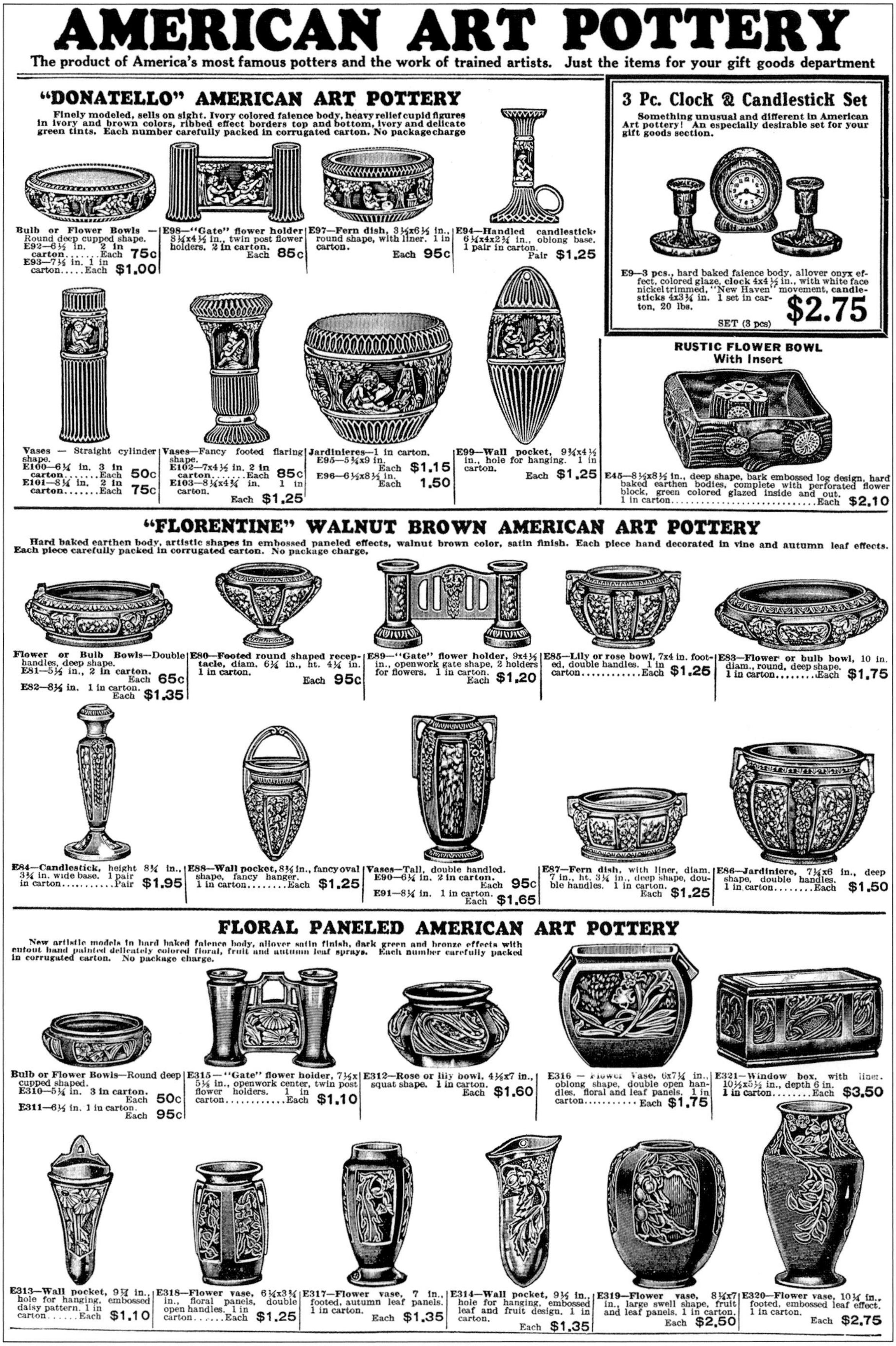

AMERICAN ART POTTERY

The product of America's most famous potters and the work of trained artists. Just the items for your gift goods department

"DONATELLO" AMERICAN ART POTTERY

Finely modeled, sells on sight. Ivory colored faience body, heavy relief cupid figures in ivory and brown colors, ribbed effect borders top and bottom, ivory and delicate green tints. Each number carefully packed in corrugated carton. No package charge

Bulb or Flower Bowls — Round deep cupped shape. E92—6½ in. 2 in carton.......Each 75c E93—7½ in. 1 in carton.....Each $1.00

E98—"Gate" flower holder 8¼x4½ in., twin post flower holders. 2 in carton. Each 85c

E97—Fern dish, 3½x6½ in., round shape, with liner. 1 in carton. Each 95c

E94—Handled candlestick, 6¼x4x2¾ in., oblong base. 1 pair in carton. Pair $1.25

Vases — Straight cylinder shape. E100—6¼ in. 3 in carton.......Each 50c E101—8¼ in. 2 in carton.......Each 75c

Vases—Fancy footed flaring shape. E102—7x4½ in. 2 in carton.......Each 85c E103—8¼x4¾ in. 1 in carton. Each $1.25

Jardinieres—1 in carton. E95—5¾x9 in. Each $1.15 E96—6½x8½ in. Each 1.50

E99—Wall pocket, 9¾x4½ in., hole for hanging. 1 in carton. Each $1.25

3 Pc. Clock & Candlestick Set

Something unusual and different in American Art pottery! An especially desirable set for your gift goods section.

E9—3 pcs., hard baked faience body, allover onyx effect, colored glaze, clock 4x4½ in., with white face nickel trimmed, "New Haven" movement, candlesticks 4x3¾ in. 1 set in carton, 20 lbs.

SET (3 pcs) $2.75

RUSTIC FLOWER BOWL With Insert

E45—8½x8½ in., deep shape, bark embossed log design, hard baked earthen bodies, complete with perforated flower block, green colored glazed inside and out. 1 in carton.............................Each $2.10

"FLORENTINE" WALNUT BROWN AMERICAN ART POTTERY

Hard baked earthen body, artistic shapes in embossed paneled effects, walnut brown color, satin finish. Each piece hand decorated in vine and autumn leaf effects. Each piece carefully packed in corrugated carton. No package charge.

Flower or Bulb Bowls—Double handles, deep shape. E81—5½ in., 2 in carton. Each 65c E82—8½ in. 1 in carton. Each $1.35

E80—Footed round shaped receptacle, diam. 6¼ in., ht. 4¼ in. 1 in carton. Each 95c

E89—"Gate" flower holder, 9x4½ in., openwork gate shape, 2 holders for flowers. 1 in carton. Each $1.20

E85—Lily or rose bowl, 7x4 in. footed, double handles. 1 in carton............Each $1.25

E83—Flower or bulb bowl, 10 in. diam., round, deep shape. 1 in carton.........Each $1.75

E84—Candlestick, height 8¾ in., 3¾ in. wide base. 1 pair in carton...........Pair $1.95

E88—Wall pocket, 8¾ in., fancy oval shape, fancy hanger. 1 in carton........Each $1.25

Vases—Tall, double handled. E90—6¼ in. 2 in carton. Each 95c E91—8¼ in. 1 in carton. Each $1.65

E87—Fern dish, with liner, diam. 7 in., ht. 3¼ in., deep shape, double handles. 1 in carton. Each $1.25

E86—Jardiniere, 7¼x6 in., deep shape, double handles. 1 in carton........Each $1.50

FLORAL PANELED AMERICAN ART POTTERY

New artistic models in hard baked faience body, allover satin finish, dark green and bronze effects with cutout hand painted delicately colored floral, fruit and autumn leaf sprays. Each number carefully packed in corrugated carton. No package charge.

Bulb or Flower Bowls—Round deep cupped shaped. E310—5¼ in. 3 in carton. Each 50c E311—6½ in. 1 in carton. Each 95c

E315—"Gate" flower holder, 7½x5⅛ in., openwork center, twin post flower holders. 1 in carton............Each $1.10

E312—Rose or lily bowl, 4⅛x7 in., squat shape. 1 in carton. Each $1.60

E316 — Flower Vase, 6x7¼ in., oblong shape, double open handles, floral and leaf panels. 1 in carton...........Each $1.75

E321—Window box, with liner. 10½x5½ in., depth 6 in. 1 in carton........Each $3.50

E313—Wall pocket, 9⅞ in., hole for hanging, embossed daisy pattern. 1 in carton......Each $1.10

E318—Flower vase, 6¼x3¾ in., floral panels, double open handles. 1 in carton......Each $1.25

E317—Flower vase, 7 in., footed, autumn leaf panels. 1 in carton. Each $1.35

E314—Wall pocket, 9½ in., hole for hanging, embossed leaf and fruit design. 1 in carton. Each $1.35

E319—Flower vase, 8¼x7 in., large swell shape, fruit and leaf panels. 1 in carton. Each $2.50

E320—Flower vase, 10¼ in., footed, embossed leaf effect. 1 in carton. Each $2.75

Butler Brothers catalog, November 1926.

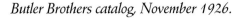

AMERICAN ART POTTERY
25 Piece Assortment—No Two Alike
Beautifully Hand Decorated Pieces that Readily Sell at $5.00 Each

Fine quality hard baked faience or earthen body, artistic shapes, heavily embossed floral figures, panels and a variety of art designs, **all hand painted and hand colored**, colors and decorations **burnt-in**, will not wash off. Every piece colored and glazed both inside and out in soft matt finish, guaranteed not to leak.

1. 8x8¼ in. footed urn shape Florentine vase, embossed panels in brown tones.
2. 10¼ in. flower vase, dark satin green with high art figures and cut-out relief effects.
3. 10½ in. Florentine footed vase with brown tone panel effect design.
4. 8½x8¼ in. double handled Florentine jardiniere, embossed panels, brown tone finish.
5. 12x6¼x5¼ in. deep oblong window box with removable earthen lining, ivory, green & brown cupid scenes and panel relief.
6. 8x7 in. jardiniere, dark mahogany, grape and leaf embossing in light and dark tan shades.
7. 8½x8 in. massive jardiniere with dogwood blossoms in heavy relief.
8. 12 in. fruit or flower bowl, rich ivory with panel scenes and relief.
9. 10x9¼ in. Rozane jardiniere, ivory body in rich stippled effect, heavy rose and leaf embossing, filled-in pink, yellow and green colorings.
10. 12 in. massive flower vase, green & ivory ribbed design with cupids and relief panels.
11. 10¼ in. extra large vase, dark bronze finish, with vintage panels and cut-out effect design.
12. 10 in. Florentine footed comport or fruit bowl, brown tone panel design.
13. 9½ in. deep round fruit or bulb bowl with 3¾ in. removable perforated flower block, green & ivory blends with dogwood blossoms.
14. 10½ in. massive flower vase, ivory and green shades dogwood blossoms in heavy relief.
15. 9x6 in. deep hanging flower basket, ivory & green ribbed panel, fruit and floral decorations, complete with removable earthen lining and brass chain hanger.

The following pieces are included with above 15 pieces in the E4 asst. but are **NOT ILLUSTRATED.**

8½ in. Florentine hanging basket with inside liner and brass chain hanger, brown tone panel effect design.
8½ in. swell shape vase, rich bronze finish, cut-out fruit panel effect.
Mammoth cylinder shape flower vase, ht. 12½ in. diam. of top 7¼ in., ivory with green ribbed panels, decorated fruits and flowers in heavy embossed effect.
10½ in. Florentine footed double handled urn shaped vase, brown tone and panel effect design.
9½ in. Florentine fruit or flower bowl with double open handles and 3¾ in. removable perforated earthen flower block.
9½x8 in. jardiniere, ivory body, green and brown tints, ribbed panels and cupid figures in heavy relief.
7½ in. high footed comport or fern dish with removable earthen liner, ivory, green & brown, cupid figures and relief decoration.
10 in. covered vase or rose jar, 2 tone green floral and relief cutout panels.
8½x7 in. deep hanging basket with liner and brass chain hanger, ivory & brown with relief cupid panels.
8½x8 in. Corinthian jardiniere, green & ivory ribbed panel, fruit and floral embossing.

E4— American Art Pottery Assortment.

25 pieces in crate, 90 lbs.

EACH PIECE **$2.50**

Butler Brothers catalog, November 1926.

*"The criterion of true beauty is,
that it increases on examination."* — GREVILLE

A FEW art objects, discreetly placed, add so much to a home! Not the hit-and-miss massing of Victorian days, but the tasteful arrangement of 1928.

And just here it is that Roseville serves so incomparably! Charming Roseville Pottery, created with that touch of genius by men and women who love their craft.

Beauty that grows as you live with it, such is the essence of Roseville Pottery. For instance, the jar and vases pictured here. Adorable they are, in delicate tints, daintily decorated with arrowheads.

These pieces and a diversity of other designs . . . bowls, jars, vases, candlesticks in a wide selection of sizes, shapes and colors . . . can be seen at good stores. For the home or as gifts they have a distinction of their own.

You will want a copy of the interesting booklet, "Pottery." Write for it.

THE ROSEVILLE POTTERY CO., *Zanesville, Ohio*

ROSEVILLE POTTERY

House & Garden, *April 1928.*

*"Ever-varying features of the
enrapturing spirit of beauty."* — ANON

YOU WILL LOVE these new creations of the Roseville potteries in the delightful *Futura* design. Done in the modern manner, they exhibit the vogue of today and breathe the spirit of tomorrow.

In this Futura pottery by Roseville, there is an abundance of sizes and shapes to choose from, scarcely any two alike. There are vases, bowls, candlesticks, wall-pockets, jardinieres, hanging baskets—all with the youthful verve and daring of these our times.

And how exquisitely colored! Blue, gray, tan, rose, green—harmonies of pleasing, soft tints that render more fascinating the flares, curves and angles of Futura.

Picture to yourself the charm of Futura in your home. Futura pottery brings the tang of the modern, strikes the key of the recent in decorative schemes. And nothing could be more original or intriguing for gifts. Ask to see the displays in leading stores.

For the interesting story of pottery, write us to send you a free copy of the profusely illustrated booklet, "Pottery".

THE ROSEVILLE POTTERY CO., *Zanesville, Ohio*

ROSEVILLE POTTERY

House Beautiful, *October 1928.*

"Beauty is created by the emotion of the artist"—SCHOEN

ADVENTUROUS... modern... intriguing... are these creations of Roseville craftsmen. In them you see expressed through fascinating form the spirit of vital artistry... fashioned with today's appreciation of beauty.

How you will adore these Futura shapes! Picture flowers in them... wonderfully exquisite in your home...a touch of dashing charm in your living-room or hall or library... yes, in any number of places.

Many are the kinds of pieces to choose from... in several soft harmonies of delicate coloring... with tastefully modeled decorations... superb... distinctive... vastly interesting!

There are jars, vases, bowls, hanging baskets, jardinieres, window boxes, wall pockets, candlesticks... scarcely any two alike. Displayed at leading stores, where you may make a selection for yourself, or remember some one with a cherished gift.

We will gladly send you a free copy of the beautifully illustrated booklet, "Pottery". Write for it.

THE ROSEVILLE POTTERY CO., *Zanesville, Ohio*

ROSEVILLE POTTERY

House & Garden, May 1929.

POTTERY that you will love as the years come and go is so enticingly created by Roseville master craftsmen.

How graceful are the curves, the angles, the proportions and the exquisite modeling! The colors are delightful, too... and tastefully rich! You will be glad that you knew about this wonderful pottery.

Fascinating and adorable... Roseville Pottery is always new, unusual, distinctive. Into your home these lovely pieces bring a beauty that never ceases to be admired... and you will find they are wonderfully appreciated as gifts.

Vases, flower bowls, jars, candlesticks, wallpockets... mighty interesting selections await you at leading stores. Ask to see the displays of Roseville Pottery.

A copy of the richly illustrated booklet, "Pottery," will be mailed you free on request. Write for your copy.

THE ROSEVILLE POTTERY COMPANY, *Zanesville, Ohio*

ROSEVILLE POTTERY

House Beautiful, October 1929.

Fascinating for gifts and bringing warmth of color and beauty of proportion into your home. Delightful variety of shapes and sizes. See them at leading stores.

ROSEVILLE POTTERY
Zanesville, Ohio

House Beautiful, *December 1931.*

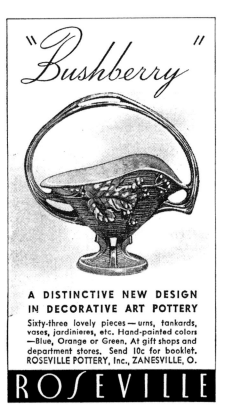

"*Bushberry*"

A DISTINCTIVE NEW DESIGN IN DECORATIVE ART POTTERY

Sixty-three lovely pieces — urns, tankards, vases, jardinieres, etc. Hand-painted colors —Blue, Orange or Green. At gift shops and department stores. Send 10c for booklet. ROSEVILLE POTTERY, Inc., ZANESVILLE, O.

ROSEVILLE

Good Housekeeping, *September 1941.*

PEONY

DECORATIVE ART POTTERY BY

ROSEVILLE

One of our loveliest floral patterns. Beautifully rounded Peony blooms in bold relief against a rich wood-texture background. Sixty-five exquisite shapes; three handpainted colors — Sienna Brown, Nile Green, Coral. At gift shops and dep't stores.

Send 10c for Roseville booklet.

ROSEVILLE POTTERY, INC.
Dept. HG-112, Zanesville, Ohio

House & Garden, *November 1942.*

ROSEVILLE
DECORATIVE ART POTTERY

Foxglove

A new, beautifully rich floral motif in 55 lovely hand-painted pieces— Red, Blue or Green. At gift shops and department stores. Send 10c for booklet on Roseville Pottery. ROSEVILLE POTTERY, INC. Dept. G-32, ZANESVILLE, OHIO

Good Housekeeping, *March 1942.*

House & Garden, *November 1942.*

House & Garden, *July 1943.*

Good Housekeeping, *October 1945.*

Good Housekeeping, *March 1947.*

Experiments with pottery began at Tiffany Furnaces in Corona, New York, as early as 1898. A few pieces of pottery were shown at the Louisiana Purchase Exposition in St. Louis in 1904. However Tiffany's Favrile pottery was not offered for sale to the general public until 1905, in conjunction with the opening of the new Tiffany's store on Fifth Ave. in New York City. Tiffany's had a large display of Favrile when they opened. No doubt they took advantage of the grand opening opportunity to publicize their new pottery products.

The vast majority of the products were molded with decorations of native flora. A few were hand thrown. The body was made of white clay which was very high fired. The original glazes were a light yellow-green shading to dark. In 1906 green tints were introduced. By 1908 "Favrile Bronze" was introduced. This bronze finished pottery was glazed on the inside and had an exterior metal coating similar to that pro-

duced at the Clewell Pottery. Some bisque or unglazed products were also sold.

Tiffany's art pottery sales ceased about 1918. However, production might have stopped long before then. Pottery production was small, and examples are scarce today.

All Tiffany pottery is signed with the LCT cipher incised. In addition, "L. C. Tiffany," "Favrile Pottery," or "Bronze Pottery" were sometimes etched into the bottom. No artist marks were used.

The 3¼" vase shown here was hand thrown. The glaze is a semi-mat green with streaks of brown and glossy amber inclusions. The bottom has the LCT cipher and some codes including C5, all incised in the white clay.

TIFFANY FAVRILE BRONZE POTTERY

A unique art product; a combination of Favrile glass, pottery and metal; the result of several years' study in the treatment of porcelain bodies with metals, creating rich color effects, and novel expressions of low relief and other forms of decoration.

TIFFANY FURNACES
LONG ISLAND, NEW YORK

The ad, from the November 1908 issue of International Studio, *confirms the introduction date of the bronze products. Previously, all resources reported a later date.*

Trent Tile Co.

In 1882 the Harris Manufacturing Company was organized for the production of tiles, and shortly afterwards the name was changed to the Trent Tile Co. In 1883 Isaac Broome, who had formerly been connected with the Etruria Pottery of Trenton, returned to that city to become the designer and modeler for this new company. Broome stayed for two years before leaving to assist with the forming of the Providential Tile Works.

In 1886 William Wood Gallimore was hired as the designer and modeler. Gallimore had 30 years experience as a potter and designer, and had earned an enviable reputation as a modeler of portrait busts and vases. He had been at the Belleek potteries in Ireland for six years, where he lost his right arm by the bursting of a gun.

By 1892 the Trent Tile Co. was operating 20 kilns. Mosaic tiles were produced in white and colors. They had developed and patented a dull glaze finish for tiles in relief which are treated by sand-blasting after glazing. The result of this process was a soft, satin-like finish. Six by eighteen inch panels with decorations in relief were manufactured extensively. They also produced soda-water fountains with modeled panels.

Employment reached 300 in 1910. But two years later they had financial difficulties and were forced into receivership. The court appointed receiver, Thomas Thropp, purchased the property in 1916. He rebuilt the organization and became the president and general manager. Thropp died in 1931. The company continued to operate for several years, reaching an annual rated capacity of 8,000,000 square feet. In the late thirties the plant was closed. In 1940 the property was purchased by the Wenczel Tile Co. of Trenton.

There were two common marks used by the Trent Tile Co. One has the impressed words on three lines, "Trent Tile – Trenton, N.J. – U.S.A." These words are framed within two parallel lines just inside each of the tiles' edges. A second mark, common to trim and stove tiles, but not uncommon to tiles up to 6", is the word "Trent" in raised letters. Both marks were made by the back die in the stamping process. While at Trent, Isaac Broome used either his last name or the letter B to sign some of his work.

B

BROOME

1927 photo of Trent factory.

Isaac Broome modeled this pair of portrait tiles during his 1883 to 1885 tenure at Trent. The 4¼″ square tiles are signed on the backs with the impressed factory mark. The female portrait has an impressed "B" on her left shoulder. The male figure tile has an unusual raised "B" in the lower left corner. Like many of the Broome designs, the backgrounds of these tiles are busy with decoration. $300.00 – 400.00 the pair.

The Murdock Parlor Grate Company was the exclusive agent for Trent in Boston. The advertising paperweight shown here was made by Trent for Murdock. The 2⅞″ x 4¼″ piece shows a woman seated at one side of the hearth watching as a playful dog knocks over the fireplace tools. The inscription reads, "May God Betide Our Ain Fireside, Murdock Parlor Grate Co." Unsigned. $200.00 – 250.00.

This 3″ x 5″ advertising paperweight also serves as an ink blotter. Made for the "Manganese Steel Safe Co., New York, The Safe to Trust," the bottom has a convex surface for attaching a blotter. An unsigned attribution. $175.00 – 225.00.

The tiles in this cast-iron stove are signed with the raised Trent factory mark. The stove was made by "Bridgeford & Company, Louisville, Ky., 1888." The sliding door with windows has a patent date of 1886. The castings on the back of the stove are as detailed as the front. The tiles are 3¼" in diameter. $75.00 – 100.00 each. $600.00 – 800.00 for the stove with tiles.

A group of stove tiles from 2½" to 4" in diameter. All are signed with the raised factory mark. $75.00 – 150.00 each.

These Dutch Renaissance portrait pairs are 6" square, and signed with the impressed factory mark. Many relief tiles have a small amount of intaglio modeling. However, these are unusual because a large part of the decoration is in intaglio. $300.00 – 350.00 pair. Framed, $350.00 – 400.00 pair. Signed "Broome," $400.00 – 450.00 pair.

This set of four 1½" x 6" tiles is shown in the 1905 catalog with the numbers 872 through 875. Signed with raised letters. $30.00 – 45.00 the set.

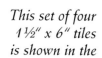

The center panel of this pastoral set is pictured in E. A. Barber's publication, The Pottery and Porcelain of the United States, *published in 1893. Barber states the set was done by W. W. Gallimore. Trent made a special effort to assure all small tiles, even 1" trim tiles, were signed with a factory mark. However, I have never seen a Trent tile over 6" square with a factory mark. Unsigned and framed. $1,200.00 – 1,600.00 the set.*

Another design pictured in the Barber book and credited to W. W. Gallimore is this 9" x 18" panel. Barber wrote of Gallimore, "Mr. Gallimore is a versatile and prolific sculptor, and an artist of fine ability. His style is vigorous and characteristic; his portrayals of boys and Cupids are especially pleasing." This outstanding example shows an extensive amount of detailed modeling in the subjects and in the background. Unsigned. $1,200.00 – 1,600.00.

The painter Emmanuel Benner created the full length portraits of "Summer" and "Autumn." A sculptor at the Trent works did excellent reproductions for a mantel facing set on 18″ x 6″ tile panels. The 1905 factory catalog calls the facing "Seasons," and shows the other two seasons on the horizontal panel. Unsigned and framed. $600.00 – 800.00 the pair.

Another panel shown in the 1905 catalog, this 9″ x 12″ tile was used as an upper corner tile in a mantel facing. The panel decoration and border frame is trimmed with gold overglaze. The facing is designated "No. 2006." Unsigned. $150.00 – 200.00.

This unusual pine cone tile was designed to extend its decoration in any of four directions. Signed with the raised mark. $40.00 – 60.00.

The 6" square tile depicting a woman with a falcon, and the four 3" square companions were part of a mantel facing. Covered with a mottled burgundy and green tinted glaze, all have the raised Trent mark. Framed. $200.00 – 250.00 the set.

This portrait of Michelangelo is so like one modeled by Broome, while he was at the Providential Tile Works, it takes close examination to see the difference. This 6" square tile has the raised mark. $200.00 – 250.00.

This is a beautifully detailed tile done in very low relief. The tile is 6" square and has the impressed mark. Framed. $65.00 – 85.00

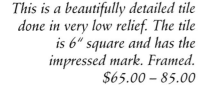

Century, *August 1886.*

       ✄ ✄

FAIENCE MANTELS IN "DELLA ROBBIA"   Sometime in the near future the Open Door hopes to present reproductions in half-tone of the beautiful designs in Faience Mantels done in the "Della Robbia" tile by The Trent Tile Company. Three of these color symphonies are shown in the Company's illustrated catalogue, which by the way, is an art publication well worth sending for. These mantels have been modeled with great care and with due regard for the structural features in their easy and secure setting. Some of the finest artistic effects are obtained by having the modeled or embossed parts in dull glazes that have all the advantage of brilliant glazes as regards color, yet possess a charm of their own in the soft sheen of their surface. Thus treated, and with the field in "Della Robbia" glazes, it is only requisite to evolve a color scheme in contrasting but harmonious tones to produce a combination that will lend a charm and elegance to the house or hall. The "Della Robbia" glaze tiles for wall and fireplace are made in twenty-five choice colorings and the dull Crystalline or fruit-skin glazed tile, plain or embossed, in fifteen colors, as soft and velvety as a rose leaf. The Trent Tile Company will gladly submit designs and color schemes, with estimates for tile work of all kinds, and are always open for a discussion of the subject with architects, decorators or home-builders.

The Craftsman, *March 1906.*

The above half-tone illustrates a Dining-room wainscoted in six inch square tile in our latest production, "Della Robbia" glazed tile.

The color selected was our number 300, a beautiful tint of variegated Moss Green. The leading decorators of Germany, France and England are discarding Marbles, and Tiles of all colors and sizes are being used almost to the exclusion of all other materials for Wall and Floor work.

Foreign literature devoted to the exploitation of interior decorations is replete with illustrations and descriptions of the tile work now being installed in the structures of Germany and France, views of the interiors of Public Buildings and of Residences showing Walls and Floors of Corridors, Vestibules, Reception Halls, Dining-rooms, Bathrooms and Kitchens are given in which the tile work possess such an artistic charm that at a glance it wins our admiration.

Trent Tile are being employed in foreign lands to do some of this elegant work, why cannot we at home "Attain unto it."

Ask your nearest tile dealer to show you samples of "Della Robbia" glazed tile, we make them in colors that will harmonize with any color scheme that may be selected.

Designs without cost upon application. Tile for "Everywhere and Anywhere."
Write Dept. C. for Brochure.

Trent Tile Company,

MAKERS OF WALL AND FIRE PLACE TILE, VITREOUS ASCEPTIC FLOOR TILE AND CERAMIC MOSAICS

Office and Works, Trenton, N. J., U. S. A.

BATHROOM IN THE RESIDENCE OF MR. WM. H. WAKEFIELD, KANSAS CITY, MO.

OF the above illustrated bathroom MR. SELBY H. KURFISS, the architect, says: "The special feature of the second floor is the large bathroom to which is added a Rain Bath, which is made in circular form. The door and window casings, walls, ceiling and tub are all of "Della Robbia" glazed tile, floor being in Ceramic Mosaic in colors to harmonize with the walls. The color of the wainscoting, including decorated cap, is shades of jade stone; the frieze and cove, old ivory with jade, light green and old rose decorations; the ceiling, old ivory with jade buttons. The design is so artistic and the blending of colors is so soft, being all mezzo tones, that it forms a beautiful picture as well as a perfect bathroom, and is a happy realization of the architect's desires."

¶ Ask your nearest tile dealer to show you samples of "Della Robbia" glazed tile. Designs without cost upon application. Tile for "everywhere and anywhere." Write Dept. C for brochure.

TRENT TILE COMPANY

Makers of WALL AND FIRE PLACE TILE, VITREOUS ASEPTIC FLOOR TILE, CERAMIC MOSAIC

Office and Works: TRENTON, N. J., U. S. A.

L'ART NOUVEAU FIRE PLACE

THE latest foreign literature on Architecture and Interior Decoration is replete with illustrations of interiors that are charming for their elegance and simplicity, and in all L'Art Nouveau predominates. All illustrations show an extensive use of Tile and Architectural Faience. **Marbles are conspicuous by their absence.** ❡ We particularly note the abandonment of oblong tile, and the exclusive use of the square shapes, the prevailing size being a six inch square with an occasional illustration showing a four or three inch square. ❡ For walls, wainscotings and fireplace work our "Della Robbia" and Mat Glazed Tile are in exact accord with the movement above mentioned.

ASK YOUR NEAREST TILE DEALER TO SHOW YOU SAMPLES
TILE FOR "EVERYWHERE AND ANYWHERE"
SPECIAL DESIGNS UPON APPLICATION WITHOUT COST
Write Dept. B for Catalogue

We make Wall and Fire-place Tile, Non-absorbent Floor Tile and Ceramic Mosaics for Churches, Banks, Office Buildings, Hotels, Theatres, Railroad Stations, Restaurants, Cafés, Private Residences, Porch Floors and Architectural Faience.

TRENT TILE COMPANY   Office and Works   TRENTON, N. J.

United States Encaustic Tile Works

The United States Encaustic Tile Company was organized in Indianapolis, Indiana, in 1877, by Frederick H. Hall, James G. Douglass, William H. Lyons, Reginald R. Parker, Alfred Harrison, and William S. Barkley. Douglass became president, Lyons the secretary and treasurer, and Hall the superintendent.

The next year and a half was devoted to erecting a plant, and conducting experiments to develop encaustic floor and wall tiles. Hall had been instrumental in the founding and the product development of the American Encaustic Tile Co.

In 1879 the factory burned and was rebuilt. Hall completed the testing, and had successfully developed the products. Marketing began, and Hall died unexpectedly. William Barkley became the superintendent. The plant manufactured colorful encaustic tiles. An 1884 article, "History of Indianapolis and Marion County," describes the process used at this factory.

"An encaustic tile, properly speaking, is one that is made of two kinds of clay — a red base, with a face of finer clay, which bears the ornamental pattern, and strengthened at the base with a thin layer of different clay to prevent warping. It is made both by the dry and plastic processes. In the latter the clay is damp. The workman, taking what he needs, cuts off a square slab, upon which the facing of finer clay is slapped down, a backing is put on the other side to make the requisite thickness. It is then put in a press, and the pattern in relief, usually made of plaster of Paris, is brought down upon the face of the tile, and the design is impressed into the soft-tinted clay. The hollows thus formed are filled with a semifluid clay of a rich or deep color, poured into them and over the whole surface of the tile. In twenty-four hours this has become sufficiently hard to admit of the surplus clay being removed, which is skillfully done by the operator, and the whole pattern and ground are exposed. The surface is perfectly smooth, but the baking brings out the indentations or ridges of the patterns."

Robert Minton Taylor, an English tile maker, was employed from 1881 to 1883. Taylor was an accomplished artist and previous business owner. He undoubtedly made significant contributions to the business. In 1884 he co-founded the Taylor Ceramic Company, which soon became the Hamilton Tile Works Company.

Three hundred workers were employed in 1884. The rated annual capacity was 2,000,000 square feet of tile.

In 1886 the bank affiliated with the U.S.E.T.Co., failed. The company entered into receivership and was reorganized as the United States Encaustic Tile Works.

Eighteen kilns were in operation in 1893, producing plain, encaustic, enameled, and embossed tiles. Miss Ruth Winterbotham, an artist and modeler employed at this works, was invited to exhibit some of her work in the Women's Building at the World's Columbian Exposition in Chicago. Her display included a series of panels with female figures in

The very high relief decoration on this tile might identify it as an early product. Some of the early production at several art tile works was done in very high relief, Chelsea, A.E., and Hamilton included. This 6" square tile with an apple decoration is the only one of this group with the circular High Art Majolica mark pictured here. The tile appears to have been made for the upper corners of a mantel facing, for the stem enters and exits the tile at a 90° angle. $60.00 – 90.00.

relief representing the March Zephyrs, and a 15" diameter plaque, a copy of the Indiana State seal. Also in this year, this works made the first mat finish glaze installation in America. The mat glaze was fired on brick and installed in a prominent hotel in Indianapolis, just north of the State House.

An expansion program was started just three months prior to the stock market crash of 1929. Loans amounting to $125,000, taken for the expansion, contributed to the company entering receivership in 1931. A new company was formed in 1932 under the name of the U.S. Tile Corporation, but it closed in 1939.

Tiles manufactured by this firm are usually well marked. Of the 19 tiles shown here, only the portrait of Ophelia has the simple, one line "U.S.E.T.W." raised letter mark. All the others have marks that cover their backs. I have only seen one unsigned relief tile attributed to this works. In an article, "High Art Majolica Tiles of the United States Encaustic Tile Works" by Barbara White Morse, published in the Mar./Apr. '82 issue of *Spinning Wheel,* and reprinted in the Jan./Mar. '93 issue of *Flash Point,* she pictures a full-length portrait of a female and suggests it's in the style of Ruth M. Winterbotham. Indeed, the facial features, hands, and proportionally small feet are all characteristics similar to the pair of female portraits shown on page 233. Relief tiles signed "Company" and "High Art Majolica" were made prior to the reorganization of 1886. Tiles marked "Works" were made after the reorganization, and the "High Art Majolica" mark disappeared.

The portrait of a girl with a Dutch hat is in high relief. The 6" tile is signed with the five line High Art Majolica mark. $175.00 – 225.00.

This pair of cavaliers are each signed with the four line High Art Majolica mark. The tiles are 4⅜" square. $200.00 – 250.00 the pair.

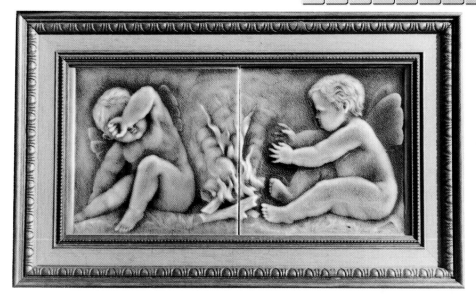

Winged putti warm themselves under a dark golden amber glaze. Two High Art Majolica tiles make this 6" x 12" panel. Framed. $350.00 – 400.00.

Lattice work provides a perch for this pair of birds. The 6" tile is one of a set for a mantel facing. The tile is signed with the five line High Art Majolica mark. $50.00 – 75.00.

The U.S.E.T.Wks made the companion tile of Hamlet to go with this portrait of Ophelia. This 6" tile has the U.S.E.T.W. mark. $150.00 – 200.00.

The decoration of a girl in a bonnet is in low relief. This 4¼" tile has the four line Wks mark. $125.00 – 175.00.

This tile is shown in an undated factory catalog as item T T 49. This hunting dog tile is 6" square and has the five line Wks mark. $175.00-225.00 if perfect.

Decorated with cherries, this tile is part of a mantel facing. The 6" tile has the five line Wks factory mark. $35.00 – 50.00.

This self-framed bird tile was removed from a mantel facing installation along with the five-piece panel shown here. All the 6″ tiles have the five line Wks mark. $150.00 – 200.00 for the corner tile. $300.00 – 400.00 for the five tile panel.

This pair of semi-nude females is probably the work of Miss Winterbotham. Both 6″ tiles have the five line Wks mark. Framed. $300.00 – 500.00 the pair

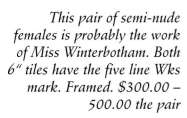

Artus Van Briggle left the employment of the Rookwood Pottery in 1899 to establish his own pottery in Colorado Springs, Colorado. Van Briggle suffered from tuberculosis and decided the drier air of the west was a better environment for his worsening condition. He continued experimenting, modeling, and painting.

Anne Gregory, Van Briggle's fiancee, arrived in Colorado Springs in 1900, and took the position of art instructor in a local high school.

Although Van Briggle had left Rookwood, he still maintained the admiration of Maria Storer, the founder of Rookwood. She provided moral and financial support. By 1901 Van Briggle had developed his dead mat glazes and forms in modeled relief. Three hundred pieces were displayed locally, and all were sold.

In 1902 a stock company was formed and it was named the Van Briggle Pottery Company. The capital from the sale of stock was used to increase the size of the facility, and for the purchase and installation of a large and two small gas fired kilns. The work force was increased.

The products were carved designs in relief, coated with mat glaze colors. Sculptured designs were influenced by Art Nouveau, and decorations were of Colorado plants and insects. Initially all pottery was sold locally. Cash was needed immediately to pay wages. But by the end of the year pottery was being shipped to major cities nationwide.

Artus Van Briggle and Anne Lawrence Gregory were married in June of 1902. Van Briggle's health was still declining and the company was growing. Anne, a talented and capable artist, assumed more and more of his responsibilities while Artus passed on his formulas and methods.

In July of 1904 Artus died. Anne continued to run the pottery that had grown to include 14 employees.

A new plant was constructed in 1907. By the fall of 1908 they were making art pottery, terra cotta mantels, tiles, and garden flower pots and ornaments. The pottery was reorganized in 1910 as the Van Briggle Pottery and Tile Company. The operation had lagging sales and went bankrupt in 1913.

The pottery has changed ownership several times and is still operating. New designs and reproductions of the old are being sold at the pottery.

Identifying Van Briggle pottery is relatively easy. The double A within a box has been used consistently. Very early pieces were dated. However, dating became inconsistent and was discontinued after 1919. The identification of time periods of the manufacture of undated examples can be done by examining the shapes, style of bottom marks, and bottom glazing. Tiles and terra cotta were signed with the company initials, VBPCo., impressed. Anyone interested in the products of this company should obtain copies of *A Collector's Guide to Van Briggle Pottery* by Nelson, Crouch, Demmin, and Newton, and a copy of *The Collector's Encyclopedia of Van Briggle Art Pottery* by Sasicki & Fania.

VAN BRIGGLE
POTTERY
COLORADO SPRINGS-COLO

TWO GOLD MEDALS
UNIVERSAL EXPOSITION
ST. LOUIS-1904

McClure's, *December 1904.*

The mug shown here was made in the 1907 – 1912 period. Artus designed this shape #28 in 1901. The mug is 4¾" tall. $300.00 – 400.00.

This 8" tall elephant is from the 1940 – 1960 period. $80.00 – 120.00.

VAN BRIGGLE POTTERY FROM MONUMENT VALLEY PARK.

THE VAN BRIGGLE POTTERY
COLORADO SPRINGS, COLO.

WORLD FAMOUS VAN BRIGGLE POTTERY — COLORADO SPRINGS, COLORADO

The sepia photo postcard and the postcard showing the colored pots were introduced around 1910. The postcard of the "World Famous Van Briggle Pottery" was used during the '20s to the mid '50s. I have no idea when the "Free Trip" visitors pass was used.

VAN BRIGGLE ART POTTERY, COLORADO SPRINGS, COLO.

We Hope You Will Enjoy Our Popular "Free Trip" Through the Van Briggle Art Pottery

Van Briggle Art Pottery has achieved world fame and recognition. *Nowhere else in all the world is there another Van Briggle Art Pottery.* Nowhere else in all the world is there even a place where Van Briggle Art Pottery can be purchased. *Van Briggle Art Pottery is sold only where it is created.*

"When you think of Gifts . . . Think of Van Briggle"

Van Briggle Is Ideal for Weddings and Birthdays . . . . Perfect for Christmas

Weller Pottery

In 1872, at the age of 21, Sam Weller established the Weller Pottery in Fultonham, Ohio. In 1882 he moved the business to Zanesville. Mr. Weller visited the Chicago World's Fair of 1893. While at the fair he was very impressed with the products displayed by the Lonhuda Pottery of Steubenville, Ohio. Mr. Weller promptly made an offer to Mr. William Long, owner and founder, to purchase his pottery. The following year Mr. Long decided to accept Mr. Weller's offer. He also agreed to work at the Weller Pottery. The Lonhuda product name continued at the Weller Pottery, and it catapulted the business into the art pottery market.

In 1896, after Long left Weller, Sam Weller changed the name of the Lonhuda line to Louwelsa.

This 8" tall, three handled, and three footed vase was decorated by Elizabeth Ayers and is signed with her hand-incised monogram and the die-stamped Lonhuda Faience shield mark used at the Weller Pottery. Seven fish painted in shades of green and one fish in shades of orange encircle the vase. $700.00 – 900.00.

LONHUDA

Hunter

Nearly all the signed products have the word Weller in the mark. However, the Lonhuda, Sicard, and Hunter lines do not.

268

237

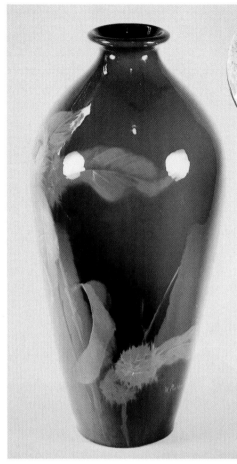

Artist signed "H. Pillsbury" on the side, this vase is 18½" tall and 9" wide. Hester Pillsbury decorated the front with opening chestnuts, the back with closed chestnuts. The bottom is marked with a die-impressed Louwelsa Weller half circle seal. $1,100.00 – 1,400.00.

The wild rose decoration on this 13⅝" vase was painted by Levi J. Burgess and is signed "L.J.B." in slip, on the side. A die-impressed Weller Louwelsa half circle seal is on the bottom. $500.00 – 600.00.

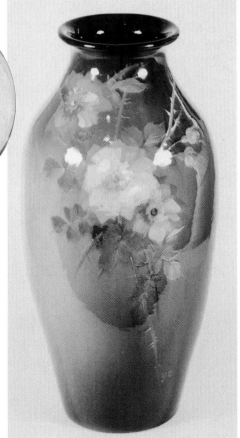

Weller expanded the standard glaze Louwelsa line to include Blue Louwelsa, Red Louwelsa, and Green Louwelsa. Blue Louwelsa was decorated in shades of a blue background with white designs. Red Louwelsa was a burgundy decoration over a deep red background. Green Louwelsa was painted in shades of green, sometimes with a little white. Examples of Blue or Red Louwelsa are scarce, and Greens are rare.

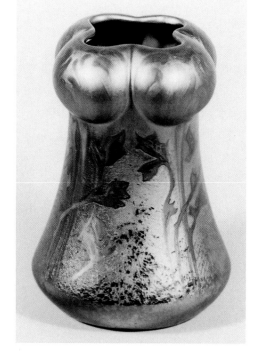

The Sicard line was produced from 1903 until 1907, when Sicard left to return to France. This 6" example is decorated with thistles, the blossoms encircling the four puffed out areas at the neck. Sicard is most commonly signed on the side. This vase is unsigned. $500.00 – 600.00.

This 7½" tall Blue Louwelsa vase was decorated with lily of the valley. The artists initials, "M L" for M. Lybarger, have been incised by hand in the bottom. The bottom also has the die-impressed Louwelsa Weller single circle seal. Examples of Weller with the single circle seal are scarce. An X over the number 348 has been die stamped in the center of the circle. $600.00 – 750.00.

A reddish brown clay, similar to that used in the manufacturing of some Weller lines of tiles, plaques, and souvenirs for the 1904 St. Louis World's Fair, was used to make this 8" example of Red Louwelsa. The concave bottom of the vase is marked with a hand-incised "Weller" in crude block letters. This vase and the Blue Louwelsa example are uncrazed, an attribute not uncommon with Blue, Red, and Green Louwelsa. $400.00 – 500.00.

Weller introduced the first line of Dickensware in 1897. Dickensware I differs from the standard line of Louwelsa only in its background coloring. Dickensware I has backgrounds of dark, non-shaded colors of brown, blue, green, or black. This 11" tall, 14" wide overall jard is signed with the die-impressed "Dickensware Weller" mark. Peach colored blossoms on green foliage over a black background surround this large jard. An unknown artist's monogram of an E within an O is painted in slip on the side. $450.00 – 600.00.

The die-impressed mark "Designed by J.W. Brooks Jr." has been found on several different squat shaped oil lamps in both the Louwelsa and Dickensware I lines. The mark is in the form of the common Weller Dickensware mark. The example shown is 6½" tall by 13" wide. It has been decorated and signed by W.F. Hall. The fount is signed Bradley and Hubbard. $450.00 – 600.00.

Eocean was another successful line for Weller. Starting in 1898, it was promoted through the mid 1920s. Eocean is more commonly found with backgrounds of gray or olive green shading to ivory. Eocean Rose had a light rose tint over the ivory background. Most pieces are signed on the bottom with either a die impressed double circle seal or a hand-incised Eocean or Eocean Rose. Some examples have Eocean or Eocean Rose hand incised on the side.

This Eocean Rose vase is 4¾" tall. The bottom markings include the die-impressed numbers 9055 and hand-incised Eocean Weller. Although this vase is not marked Eocean Rose, it does have a rose tint over the ivory background. The fish decoration appears to have been done by Charles Chilcotee (see All About Weller, *color plate C-1). $500.00 – 600.00.*

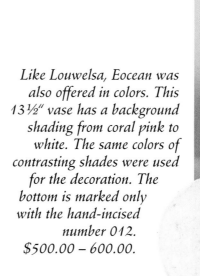

Like Louwelsa, Eocean was also offered in colors. This 13½" vase has a background shading from coral pink to white. The same colors of contrasting shades were used for the decoration. The bottom is marked only with the hand-incised number 012. $500.00 – 600.00.

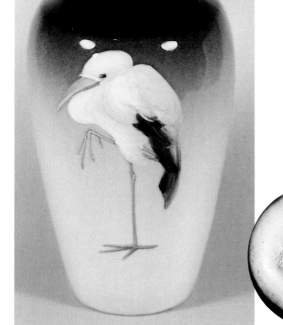

Eocean is hand incised on the bottom of this 8" vase, along with the artist's large S monogram. The decoration of a stork has been painted. $700.00 – 900.00.

Grotesque but beautiful, this jardiniere and pedestal set appeared in the July 1901 issue of House Furnisher: China, Glass and Pottery Review. *A reprint is shown in* All About Weller, *which also shows the ped in the Weller residence in the Gold Room, to the right of the fireplace, but with a Sicard glaze. This set is 36" tall. The jard has a 12" opening and is decorated all around with swans. The ped is made of four individually molded pieces fired together. The top, or jard platform, is covered underneath with floral garlands. The base has four feet of alternating dolphins and lion heads. The vertical support is a sea monster originally molded in left and right sides. Both pieces of the set are covered with a blended pink to green to brown gloss glaze. Large old sets like this are very difficult to find in excellent condition. This one is mint, and rare! $1,000.00 – 1,350.00.*

Louwelsa Perfecto appeared in 1903. The decorations were done in very pale colors with a mat finish. Backgrounds shaded from a predominating sea green to pink, salmon, or tan. This line was discontinued in 1904, thus contributing to its scarcity today.

This 18" vase is of the Louwelsa Perfecto line, but it has been covered with a clear gloss glaze. This is one of the many examples of Weller that are variations to their line's general description. The sea green background shading to a pink center with salmon colored blossoms fits well with the trade's descriptions of this line. The gloss glaze application has however, resulted in a slight brightening of the colors. The bottom has the die-impressed number 430 with an X above and one below. On the side, about 3" above the bottom, the artist signed "L.Mitchell" in thick slip. These hollyhock blossoms reflect the artist's ability to paint depth upon a flat surface. $1,200.00 – 1,500.00.

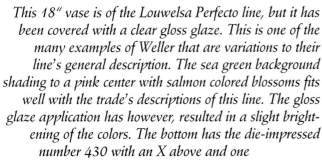

Jap Birdimal, a creation of Frederick H. Rhead, was introduced in 1904. This 10" vase with a geisha was decorated by an unknown artist who signed the initials, VMH, on the side at the bottom edge. Although the name of this artist is lost, the monogram has appeared on other Jap Birdimal products. $700.00 – 900.00.

Matt Louwelsa was introduced in 1905. It was probably a replacement of Perfecto, so Weller could continue to compete with the similar mat finished products of several other potteries. This 12⅜" tall Matt Louwelsa tankard has a background reminiscent of Perfecto's light green shading to pink in the center. However, the monk with spirits decoration and darker green overspray on the lower portion are too dark to meet the description of Perfecto's pale colors. The signature of Frank Ferrell is painted on the side in slip. The bottom has an in mold number 580 in 1" high numerals. These large numbers were nearly obliterated when the clay was still wet, so a smaller 580 was die stamped. $900.00 – 1,200.00.

Sam Weller invested greatly in promoting his pottery at the St. Louis Expo of 1904. He constructed a working pottery and sold pottery souvenirs. A series of 4¾" diameter presidential plaques, molded in white clay with a natural bisque finish, were sold. Also popular was a group of miniature vases, mugs, jards, jugs, pitchers, and teapots. This series used existing molds to form a red clay product with a bisque finish. These red clay souvenirs were then decorated in slip with children, angels, Oriental, and Indian figures. Sometimes the decorator included the words "St. Louis, 1904." Most were not signed Weller.

This red clay souvenir mug is 3½" tall. There is an in-mold number 320 in the bottom. This same shape mug is shown in The Collector's Encyclopedia of Weller Pottery by Huxford, with a Sicard glaze. It also appears as another souvenir with an in-mold map of the Louisiana Purchase and "St. Louis, L.P.E., 1904." $175.00 – 225.00.

Classical figures in relief were the molded decoration of the Narona line introduced in 1909. This 9½" jard has a clear glazed interior and a smeared on exterior finish that resembles brown shoe polish. This piece of Narona is unusual because three of the eight panels have the initials J.B. at their base. The Narona line was most probably designed by the Weller artist and sculptor John Butterworth. Examples of Narona are very scarce. $400.00 – 600.00.

"Bells of San Juan is a line modeled after the old buildings of California" was written in the Jan. 13, 1910, issue of Crockery and Glass Journal. Ann Gilbert McDonald brought this pattern to light in her book All About Weller. The book shows this line with a Claywood type glaze. The example shown here is the other known glaze treatment. This 8" tall, 10" wide jard has four panels, each depicting a different California mission. There are no known signed examples of this line. $500.00 – 600.00.

Flemish or Roma line? This 7 lb. doorstop is 9½″ tall and 8¼″ wide. The very high relief molding suggests Flemish, while the pale pastel colors on a creamware background lean toward Roma. The bottom has a die-impressed Weller in block letters. $250.00 – 350.00.

Knifewood was introduced in 1921. This 11″ molded form was a colorful member of the Knifewood line. However, this example was introduced earlier, probably as a late arrival of the Burntwood line. Burntwood was unglazed on the exterior except for the upper and lower bands of dark brown. Later examples, like this one, were covered inside and out with a clear glaze. $175.00 – 250.00.

The Hudson line of pottery was introduced in the late teens, and production of about a dozen lines and variations continued well into the thirties. White and Decorated was the first line. It has a solid ivory background and is slip decorated with mostly florals, some birds, and a few rare pictorials or scenics. Blue and Decorated followed in the same style on its navy background, but with more pictorials being produced. The common, or most popular Hudson pattern, was introduced in 1919. Called just Hudson, this line has shaded backgrounds of one color or one color shading to another color. A wide variety of naturalistic florals were painted. Beautiful scenes were also painted in this line and are called Pictorials. The decorations included landscapes, people, animals, or birds. Many of this Pictorial line were similar in style to Rookwood scenics in that they were decorated all around. Two lines of Hudsons appeared with gloss instead of the standard matt glaze. One was early and it was just White and Decorated ware with a different glaze. The second gloss glaze line was introduced in 1934 with dog and cat decorations.

The Rochelle line, with floral decorations over a shaded brown background, had its debut in the twenties. Hudson Light decorations were done completely in pale colors, usually of gray, green, and ivory. The Copra line has a smear type background with florals done in the style of the Louella line. Hudson Perfecto differs from all other Hudson lines because it appears to have been painted in mineral colors rather than slip.

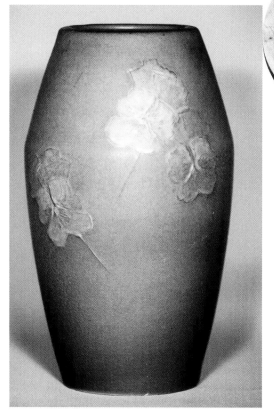

A rare variety of Hudsons were made with both the background and decoration in shades of but one color. Colors of gray, blue, or maroon were used. Here is an example of maroon on maroon with a decoration of pansy faces with disappearing stems painted over a shaded background. The vase is covered with a vellum type glaze. The bottom of this 8" vase is signed Weller in crude block letters that were hand incised with a sharp tool. Rare! $900.00 – 1,100.00.

This 13" Hudson vase was painted by the artist Kennedy. The signature appears on the narrow foot. The bottom has a die-impressed Weller in block letters. $800.00 – 1,100.00.

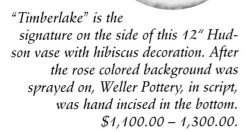

"Timberlake" is the signature on the side of this 12" Hudson vase with hibiscus decoration. After the rose colored background was sprayed on, Weller Pottery, in script, was hand incised in the bottom. $1,100.00 – 1,300.00.

A trumpet vine with pink and rose colored blossoms was painted across the front of this 15" vase. The same flowers appear on the back side, but are painted in shades of blue. The all blue decoration has the appearance of a blue on blue line product. The signature of H. Pillsbury appears on the back of the vase. The Weller Pottery script mark was incised on the bottom by hand, after the background colors were applied. $1,600.00 – 2,000.00.

The beautiful, well executed, two-color iris was done by the artist Dorothy England. She signed D England at the bottom edge of this 8½" vase. The bottom is marked with the Weller Ware Pottery ink stamp. $600.00 – 800.00.

Frosted Matt is one of several arts & crafts type glazes produced at Weller. Introduced in 1921, it was offered in a variety of colors. This melon shaped example is 8" tall and 9½" wide with a ¾" opening in the short neck. The medium green background on the neck shades quickly to yellow over the top, then back to medium green from the shoulder to the base. The background is over-glazed with a thick, light green glaze that separated or shrank during the firing process. This shrinking process of the overglaze is the hallmark of the Frosted Matt line. The separated overglaze is raised, but is smooth to the touch. An exceptional example of this line. $500.00 – 700.00.

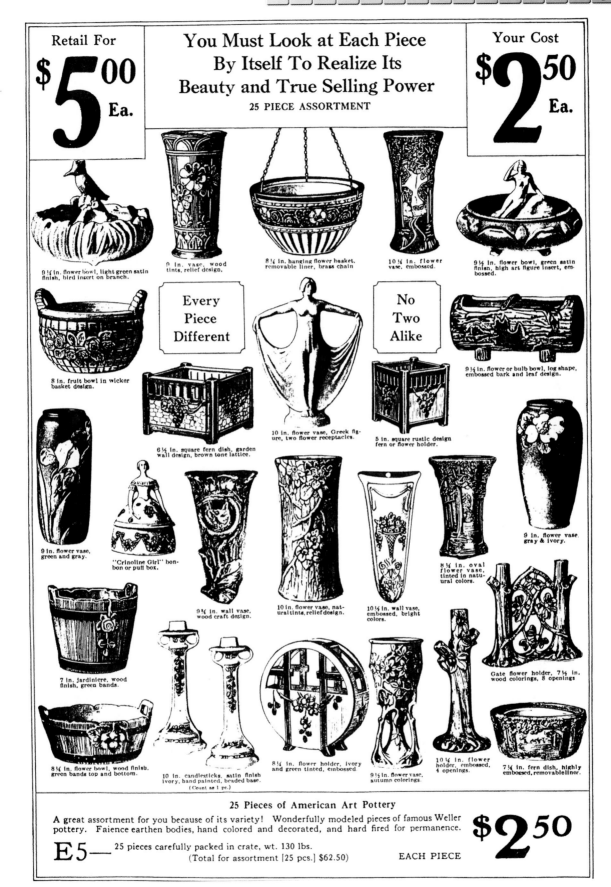

Retail For
$5.00 Ea.

You Must Look at Each Piece
By Itself To Realize Its
Beauty and True Selling Power
25 PIECE ASSORTMENT

Your Cost
$2.50 Ea.

9½ in. flower bowl, light green satin finish, bird insert on branch.

9 in. vase, wood tints, relief design.

8½ in. hanging flower basket, removable liner, brass chain.

10¼ in. flower vase, embossed.

9½ in. flower bowl, green satin finish, high art figure insert, embossed.

8 in. fruit bowl in wicker basket design.

Every Piece Different

No Two Alike

9½ in. flower or bulb bowl, log shape, embossed bark and leaf design.

6½ in. square fern dish, garden wall design, brown tone lattice.

10 in. flower vase, Greek figure, two flower receptacles.

5 in. square rustic design fern or flower holder.

9 in. flower vase, green and gray.

"Crinoline Girl" bonbon or puff box.

9¾ in. wall vase, wood craft design.

10 in. flower vase, natural tints, relief design.

10¼ in. wall vase, embossed, bright colors.

8¼ in. oval flower vase, tinted in natural colors.

9 in. flower vase, gray & ivory.

7 in. jardiniere, wood finish, green bands.

10 in. candlesticks, satin finish ivory, hand painted, beaded base. (Count as 1 pc.)

8¼ in. flower holder, ivory and green tinted, embossed.

9½ in. flower vase, autumn colorings.

10¼ in. flower holder, embossed, 4 openings.

Gate flower holder, 7½ in. wood colorings, 8 openings

8¼ in. flower bowl, wood finish, green bands top and bottom.

7¼ in. fern dish, highly embossed, removable liner.

25 Pieces of American Art Pottery

A great assortment for you because of its variety! Wonderfully modeled pieces of famous Weller pottery. Faience earthen bodies, hand colored and decorated, and hard fired for permanence.

E5— 25 pieces carefully packed in crate, wt. 130 lbs.
(Total for assortment [25 pcs.] $62.50)

$2.50
EACH PIECE

The November 1926 catalog issued by Butler Brothers featured this promotion. Butler Brothers was a large wholesale business with warehouses in New York, Chicago, St. Louis, Minneapolis, and Dallas.

This 6" example of Barcelona, sold through the 1920s, has an unusual factory mark. The mark appears to have been made by writing "Weller" with a wax pencil, then painting over the mark with the yellow/gold background color. When the vase was fired, the wax dissolved and the factory name appeared, surrounded with the yellow glaze. $125.00 – 175.00.

Weller manufactured several lines of tiles over their art pottery producing years. The early tiles were in low or high relief, some of which included intaglio decoration. These early tiles were covered with a gloss glaze of a solid color. Weller published a catalog of plaques with classical figures and designs in relief about 1905. They also manufactured tiles and plaques with Sicard and LaSa glazes. A line of colorfully decorated faience relief tiles with arts & crafts scenes were produced, and were signed with an incised "Weller Art Tiles." In 1930 they published a catalog of faience tiles with Incan decorations in relief. A variety of Hudson-decorated tiles were produced with scenes on single tiles or in sets. Although a wide variety of tiles were made, none must have been made in any significant quantity, because today, all lines of Weller tiles and plaques are scarce to rare. Tiles and panels of the Hudson line painted with scenes, animals, or birds have recently sold. A single 4½" square tile brought $1,500.00, and a 9" x 14" six-tile panel $20,000.00.

Red or terra cotta clay was used to make this 11½" diameter plaque. The clay appears similar in color to that used to make the Red Louwelsa vase and the 1904 souvenir mug previously discussed in this chapter. The plaque is covered with a brown wash glaze. Weller in small block letters is die stamped on the back. Rare! $500.00 – 600.00.

This unsigned relief plaque is 11" in diameter and may have been made by Weller. A terra-cotta clay plaque of the identical size and relief detail, but with a different border, is shown in American Art Pottery by Lucile Henzke. $400.00 – 500.00.

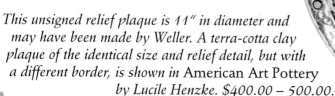

Weller tiles can also be seen in the publications *Zanesville Decorative Tiles* by E. Stanley Wires, Norris F. Schneider, and Moses Mesre; *Zanesville Art Tile in Color* by Evan and Louise Purviance; *The Collector's Encyclopedia of Weller Pottery* by Sharon and Bob Huxford; and *All About Weller* by Ann Gilbert McDonald.

Like the Hobart jard, this Hobart or Ting figurine does not appear in any other known publication. The Oriental boy kissing his goose is covered with a white mat glaze. Hobart and Ting were both creations of Rudolph Lorber. No Weller mark is visible on the small, glazed bottom. $125.00 – 175.00.

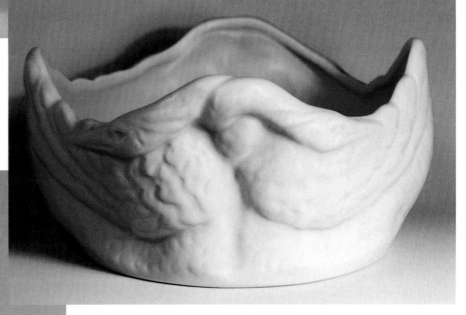

Courting geese or swans with necks entwined surround this 5" x 10" jard. The unusual shape is covered with a mono-chromatic green glaze. This is an example of the Hobart line, introduced in 1927. The bottom has the die-impressed Weller mark in block letters. $150.00 – 200.00.

This Classic line 6½" figure of a fisher boy was first intro-duced as part of the Muskota line in 1915. Later he appeared as a Hobart figure covered with solid color mat glazes. This figure and other figures from the Muskota and Hobart lines were sold as accessories to the Classic line in the '30s. $125.00 – 175.00.

Unlike Rookwood and Roseville, Weller did little advertising in the popular household magazines of the times. The following ads appeared in the late '20s.

HAVE you thought of a bird-bath or a sculptured vase as belonging only to some great terraced garden? Beautiful Graystone, the garden pottery of Weller Ware, will bring this emphasis, this added interest to your own garden. A bird-bath where the birds really revel—an urn of outpouring vines. The mellow gray contours of Graystone suggest pure pottery of the ancients, seemingly beyond price. Yet Graystone is reasonable. Reasonable, also, is Weller Ware in colors for inside your home—in art pottery and distinctive kitchen ware. Paula Morgan, authority on garden and home decoration, will give free advice regarding any decorative need. Address her in care of The Weller Potteries, Zanesville, Ohio.

WELLER WARE

TRY placing a vase of Weller Ware on a prominent table, or in clear sunlight on a sill. Its unusual luster will glow and glisten in the light. Here you will see the full splendor of its colors. For Weller Ware has all the changes of fire! Sometimes its background hues have "over-drips" of a second shade—luxurious effects never seen in other pottery. Such brilliance is in flower-pitchers, candlesticks, great peasant plates. Also in candy jars, window bowls, footed dishes for fruit. Yet prices for this decorative pottery are surprisingly in reason— as they are for the Weller cottage sets and distinctive kitchenware. . . . Paula Morgan, authority on home and garden decoration, will give free advice concerning handsome treatments of pottery for your home. Write her in care of The Department of Decorative Arts, The Weller Potteries, Zanesville, Ohio. *Established in* 1872.

WELLER ⬦ WARE

A FRUIT bowl, a candlestick, a great peasant plate—any pottery in Weller Ware comes in any color you can see in fire—in brilliant effects possible only with Weller! A piece of Weller Ware in your home has an intense shining. With flowers in a vase of it, a candy jar of it flashing on a sill—you create an arresting picture. Weller Ware quickens so glowingly under light! It glistens in bright cool shapes that are always graceful. . . . The hand-made fruit bowl illustrated, green, with over-drips of a deeper shading, has the outer green of its bowl frosted over like a leaf. Such coloring complements richly the tints of every fruit that grows. . . . Weller prices are refreshing—never beyond your reach. Ask us for free advice about decorative pottery for your home. Address the Department of Decorative Arts, The Weller Potteries, Zanesville, Ohio. *Potters since* 1872.

WELLER  WARE

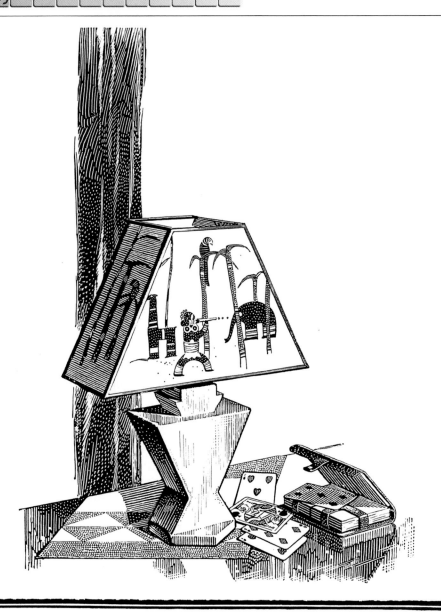

SOMETHING of the spirit of Far-Eastern wood-blocks is in these "modern" lamps of Weller pottery. They wear a similar ancient calm. Their angles are as sharply traced as though following grains of fragrant wood. But their lustres are water-like and brilliant. Weller Ware lustres—in colors from a pale cool ivory to all the changes of fire! . . . The attending shades of parchment have their colors laid on flat and bold—fresh with vitality when the light diffuses through the red curve of a parrot, or the gold vigor of a giraffe. . . . See these interesting lamps at jewelry shops, china, glass and lamp departments. Also the vases and fruit-bowls in the "modern" designs. And such less challenging shapes as Grecian urns and candlesticks. Our folders will help you select pleasing pottery for your home. Address the Department of Decorative Arts, The Weller Potteries, Zanesville, Ohio. *Potters since* 1872.

WELLER ⬠ WARE

Wheatley Pottery

Thomas J. Wheatley had previously operated his own pottery from 1879 till 1884. He had a thorough knowledge of pottery making and decoration, and had lectured some artists prior to their employment at the Rookwood Pottery. Wheatley had manufactured art pottery decorated in the Limoges style of slip underglaze, and some with applied decorations of blossoms and grasses. The factory was destroyed by flood, and production never resumed.

In 1903 Wheatley and Isaac Kahn established the Wheatley Pottery Company of Cincinnati, Ohio. A new plant measuring 50' x 200' was constructed to include work rooms, equipment, studios, and two kilns.

Modeled and molded forms covered with mat glazes were produced. Wheatley molded some forms similar to those already rated as desirable by the buying public. By doing this he captured the part of the market that could not afford the more expensive originals. He also modeled forms of his own design, some with applied decorations of flora or fauna. He covered all the forms with original flowing glazes that he created.

Sometime prior to 1909, Wheatley began to produce garden pottery after antique forms.

In 1910 the plant was destroyed by fire. They rebuilt and continued to manufacture the faience garden pottery with an expanded line, but there is no evidence that the production of art pottery ever resumed.

By the time Wheatley died in 1917, all his efforts were being given to the manufacturing of faience tiles, chimney pots, garden furniture, fountains, bird baths, vases, and boxes. The Wheatley Pottery employed 30 workers by 1921.

The Cambridge Tile Manufacturing Co. acquired the Wheatley firm in 1927. The Wheatley operations name was changed to the Wheatley Tile & Pottery Company. This same year a sales company, the Cambridge-Wheatley Company, was formed to represent both organizations. Large architectural panels and mantel facings were now being offered.

In 1929 Cambridge built a new and modern facility in Hartwell, Ohio, just north of Cincinnati. In 1931 the Wheatley operation was moved into the new plant.

Both the Cambridge-Wheatley Co. and the Wheatley Tile & Pottery Co. names were legally dissolved in 1936.

Art pottery products of the Wheatley Pottery Company were signed with a conjoined WP within a circle, either impressed or on an attached paper label. Architectural and faience products were signed "Wheatley" in block letters or had the catalog number impressed. Most art pottery products today are unsigned, the labels having been removed or the impressed marks covered with glaze.

The Cambridge-Wheatley Co. catalog of 1928 illustrates both of these 12" raised line decorated faience tiles. They are marked only with the corresponding catalog number impressed on one edge. $250.00 – 350.00 the grill tile. $800.00 – 1,200.00 the other

The tile panel shown here, recently removed from a pub within the greater Cincinnati area, is composed of 3" x 6" tiles. This panel is the only one of the five removed that survived without damage. The tiles are evidence of different attempts to influence the glaze effect. Some tiles were fired tilted, or on their end or side, to get the glaze to run in a certain direction. Others were on their backs to obtain an even separation, or breaking up. One loose tile had a splotch of orange and one of yellow applied over the green background. Others had the glaze scraped off, in a spot or two, to expose the clay. $20.00 – 30.00 each loose tile. $600.00 – 900.00 the panel.

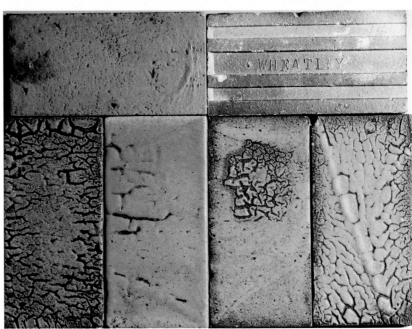

House Beautiful,
May 1917.

258

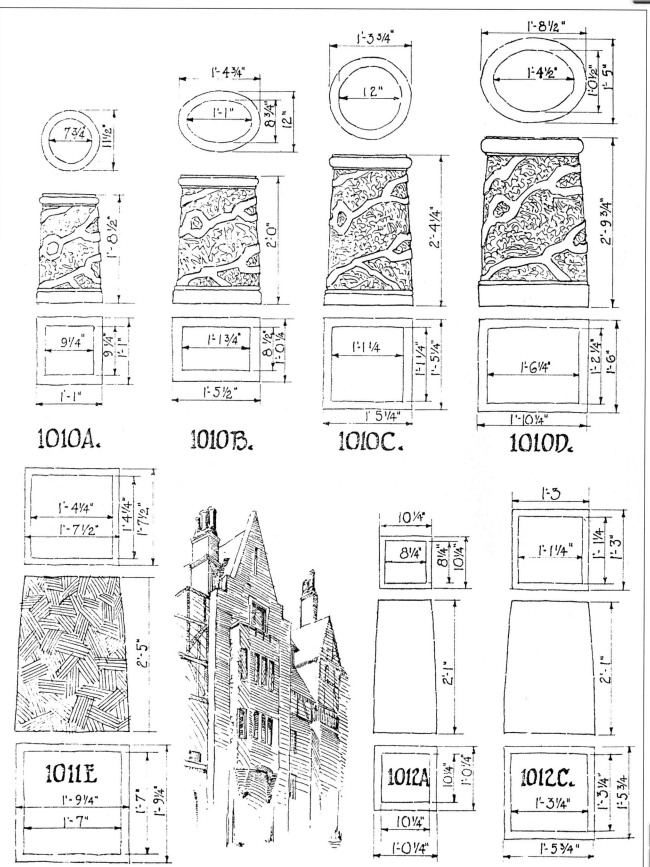

Chimney tops from undated factory catalog.

Country Life, *May 1915.*

House Beautiful,
June 1926.

Pottery that is a Part of Your Garden

The landscaping of your garden becomes most beautiful when it is in strictest accord with the architecture of your home.

The rich Old Ivory or Plymouth Grey tones of Wheatley Garden Pottery in authentic architectural designs are the artistic complements of town house or country home.

Write for catalogue showing 200 different designs of bird baths, jardiniers, fountains and boxes.

Dealers Write for Interesting Proposition and discounts on

**GARDEN POTTERY
FAIENCE TILE**

The Wheatley Pottery Company
4617 Eastern Ave.
Cincinnati, O.

House & Garden,
July 1924.

238-240
Approx. net weight
80 pounds
24 inches
Price $12.00 net

402-363
Box and stand
30 inches long,
11 inches wide,
10 inches deep
Price Complete $25.00
Approx. Weight 125 lbs.

Beautify Your Garden

WHEATLEY Garden Pottery in exquisite designs from authentic artistic sources delights the eye and immeasurably lends enchantment to the most beautiful garden.

There are pieces in Old Ivory and beautiful Plymouth Gray finishes for every conceivable landscape treatment.

Write for catalogue illustrating 200 different designs.

Dealers write for excellent proposition and discounts upon Garden Pottery and Faience Tile.

238-240
Approx. net weight 80 pounds, 24 inches high,
Price $12.00 net.

The Wheatley Pottery Company
4621 Eastern Avenue   Cincinnati, Ohio

Country Life,
July 1924.

146
Pedestal and Sundial
38 inches high, 12 inch top and base
Price complete $29.00
Approx. net weight 75 lbs.

402-363
Box and Stand
30 inches long, 11 inches wide, 10 inches deep
Price complete, $25.00
Approx. net weight, 125 lbs.

Wheatley Architectural Faience Tile

The beautiful mantle shown above is but one of almost numberless treatments obtainable with Wheatley Architectural Faience for interiors and exteriors. In black gun metal polychrome pointed with white, it is a piece of striking yet perfectly balanced contrast. Note the studied irregularity of the floor tiling. It is but one of the many artistic touches given by Wheatley artists to every design of their own origination.

The Wheatley Pottery Company will submit original designs in water color or exactly reproduce detailed renderings as presented by the architect to his client.

Pencil Points,
July 1926.

Unglazed Floor Tile

The designing of floor tile as understood by Wheatley artists and artisans is an art in itself, in which material, utility, color, balance, proportion and methods of laying must be considered as an artistic whole. Our finer floor tiles are almost exclusively hand made and decorated. Decorations are fixed and do *not* wear—a Wheatley feature.

Though we have a beautiful showing of stock designs, our ability to work with the architect and to originate has given the wonderful architectural possibilities of tiles a new and practical aspect.

The soft, harmonious tones of fine tile floors often change an average dwelling into a home of beauty. Every architect with a true sense of the beautiful should thoroughly investigate Wheatley floor tile.

It couples beauty with economy and durability while giving complete play to originality.

Write for Illustrated Catalog
Color sketches submitted upon request

The Wheatley Pottery Company
Department A-7   Cincinnati, Ohio

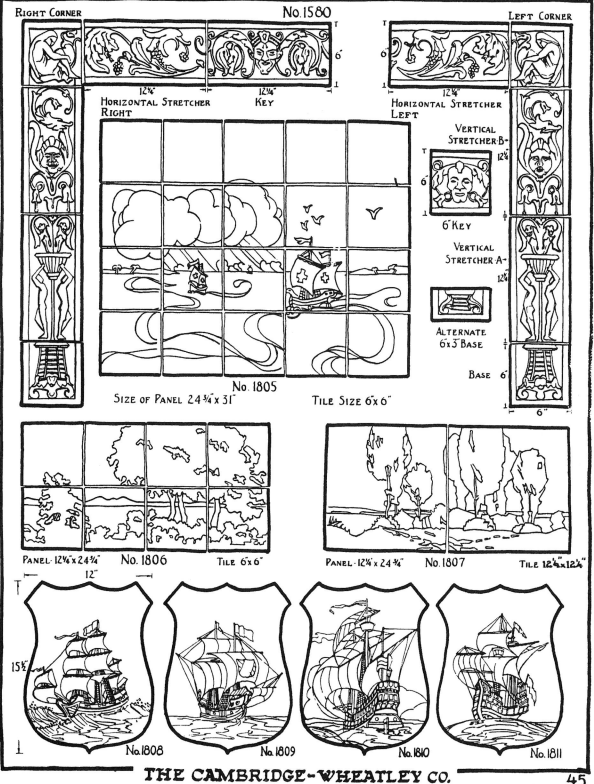

WHEATLEY FAIENCE TILE
DECORATIVE DESIGNS

RIGHT CORNER — No.1580 — LEFT CORNER

HORIZONTAL STRETCHER RIGHT — KEY — HORIZONTAL STRETCHER LEFT

VERTICAL STRETCHER·B·

6" KEY

VERTICAL STRETCHER·A·

ALTERNATE 6"x3" BASE

BASE 6"

No. 1805
SIZE OF PANEL 24¾" x 31" — TILE SIZE 6"x 6"

PANEL·12¼" x 24¾" — No. 1806 — TILE 6"x 6"

PANEL·12¼" x 24¾" — No. 1807 — TILE 12¼"x12¼"

No.1808 — No.1809 — No.1810 — No.1811

THE CAMBRIDGE-WHEATLEY CO.

45

263

Page from 1928 factory catalog.

WHEATLEY FAIENCE TILE
GRILLES ~ POLYCHROME PANELS

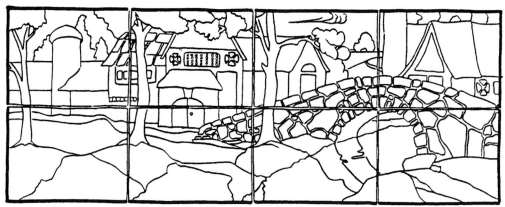

No. 1802 DECORATED PANEL   SIZE · 18¼ × 49¾   TILE SIZE · 9¾ × 12¼

NO. 1902   GRILLE
SIZES · 6 × 6; 4˝ × 4˝

NO. 1804 DECORATED PANEL
SIZE · 12½ × 21˝   TILE SIZE · 4 × 4˝

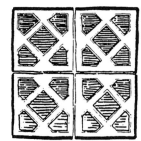

NO. 1903   GRILLE
SIZES · 6 × 6; 7 × 7˝

NO. 1901   GRILLE
SIZES · 6 × 6; 4˝ × 4˝

NO. 1803 DECORATED PANEL
SIZE · 16¾ × 16¾ TILE SIZE · 8¼ × 8¼

NO. 1904   GRILLE
SIZE · 12˝ × 12˝

NO. 1905   GRILLE
SIZE · 4˝ × 4˝

NO. 1813 OUTLINE INSERT

NO. 1581 OUTLINE DESIGN

NO. 1812 R   NO. 1812 L
OUTLINE INSERTS

46

THE CAMBRIDGE-WHEATLEY CO.

Page from 1928 factory catalog.

Tile for Every Purpose

In addition to the wide variety of tile and tile products shown and listed herein, THE CAMBRIDGE-WHEATLEY COMPANY produces a large number of complete units for mantels, fire frames, mantel arches, fountains of all types, and similar installations.

New Catalogues on Request

Our complete new catalogues of tile and hand-fashioned garden pottery will be forwarded upon request.

Specification sheets and full information on any specific items of the Cambridge-Wheatley line also gladly furnished at any time.

Service

Designers are maintained at our New York and Chicago headquarters, and at our factories, in the interest of service to architects and contractors.

A Cambridge-Wheatley Mantel of Artistically Unique Design

Cambridge-Wheatley Fountain

With figure of intriguing quaintness, modeled by a noted sculptor

Cambridge-Wheatley Hand Fashioned Garden Pottery

Blends harmoniously with the landscape, adding charm and distinction to any grounds

Decorative Window at Permanent Building Material Display, New York, N. Y.

Typical of the beautiful designs that may be obtained in Cambridge-Wheatley Tile

A Memorial Drinking Fountain

There is no more appropriate medium for commemorating some outstanding event or perpetuating the memory of a noteworthy individual

Zanesville Majolica

The Zanesville Majolica Company was established in Zanesville, Ohio, by John Heilmann, a grocer, in the spring of 1883. The operation was small, for the manufacturing was done in the J. and G. Pyatt pottery. By the end of July the company exhibited samples of their products at Hatton's Drug Store. The exhibit got a very favorable response. In September they had a display at the Eleventh Cincinnati Industrial Exposition, and they were awarded a gold medal for artistic design and execution, originality, and fine glaze.

The company soon received written admiration of their products from Matt Morgan, president of the Matt Morgan Art Pottery, Palliser, Palliser and Co., an architectural firm in Bridgeport, Connecticut, and in an article published in Frank Leslie's *Illustrated Newspaper*. Success seemed inevitable.

The business was incorporated on November 27, 1883. Heilmann, Charles F. Hatton, Edgar M. Hatton, William S. Harlan, and William M. Shinnick organized the stock company.

On the night of January 20, 1884, the one story wood frame building of the Pyatt brothers was totally destroyed by fire. Although the Pyatt brothers began rebuilding their pottery in May, Zanesville Majolica never recovered.

Records of the name of the modeler or modelers who had designed more than 45 different plaques, and the reasons this promising company failed, have yet to be found.

In an article, "Zanesville Majolica" by Michael Sims, published in the January – March 1992 issue of *Flash Point,* a panel pictured has the marks of Adolph Metzner and the Hamilton Tile Works Company, and shows a striking similarity to those produced at Zanesville Majolica. There is no evidence of a relationship between Metzner and Zanesville Majolica, and there is little similarity between other products of these works. However, Metzner was in the process of starting his Hamilton works when the Zanesville Majolica operation burned. He would obviously have needed designs, and may have purchased dies of the defunct Zanesville works, or simply reproduced a mold from a bisque example. Bisque and wash glazed examples are known to exist.

The only known mark for Zanesville Majolica is shown here. The mark is from the back of this 6¼" x 11⅞" panel. The majority of the few known examples of this factory are unsigned. Examples are rare, signed examples are very rare.
$800.00 – 1,200.00 framed.

Atomize – spray on, shower of fine droplets.

Aventurine – containing auriferous particles, resembling gold.

Backdie – a device for stamping in a press, as a design on the back of a coin.

Barbotine – pottery painted with liquid clay, the underglaze decorations being more or less in relief, similar to the method used by an artist painting on canvas. Sometimes used on applied or sculpted decorations.

Belleek – a thin porcelain.

Biscuit – pottery or porcelain which has been fired once, but not glazed — sometimes bisque.

Bisque – see biscuit.

Crazing – the crackling of glaze, produced by unequal expansion and contraction of glaze and body.

Crystalline – a glaze showing crystallizations, in various colors.

Embossed – a decoration in relief, made by molding or pressing.

Enamel – a color tinted glaze fused to pottery.

Encaustic – a tile with the pattern inlaid in clay a different color from the ground, and burned in, usually unglazed and used for floors.

Faience – a general term referring to all kinds of earthenware, came to mean architectural ceramics in particular.

Impressed – a mark made by pressure, an indentation in the clay.

Incised – a mark made in wet clay by hand, usually with a nail or simple cutting instrument.

Intaglio – an indented pattern, sunken decoration, reverse of relief, opposite of cameo.

Mantel Facing – a fireplace surround.

Mat, Matt, or Matte – a dull glaze, without gloss.

Mint – in the same condition as when it left the factory or studio.

Mosaic – small pieces forming a pattern or decoration, or the appearance of.

Pooling – a puddling or accumulation of glaze at the lowest spot when fired in the kiln.

Relief – embossing done by molding or pressing.

Slip – a preparation of fluid clay, colored engobe (mineral slip).

Stamped – a method of applying an ink mark, impressed, by hand or machine. A die impressed mark.

Sweet's – annual architectural catalogs.

Terra Cotta – for architectural decorating purposes, a hard dark red to red-brown vitrified pottery, glazed or unglazed, garden pottery.

Tiger Eye – an aventurine glaze resembling the luminous appearance of a tiger's eye.

Transfer Printing – the art of transferring engraved patterns to the surface of pottery or porcelain by means of tissue paper with prepared ink.

Underglaze Decoration – the ornamentation of a vessel, tile, etc., by painting designs on the biscuit before it is glazed.

Vitreous or Vitrified – non-porous, will not absorb moisture.

Bibliography

Books and Exhibition Catalogs

Barber, Edwin Atlee. *The Pottery and Porcelain of the U. S. and Marks of American Potters.* NY: J & J Publishing, 1976.

Barnard, Julian. *Victorian Ceramic Tiles.* London: Studio Vista Publishers, 1972.

Bell, Frederic. *Notes on a 50-Year Revolution.* Rahway, NJ: Quinn & Boden Co. Inc., 1973.

Blasberg, Robert W. *Grueby.* Syracuse, NY: Everson Museum of Art, 1981.

———. and Carol L. Bohdan. *Fulper Art Pottery: An Aesthetic Appreciation.* NY: The Jordan-Volpe Gallery, 1979.

Bruhn, Thomas P. *American Decorative Tiles 1870 – 1930.* Storrs, CT: William Benton Museum of Art, 1979.

Buxton, Virginia Hillway. *Roseville Pottery — for Love or Money.* Nashville, TN: Tymbre Hill Publishing Co., 1977.

Carlton, Jim and Carol. *Collector's Encyclopedia of Colorado Pottery.* Paducah, KY: Collector Books, 1994.

Cincinnati Art Museum. *The Ladies, God Bless 'em.* Cincinnati, OH: Cincinnati Art Museum, 1976.

Cummins, Virginia Raymond. *Rookwood Pottery Potpourri.* Silver Springs, MD: Cliff R. Leonard and Duke Coleman, 1980.

Darling, Sharon S. *Teco: Art Pottery of the Prairie School.* Erie, PA: Erie Art Museum, 1989.

Dietz, Ulysses G. *The Newark Museum Collection of American Art Pottery.* Newark, NJ, 1984.

Ellis, Anita J. *Rookwood Pottery — The Glaze Lines.* Atglen, PA: Schiffer Publishing Ltd., 1995.

Evans, Paul. *Art Pottery of the United States.* NY: Charles Scribner's Sons 1974.

Hibel, John and Carol, and Robert DeFalco. *The Fulper Book.* State College, PA, 1992.

Huxford, Bob and Sharon. *The Collector's Encyclopedia of Brush McCoy Pottery.* Paducah, KY: Collector Books, 1978.

———. *Early Roseville.* Paducah, KY: Collector Books, 1979.

———. *The Collector's Encyclopedia of Roseville Pottery.* Paducah, KY: Collector Books, 1976.

———. *The Collector's Encyclopedia of Weller Pottery.* Paducah, KY: Collector Books, 1979.

Johnson, Deb and Gini. *Beginner's Book of American Pottery.* DeMoine, IA: Wallace-Homestead Book Co., 1974.

Kovel, Ralph and Terry. *Kovel's American Art Pottery.* NY: Crown Publishers, 1993.

Lehner, Lois. *Lehner's Encyclopedia of U. S. Marks on Pottery, Porcelain & Clay.* Paducah, KY: Collector Books, 1988.

Lockett, Terence A. *Collecting Victorian Tiles.* Suffolk, England: Antique Collector's Club, 1979.

MacDonald, Ann Gilbert. *All About Weller.* Marietta, OH: Antique Publications, 1989.

Mercer, Henry C. *The Tiled Pavement in the Capitol of Pennsylvania.* State College, PA: The Pennsylvania Guild of Craftsmen, 1975.

Nelson, Scott H., Lois K. Crouch, Euphemia B. Demmin, and Robert Wyman Newton. *A Collector's Guide to Van Briggle Pottery.* Indiana, PA: A.G. Halldin Publishing Co., 1986.

Ormond, Suzanne and Mary E. Irving. *Louisiana's Art Nouveau — The Crafts of the Newcomb Style.* Gretna, LA: Pelican Publishing Co., Inc., 1976.

Pear, Lillian Myers. *The Pewabic Pottery.* Des Moines, IA: Wallace-Homestead Book Co., 1976.

Peck, Herbert. *The Book of Rookwood Pottery.* NY: Crown Publishers, Inc., 1968.

———. *The Second Book of Rookwood Pottery.* Tucson, AZ: Peck, 1985.

Purviance, Louise and Evan and Norris F. Schneider. *Weller Art Pottery in Color.* Des Moines, IA: Wallace-Homestead Book Co., 1971.

———, and Norris F. Schneider. *Zanesville Art Pottery in Color.* Des Moines, IA: Wallace-Homestead Book Co., 1968.

———. *Zanesville Art Tile in Color.* Des Moines, IA: Wallace-Homestead Book Co., 1972.

Roesch, Jessie. *Newcomb Pottery.* Atglen, PA.: Schiffer Publishing Ltd., 1984.

Saloff, Tim and Jamie. *The Collector's Encyclopedia of Cowan Pottery.* Paducah, KY: Collector Books, 1994.

Sasicki, Richard and Josie Fania. *The Collector's Encyclopedia of Van Briggle.* Paducah, KY: Collector Books, 1993.

Taft, Lisa Factor. *Herman Carl Mueller.* Trenton, NJ: New Jersey State Museum, 1979.

Trapp, Kenneth R. *The Arts and Crafts Movement in California: Living the Good Life.* NY: Abbyville Press, 1993.

———. *Celebrate Cincinnati Art.* Cincinnati, OH: Cincinnati Art Museum 1981.

Van Lemmon, Hans. *Tiles — 1000 Years of Architectural Decoration.* NY: Harry N. Abrams, 1993.

Articles

Blasberg, Robert W. "Grueby Art Pottery." *Antiques,* Aug. 1971.

———. "Moravian Tiles: Fairy Tales in Colored Clay." *Spinning Wheel,* June 1971.

———. "Twenty Years of Fulper." *Spinning Wheel,* Oct. 1973.

Coleman, Oliver. "The Mercer Tiles and Other Matters." *The House Beautiful,* July 1903.

Darling, Sharon. "Chicago Ceramics and Glass." *Spinning Wheel,* Mar. – Apr. 1980.

Fox, Claire Gilbridge. "Henry Chapman Mercer: Tilemaker, Collector, and Builder Extra Ordinary." *Antiques,* Oct. 1973.

Graham, Jim. "Thomas Wheatley's Arts and Crafts Pottery." *Journal of the A.A.P.A.* May – June 1996.

Hendeson, Helen. "Color and Design — the Legacy of the C. Pardee Works." *Antique Week,* June 1996.

Jaques, Bertha. "Our American Potteries — The Pauline Pottery." *The Sketch Book,* June 1906.

Main, Sally. "Newcomb Pottery: The Trend of Education." *Journal of the American Art Pottery Assoc.,* Mar./Apr. 1996.

Meline, Elva. "Art Tile in California — The Work of E.A. Batchelder." *Spinning Wheel,* Nov. 1971.

Messineo, Jim and Mike Witt. "Buyer Beware!" *Journal of the A.A.P.A.,* Mar./Apr. 1996.

Millet, Frank D. "Some American Tiles." *Century Illustrated,* Apr. 1882.

Morse, Barbara White. "Art Tiles and Plastic Sketches of Arthur Osborne." *Spinning Wheel,* Apr. 1979 and May 1979.

———. "Buying a Low Art Tile Stove." *Spinning Wheel,* Nov. 1970 and Dec. 1970.

———. "Chelsea Ceramic Charm and Comfort." *The Antiques Journal,* Oct. 1972.

———. "High Art Maiolica Tiles of the United States Encaustic Tile Works." *Spinning Wheel,* Mar./Apr. 1982.

———. "John Gardner Low and His Original Art Tile Soda Fountain." *Spinning Wheel,* July/Aug. 1971 and Sept. 1971.

———. "Tiles made by Isaac Broome, Sculptor and Genius." *Spinning Wheel,* Jan./Feb. 1973.

———. "Tiles to Treasure, Low Art Tiles." *Spinning Wheel,* Mar. 1969.

"Picture Fireplaces, Illustrating Stories for Sitting Room, Library and Nursery." *The Craftsman,* Dec. 1916.

Pilling, Ronald. "W. Henry Chapman Mercer and the Moravian Tile Works." *American Art & Antiques,* Nov./Dec. 1979.

Rago, David. "American Art Pottery." *The Antique Trader,* May 9, 1983.

Robinson, Edward Wanton. "A Word on Faience." *The Craftsman,* Nov. 1908.

Sasicki, Richard. "Van Briggle Tiles — Delightful Textures." *Journal of the A.A.P.A.,* Mar./Apr. 1994.

Shull, Thelma. "The Pauline Pottery." *Hobbies,* Oct. 1943.

Townsend, Everett. "Ceramic History." *Bulletin of The American Ceramic Society,* May 1943 and Aug. 1943.

Volpe, Todd M. and Robert W. Blasberg. "Fulper Art Pottery: Amazing Glazes." *Art & Antiques,* July/Aug. 1978.

Watkins, Lura Woodside. "Low's Art Tiles." *Antiques,* May 1944.

Whyte, Bertha Kitchell. "Pauline Pottery of Edgerton, Wisconsin." *Spinning Wheel,* Apr. 1958.

Articles in Flash Point

Bazil, Melanie. "Art is Born in Pewabic Tiles." Apr./June 1990.

Darling, Sharon S. "Architectural Terra Cotta in Chicago." A 1992 colored pamphlet.

Koehler, Vance A. "Henry Chapman Mercer, Tile Maker." Special Edition 1991.

Knauf, Sandra. "The Van Briggle Connection." Apr. – June 1992.

Morse, Barbara White. "Soda Fountains: Low Art Tiles." Apr. – June 1992.

———. "Poems in Clay: Low Art Tiles." Oct. – Dec. 1990.

"Ohio Features Ceramic Genius." Apr. – June 1991.

Sims, Michael S. "F. H. Hall — Pioneer and Enigma of the American Tile Industry." Summer 1996.

———. "Tiles of Zanesville, Ohio." July – Sept. 1993.

———. "Zanesville Majolica — Gold Medal Winner of the Clay City." Jan. – Mar. 1992.

Taylor, Joseph A. "Ernest Allen Batchelder — Craftsman Turns Entrepreneur." Oct.-Dec. 1992.

Tunick, Susan. "American Decorative Tiles." A 1991 colored pamphlet.

Index

271